lonely planet

BEST ROAD TRIPS

# GERMANY, AUSTRIA & SWITZERLAND

### ESCAPES ON THE OPEN ROAD

MARC DI DUCA, BECKI ENRIGHT, ANTHONY HAM

# Contents

## PLAN YOUR TRIP
Welcome to Germany,
Austria & Switzerland.................4
Our Picks.................................6
When to Go............................14
Get Prepared for Germany,
Austria & Switzerland..............16

## ROAD TRIPS ..................18

## NORTHEASTERN
GERMANY ............................21
Along the Baltic Coast ............24
Design for Life:
Bauhaus to VW.......................30
Lakes & Treasures
of Mecklenburg–
Western Pomerania................34
Highlights of Saxony...............38
Central Germany's
Castles & Palaces...................44
Berlin & the Jewels of
Eastern Brandenburg..............48
Via Regia................................52
German Avenues Route.........60

## NORTHWESTERN
GERMANY .............................73
North Sea Coast.....................76
German Fairy Tale Road.........82
Cologne & the Ruhr Valley.....90
Romantic Rhine......................94
Moselle Valley......................102
German Wine Route.............106

## SOUTHERN GERMANY .....111
Bergstrasse..........................114
German Castle Road............118
The Romantic Road..............124
Glass Route.........................132
German Alpine Road............136
Lake Constance...................144
Fantastic Road ....................148
Schwarzwaldhochstrasse.....152

## AUSTRIA ............................157
Along the Danube................160
The High Alpine Trio –
Grossglockner to Silvretta....164

Mountain Valleys of
Tyrol & Vorarlberg................170
Castles of
Burgenland & Styria............. 176
Salzkammergut....................182
Carinthian Lakes..................188

## SWITZERLAND.................193
Northern Switzerland ...........196
Lake Geneva &
Western Switzerland............200
Geneva to Zürich..................204
The Swiss Alps.................... 210
Graubünden & Ticino...........218

## TOOLKIT .......................225
Arriving................................226
Getting Around....................227
Accommodation ..................228
Cars.....................................229
Health & Safe Travel............230
Responsible Travel..............231
Nuts & Bolts........................232

# Welcome to Germany, Austria & Switzerland

Occupying a vast swathe of the continent, from the blustery flats of the North Sea coast to the highest peaks of the Alps, the character-packed trio of Germany, Austria and Switzerland are Mitteleuropa at its finest. And the good news is that when it comes to touring in your own vehicle, there may be nowhere better on the planet. The German-speaking nations' knack for laying decent asphalt means quick zips along the autobahn deliver you deep into a region before veering off onto the high road for slower exploration. And in this part of Europe, not a minute passes without some distraction from the windows – a castle perched high on a mountain top, a gingerbread house bedecked in flower boxes bursting with geraniums, grapes ripening in the sun or a cable car ascending a limestone rock face. So pack up and fill up for a European road trip of a lifetime.

**Lauterbrunnen (p214), Switzerland**
ANDREW_MAYOVSKYY/GETTY IMAGES

# Our Picks

## BEST WINE & FOOD DRIVES

That seatbelt may be feeling a little stretched by the time you get through central Europe – road trips in this part of the world seem to be an endless culinary autobahn of sausages and dumplings, Black Forest gateau, Swiss chocolate and creamy Alpine cheeses. Wash it all on its way with some of best wines produced north of the Alps and the world's best beers.

**TOP TIP**

The unique fusion cuisine of Switzerland's Ticino canton is known for its polenta, risottos, semi-hard Alpine cheeses and charcuterie.

### 1 German Wine Route

Explore the vine-carpeted slopes, picture-book villages and thermal springs along this well-established touring route.
**P106**

### 2 Moselle Valley

Vineyards and south-facing slopes galore line this route through Germany's most famous wine-producing region.
**P102**

### 3 Schwarzwaldhochstrasse

Sample traditionally earthy, seasonal flavours in one of southern Germany's most celebrated foodie regions.
**P152**

### 4 Mountain Valleys of Tyrol & Vorarlberg

Schnapps, Alpine cheeses, wild meadow honey, beer and Mozartkugeln sweets abound on this tastily tempting route.
**P170**

### 5 Graubünden & Ticino

This route gives you a genuine taste of Italy's supreme cuisine without setting foot in the *bel paese*.
**P218**

**TOP TIP**

Swiss wine is a thing, but is hardly ever found outside the country's borders, making it an unusual souvenir.

Alpine cheese

Moselle Valley (p102), Germany

**TOP TIP**
Black Forest gateau is an irresistible blend of chocolate sponge layered generously with whipped cream and kirsch cherries.

**TOP TIP**

Unless in a hurry, try to take routes that avoid the many tunnels through the Alps. These are sometimes expensive and you see nothing.

# Our Picks

## BEST MOUNTAIN DRIVES

Especially in the south of the region, where the Alps create one of the world's most famous natural barriers, it will be time to buckle up for Europe's greatest mountain journeys. Take the high road across passes, the valley motorways or, if you are in a hurry, tunnels that burrow through entire mountain ranges. On sunny days, icy peaks and shimmering white glaciers are spellbinding. Keeping your eyes on the road can be hard in these parts.

**TOP TIP**

Many locals in Central Europe leave their winter tyres on their vehicles well into May, just in case.

**TOP TIP**

It's always a good idea to have wheel chains in your car between 1 November and 31 March.

Grossglockner High Alpine Road (p164), Austria

### ❶ The Swiss Alps
Tour the biggest names in the Alps, such as the Matterhorn, Eiger, Mönch and Jungfrau.
**P210**

### ❷ Bergstrasse
A 2000-year-old Roman trade route, Germany's historic 'mountain road' shadows the forested Odenwald range.
**P114**

### ❸ German Alpine Road
Bavaria's sliver of the Alps action is one packed with snow-dusted peaks and serene mountain lakes.
**P136**

### ❹ Salzkammergut
Discover the Alps of *Heidi* and *The Sound of Music* on this odyssey out of Salzburg.
**P182**

### ❺ The High Alpine Trio – Grossglockner to Silvretta
A feat of 1930s engineering, this road swings giddily around 36 switchbacks through the Austrian Alps.
**P164**

Matterhorn (p217), Switzerland

# Our Picks

## BEST LAKE & RIVER DRIVES

You're gonna need a lot of superlatives to describe some of Central Europe's watery parts. Few regions of Europe claim so many of the longest, biggest, deepest… The queen of all European rivers – the Danube, which drains much of the Alps – dominates Germany and Austria. Europe's highest mountains trap some picture-perfect bodies of water that will make for some of the most attractive photographs you'll get anywhere.

**TOP TIP**
The Danube has its source in the Black Forest and ends 10 countries and 2850km later in the Black Sea.

**1 Lakes & Treasures of Mecklenburg–Western Pomerania**
Germany's flatlands and plains have created a string of beautiful lakes.
**P34**

**2 Romantic Rhine**
Powerhouse riverside cities and castle-capped cliffs; this German journey along Europe's longest river is epic.
**P94**

**3 Along the Danube**
Follow the Austrian edition of Europe's longest watercourse for abbeys, castles and a resplendent capital.
**P160**

**4 Lake Geneva & Western Switzerland**
Vineyards, villages, beaches and castles embellish Europe's largest Alpine lake shared between Switzerland and France.
**P200**

**5 Lake Constance**
A circular, shore-hugging journey visiting the pick of the bunch of sights on Germany's largest lake.
**P144**

**TOP TIP**
Electric tour boats ply Bavaria's eye-candy Königssee but no other craft are allowed onto this pristine Alpine lake.

Château de Chillon (p202), Lake Geneva, Switzerland

PETER STEIN/SHUTTERSTOCK

BEST ROAD TRIPS: GERMANY, AUSTRIA & SWITZERLAND

# Our Picks

## BEST HISTORY DRIVES

Visitable history goes back millennia in these parts, the Romans having occupied the Alps and some regions north of them. Central Europe is littered with reminders of an often turbulent past from the ancient to the uncomfortably recent. There really is something for everyone here, from neoclassical palaces to Cold War relics, Roman walls to baroque churches and centuries-old breweries to 20th-century sites that witnessed the rise of the Nazis.

**TOP TIP**

The Limes is a UNESCO-listed site stretching 600km through southern Germany, Austria and Slovakia that formed the border of the Roman Empire.

### Berlin & the Jewels of Eastern Brandenburg

WWII comes hauntingly alive in a concentration camp and on the largest battlefield on German soil.

**P48**

### Cologne & the Ruhr Valley

This drive in northwest Germany delivers you to the Romans amid 20th-century postindustrial rejuvenation.

**P90**

Brandenburg Gate, Berlin (p48), Germany

### Moselle Valley

Southern Germany has many Roman relics but some of the finest are visited by this wine-scented drive.

**P102**

### The Romantic Road

The concentration of medieval walled towns in Bavaria's eastern flank is like nothing else you've seen.

**P124**

### Via Regia

Trans-Germania west-east autobahn odyssey that visits many cities that still bear the hallmarks of the old GDR.

**P52**

# Our Picks

## BEST CASTLE DRIVES

If there's something Mitteleuropa does particularly well, it is romantic castles and high-perched fortresses. In some parts of the region, hilltops seem almost naked without an erstwhile feudal residence or crumbling ruins. These noble piles dating from every architectural era set the perfect backdrop for any Europe road trip and also serve as fascinating and informative repositories of the region's past. The only problem is which of the thousands to choose from.

**TOP TIP**
Some castles in Europe close for visitors over the winter so check before you base an itinerary around them.

### Central Germany's Castles & Palaces
Drive between mysterious ruins, draughty fortresses and swish palaces on this scenic trip.
**P44**

### German Fairy Tale Road
A dreamy trip straight out of a Brothers Grimm fairy tale linking places that look like they were AI-created.
**P82**

### German Castle Road
Castle-hop in southern Germany along 600km of scenic road and a thousand years of history.
**P118**

### Castles of Burgenland & Styria
There are castles galore on this drive through eastern Austria's borderland wine country.
**P176**

### Highlights of Saxony
Visit aristocratic homes of all shapes and sizes across the eastern German state of Saxony.
**P38**

**TOP TIP**
Saxony's Schloss Moritzburg was a location for the most watched film from Eastern Europe – the Czechoslovak-GDR version of *Cinderella*.

Schloss Moritzburg (p42), Germany

Schloss Neuschwanstein (p130), Germany

**TOP TIP**
Bavaria's Neuschwanstein Castle is said to have been the inspiration for Walt Disney's fairy tale fortress.

# When to Go

Across this huge region there's no season that would be off-limits to motorists but each time of year brings challenges.

## I LIVE HERE

### FAIRY TALE DRIVING ROUTES

**Marc Di Duca,
Lonely Planet writer**

With clogged roads, endless roadworks on Germany's autobahns and queues at tunnels, heading south during the European summer hols rarely brings motoring joy. That is, until you arrive in Switzerland's Italian-speaking canton of Ticino. Driving into the region's many narrow valleys on almost single-lane roads, the tourist crush never appears as the ribbon of grey tarmac undulates through the limestone peaks, chestnut forests and stone-built hamlets. Other cars are rare and everyone is doing 50km/h, just slow enough to admire the fairy tale scenery. Stopping by the road for a dip in the chilly waters of Ticino's rivers is the icing (literally) on the motoring cake.

From the North Sea coast to roads heading over Alpine passes and from the plains of Bavaria to the valley of the Danube, this chunk of Central Europe has varied weather, to say the least. While spring flowers are pushing through the soil in Munich, the snow may still be falling in the Alps and an icy wind blowing in Germany's north. Preparing your vehicle and your gear for the climate really does depend on where you are going and when.

Spring flowers, Munich (p140), Germany

## Weather Watch (Munich)

| JANUARY | FEBRUARY | MARCH | APRIL | MAY | JUNE |
|---|---|---|---|---|---|
| Avg daytime max: 3°C | Avg daytime max: 4°C | Avg daytime max: 9°C | Avg daytime max: 14°C | Avg daytime max: 18°C | Avg daytime max: 21°C |
| Days of rainfall: 9 | Days of rainfall: 8 | Days of rainfall: 10 | Days of rainfall: 10 | Days of rainfall: 11 | Days of rainfall: 11 |

Grossglockner High Alpine Road (p166), Austria

### WINTER WARNING

Austria, Switzerland and Germany's south are almost guaranteed snow between December and March. Think winter tyres, snow chains, ice scrapers, emergency shovels, extra food and blankets.

## Accommodation

The European summer holidays (July and August) are the time when accommodation is at its priciest and that holds true across the entire region. There are also spikes around Christmas and New Year. Wherever there is skiing, expect January to March to be more expensive. Lowest rates in towns come in November, March and possibly May. Standards are high across the board but bargains are largely a thing of the past.

### SUN & SIZZLE

Summers can be hotter than many imagine here, especially on the plains. The south side of the Alps can fry even at relatively high altitudes and the flats of Bavaria can be muggy. High in the Alps the sun's rays are stronger, so slap on sunscreen.

### THE MAIN FESTIVALS

Some six million visitors pitch up in Munich in late September for the two weeks of lager drinking and merrymaking that is the famous **Oktoberfest**, the world's biggest beer festival. **September-October**

**Donauinselfest**, the world's biggest free music festival, takes place in Vienna and attracts around three million visitors. It is held on an island in the Danube. **June**

The most famous jazz festival in the world, **Montreux Jazz Festival**, takes place in the unlikely setting of this Swiss town and draws in around 300,000 foot tappers over the two weeks it takes place. **July**

**Karneval der Kulturen (Carnival of Cultures)** is an international street festival that occupies the Kreuzburg neighbourhood of Berlin for four days, attracting a million revellers. **May-June**

### SUMMER STORMS

After sultry days, big storms can rumble down the valleys in the Alps, the same valleys that motorways and other major roads use to snake their way through the mountains. If a storm hits, slow down in reduced visibility or even pull over at a service station.

| JULY | AUGUST | SEPTEMBER | OCTOBER | NOVEMBER | DECEMBER |
|---|---|---|---|---|---|
| Avg daytime max: **23°C** | Avg daytime max: **23°C** | Avg daytime max: **18°C** | Avg daytime max: **14°C** | Avg daytime max: **8°C** | Avg daytime max: **4°C** |
| Days of rainfall: 11 | Days of rainfall: 10 | Days of rainfall: 9 | Days of rainfall: 9 | Days of rainfall: 8 | Days of rainfall: 10 |

# Get Prepared for Germany, Austria & Switzerland

Useful things to load in your bag, your ears and your brain

## Clothing

What clothing you pack depends heavily on when you are heading to Central Europe and what you intend to do there. From swimwear for the beaches of the North Sea to full winter hiking gear, packing the right attire is essential.

**Swimwear:** No matter which season you are travelling, make sure you bring your swimming things, as good for a day on the beach in northern Germany as for a thermal spa in the Alps or a dip in a cooling mountain river along the way.

**Layers:** In winter, a merino-wool base layer, a fleece and a water- and windproof jacket or down coat are pretty much must-haves everywhere. Between December and March gloves and a hat are all but indispensable.

**Sunglasses:** The sun's harmful rays can be stronger at altitude than down by the sea. Make sure your eyewear has a good UV filter.

**Smart casual:** For better-class restaurants, the theatre, lobby bars and even museums, locals in this part of the world dress smartly casual and you should, too.

**Hiking boots:** Boots or at least trail shoes are a very good idea for mountain trips. The latter are also very suitable for exploring cobbled old towns.

### WATCH

**Mike Casa**
*(mikecasacomedy.ch)*
Mike Casa is a Swiss-Ticino comedian who often performs in English, poking fun at the absurdities of life in Switzerland.

**Oktoberfest in Munich – The Wiesn Madness**
*(WELT; 2019)*
Documentary about the traditions and inner workings of the world's biggest beer festival.

**The Third Man**
*(Carol Reed; 1949)* The most famous film shot in postwar Vienna, based on the novel by Graham Greene.

Hiking, Austria (p156)

LISTEN

**Falco 3**
*(Falco; 1985)* Falco's third album features mega hits like 'Vienna Calling' and 'Rock Me Amadeus'.

**Eine kleine Nachtmusik, K 525**
*(Wolfgang Amadeus Mozart; 1787)* The most uplifting and recognisable composition for a chamber ensemble.

**Hoizhakka Pogo**
*(Hundsbuam; 1996)* This track and many others by Hundsbuam blend Bavarian folk with punk and rock.

READ

**Germania**
*(Simon Winder; 2010)* The long history of what is now Germany told in an entertaining, engaging way.

**The Magic Mountain**
*(Thomas Mann; 1924)* This novel by the German literary great immerses readers in Davos' snow-bound streets and mountains.

**A Death in Vienna**
*(Daniel Silva; 2005)* This page-turning spy thriller digs up the ghosts of WWII.

**The White Spider**
*(Heinrich Harrer; 1959)* Gripping account of the first ascent of the north face of the Eiger in Switzerland.

## Words

**Grüss Gott** *(groos-got)*: 'hello' in southern Germany and Austria

**Guten Tag** *(gooten tag)*: 'hello' in northern Germany

**Grüezi** *(grue-etsee)*, **Bonjour** *(bon-zhoor)*, **Ciao** *(chau)*: common greetings in Switzerland, depending on where you are

**Hallo/Servus** *(ha-lo/ser-vus)*: common and less formal greetings

**Auf Wiedersehen** *(owf vee-der-zehn)*: formal way of saying goodbye

**Tschüss** *(choos)*: common informal way of saying 'cheerio'

**Bitte** *(bitta)*: 'please' and can also be used to say 'you are welcome'

**Danke (schön)** *(dahn-ke (shurn))*: 'thanks (very much)' in all situations

**Wie geht es?** *(vee gayt es)*: 'how are you?'

**Ich verstehe nicht** *(ikh fer-shtay-e nikht)*: 'I don't understand'

**Prost!** *(prawst)*: 'cheers'

**Guten Appetit** *(goo-ten ah-peh-teet)*: 'bon appetit'

**Entschuldigung** *(ent-shul-di-gung)*: 'excuse me' as well as being a way of attracting attention, just like in English

BEST ROAD TRIPS: GERMANY, AUSTRIA & SWITZERLAND

# ROAD TRIPS

Rothenburg ob der Tauber (p120), Germany

# Contents

**NORTHEASTERN GERMANY 21**

**NORTHWESTERN GERMANY 73**

**SOUTHERN GERMANY 111**

**AUSTRIA 157**

**SWITZERLAND 193**

Berlin (p48)

# Northeastern Germany

**01 Along the Baltic Coast**
Explore the bracing, beautiful Baltic with superb historic towns along the way from Lübeck to Rügen Island. **p24**

**02 Design for Life: Bauhaus to VW**
Drive through the evocative industrial heart of the old East Germany (GDR) en route from Weimar to Hanover. **p30**

**03 Lakes & Treasures of Mecklenburg–Western Pomerania**
Meander among palaces and jewel-box towns on land dotted with lakes between Lüneburg and Greifswald. **p34**

**04 Highlights of Saxony**
Follow one of Germany's most storied paths, past palaces and fortresses and via Dresden on the road from Görlitz to Leipzig. **p38**

**05 Central Germany's Castles & Palaces**
Discover Germany's heartland, from Leipzig to Kassel, with castles and lavish palaces to keep you company. **p44**

**06 Berlin & the Jewels of Eastern Brandenburg**
Begin in Berlin and end at Gedenkstätte on this trip through a watery forest, WWII sites and medieval marvels in Berlin's orbit. **p48**

**07 Via Regia**
Set out from Saarbrücken bound for Görlitz along the German portion of the longest historic road link across Europe. **p52**

**08 German Avenues Route**
Get to know one of Germany's most picturesque, treelined driving routes on this loop out of Dessau-Rosslau. **p60**

# Explore

# Northeastern Germany

It can be difficult to know where to begin in Germany's northeast, so much is there to see. Along the often quiet byways that connect some of the country's most iconic cities (Berlin, Dresden, Weimar and Hanover), you'll pass through magical towns steeped in history, including Stralsund, Lübeck and Quedlinburg, to name just three. In between, you'll traverse scenic landscapes that range through farm country and forests and draw near to riverbanks and rolling hills. Along the way, you'll journey from the shores of the Baltic in the country's far north to Germany's historic and cultural heartland.

## Berlin

Germany's capital is the heartbeat of the country, rich in history and cultural significance and filled with excellent hotels, restaurants and attractions. It combines the best of both worlds, both destination in its own right and perfectly sited gateway city – you can be driving any of northeastern Germany's driving routes within little more than an hour of leaving Berlin.

## Dresden

Few cities have been so impressively reborn as Dresden. Devastated during WWII, the city now has a dynamic cultural and nightlife scene, a resurrected skyline and old town, and one of Germany's most splendid repositories of the baroque. Dresden works as both stopover and starting point, providing as it does both the necessary infrastructure for travelling around the northeast and the cultural inspiration that provides context for everything you'll see while here.

## Leipzig

One of Germany's most underrated cities, Leipzig has emerged from the GDR as from a chrysalis, showcasing museums, opening its doors to all manner of cultural celebrations, and close to beautiful natural areas just waiting to be explored. Most of the best routes through the country's northeast pass right by the city, and its relatively compact core means that you can be out and into the countryside in no time at all after leaving your downtown hotel.

### WHEN TO GO

Let's be clear: northeastern Germany is superb at any time of the year. But the best months are undoubtedly from May (some say April) until August or September, when you can expect clear skies, dry hiking trails and mild to warm temperatures. August (and, to a lesser extent, July) can be super-busy, but other months are glorious.

## Erfurt

Most people fall in love with Erfurt straight away, and those that don't usually end up doing so within the hour. Its Altstadt is superb and it's easier to drive into and out from than most large cities. It also has some excellent places to stay and eat. It also stands effortlessly at so many crossroads – between the old GDR and West Germany, between Bavaria and the country's central heartland and on into the north, all within reach of so many routes in this book.

## Hanover

If you'd like to take the pulse of modern Germany, Hanover might just be your place. A slick, together kind of place, Hanover is like a template for the modern German city with impeccable green and tech credentials, an abundance of parks and cultural sites, and the kind of quiet self-confidence that comes from knowing that this is a really cool place to live. And yes, with its fine accommodation and culinary scenes, and a central location, it's great place to rest from the road as you plan your next move.

### TRANSPORT

You could pick any of the major towns in northeastern Germany and be well set up to explore. Berlin, Dresden and Hanover in particular have lots of domestic and international air connections, with all airports having plenty of car rental companies ready to send you out onto the region's wonderful roads.

 WHAT'S ON

**Dixieland Fest**
The merriest of Dresden's festivals, held in May, with concerts on board steamships.

**Wave-Gotik-Treffen**
The world's largest Goth festival, with a pagan village, a medieval market and lots of dark music takes over Leipzig in May-June.

**Maschseefest**
Two and a half August weeks of music, food and drink in Hanover; it's Germany's largest lake festival.

**Leipziger Jazztage**
Leipzig's October jazz festival draws acts and visitors from across Europe.

 WHERE TO STAY

Hotels in all their marvellous, modern variety provide ample choice when staying along the routes of the northeast. The major cities offer everything from modern hotels (the best have slick designer decor and musical or historic themes) and apartments to grand old-world places that evoke bygone eras; wherever you stay in a city, make sure there's parking nearby. But the German tradition of lodging in a country hotel, family-run pension, or wooden-beamed *Gästehaus* is alive and well in northeastern Germany. Staying in such places, wandering the old streets after dark, could rank among your best memories of these trips.

### Resources

**Saxony** (*visitsaxony.com*)
Official tourism site for a region that includes Dresden, Leipzig and so many historic places in between.

**Berlin** (*visitberlin.de*)
Everything you need to know about one of Europe's most dynamic and exciting cities, with plenty on its hinterland, too.

# 01

# Along the Baltic Coast

**BEST FOR FAMILIES**

Riding the Molli steam train along the Baltic coast.

| DURATION | DISTANCE | GREAT FOR |
|---|---|---|
| 5 days | 417km / 259 miles | History, nature & families |

| BEST TIME TO GO | April to October for the best weather. |
|---|---|

*Molli steam train, Kühlungsborn (p26)*

The Hanseatic cities along the Baltic coast are some of the most beautiful in Germany, perfect for evocative strolling amid huge architectural treasures made from untold millions of bricks. In between, this drive takes you along the wave-tossed coast with its rugged beaches and long sandy vistas. But there are also great places to take a dip, like the fabled promenade at Binz.

## Link Your Trip

**03 Lakes & Treasures of Mecklenburg–Western Pomerania**

From Greifswald, found on both routes, discover the inland charms and surprises of the region.

**06 Berlin & the Jewels of Eastern Brandenburg**

It's only 180km south (under two hours on the A20) from Greifswald to hit this route's Kloster Chorin, a 13th-century abbey.

### 01  LÜBECK

A 12th-century gem with more than 1000 historical buildings, Lübeck's picture-book appearance is an enduring reminder of its role as one of the founding cities of the mighty Hanseatic League and its moniker as the 'Queen of the Hanse'. Behind its landmark 1464 **Holstentor** (Holsten Gate), you'll find streets lined with medieval merchants' homes and spired churches forming Lübeck's 'crown'.

The fine Gothic **Marienkirche** (St Mary's Church; st-marien-luebeck.com) has the world's highest brick-vaulted roof and was the model for dozens of churches in northern Germany. A WWII bombing

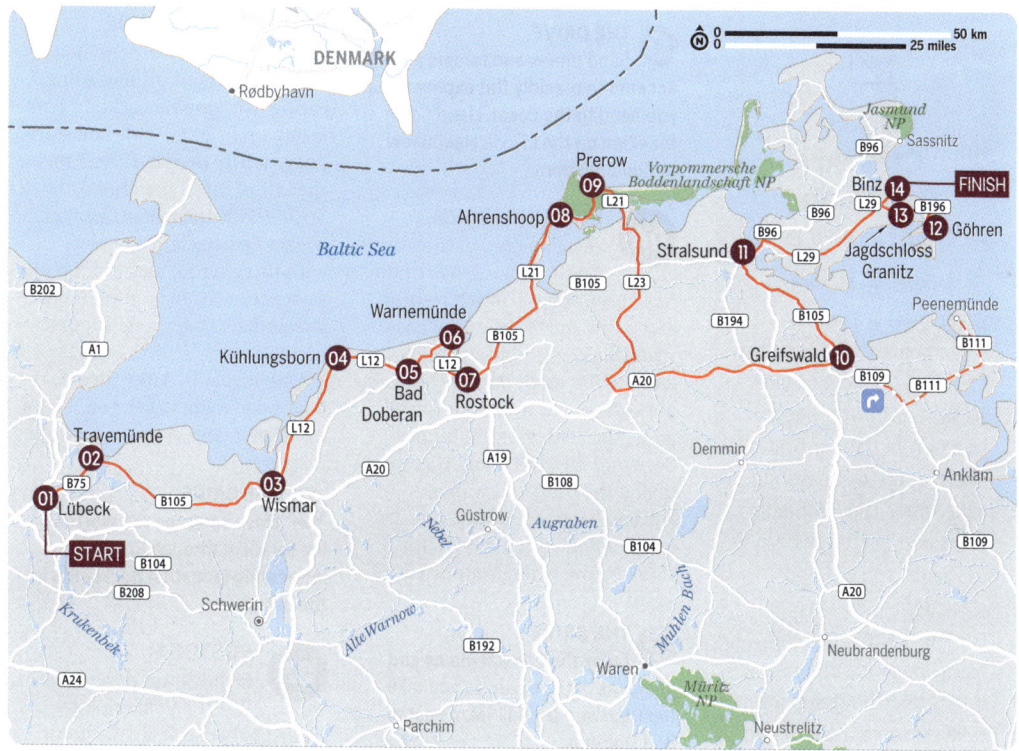

raid brought down the church's bells, which have been left where they fell in 1942 and have become a famous symbol of the city.

Thanks to a lift, everyone can enjoy panoramic views from the 50m-high platform in the tower of the 13th-century **Petrikirche** (Church of St Peter; st-petri-luebeck.de).

In the north of the old town the brilliant **Europäisches Hansemuseum** (European Hanseatic Museum; hansemuseum.eu) tells the remarkable story of the Hanseatic League, Lübeck and the region. Transfixing exhibits use every modern technology to tell a story as dramatic as anything in *Game of Thrones*.

### THE DRIVE
Take the B75 northeast for 19km to Travemünde.

### 02 TRAVEMÜNDE
Writer Thomas Mann declared that he spent his happiest days in Travemünde, just outside Lübeck (which bought it in 1329 to control the shipping coming into its harbour). Its 4.5km of sandy beaches at the point where the Trave River flows into the Baltic Sea make it easy to see why. Water sports are the main draw, along with a colourful **sailing regatta** (travemuenderwoche.com) in mid-July.

The town is all wide streets and has a certain 1960s feel. Vorderreihe on the waterfront is lined with upscale shops and cafes.

The town takes great pride in its historic four-masted sailing ship turned museum, **Passat** (rettetdiepassat.de), which used to do the run around South America's Cape Horn from the early to mid-20th century.

### THE DRIVE
Take the very short but fun car-ferry ride across the Trave River, then take the Siedlung road southeast for 10km to the junction with the B105, which you follow for 39km east to Wismar.

### 03 WISMAR
With its gabled facades and cobbled streets, this small, photogenic city looks essentially Hanseatic. But although it joined the Hanseatic trading league in the 13th century, it spent most of the 16th and 17th centuries as part of Sweden. There are numerous reminders of this era all over town. The entire **Altstadt** (old town) was UNESCO-listed in 2002.

TOP TIP:

## Classic Roadside Attraction: Karls

Gloriously hokey, **Karls** (karls.de) is a roadside attraction in the cheesiest tradition. The schtick here is fruit – strawberries to be exact. In this sprawling hodgepodge of petting zoo, shops, playgrounds, cafes and, yes, strawberry fields, you will find something for anyone in the family. The fresh-strawberry ice cream is really good. Watch them make preserves, then listen to the mechanical bears sing Elvis. Karls is about 12km northeast of Rostock.

The sober red-brick **St-Nikolai-Kirche** (kirchen-in-wismar.de) is the largest of its kind in Europe. Its linden-tree-shaded churchyard is next to a small canal and is Wismar's loveliest spot.

Dominating the middle of the **Markt** is the 1602-built Wasserkunst (waterworks), an ornate, 12-sided well that supplied Wismar's drinking water until 1897. Today it remains the town's landmark. The large **Rathaus** (Town Hall) at the Markt's northern end was built between 1817 and 1819.

### THE DRIVE
Sand dunes and forests add accents to placidly flat expanses as you head to the coast. Head north for 42km on the L12 via Neubukow to Kühlungsborn.

### 04 KÜHLUNGSBORN
Get some beach time in Kühlungsborn, one of the most atmospheric beach resorts along this starkly beautiful coast.

**Molli** (Mecklenburger Bäderbahn Molli; molli-bahn.de) is a popular tourist train that travels along the coast from Kühlungsborn and Bad Doberan. Alternate taking the train and walking between stops for a gorgeous day out along the often-wild Baltic shore before you set out driving again.

### THE DRIVE
Enjoy the coastal plains and glimpses of the Baltic as you take the Pfarrweg and L12 16km east to Bad Doberan.

### 05 BAD DOBERAN

The former summer ducal residence of Bad Doberan was once the site of a powerful Cistercian monastery and is now home to a fantasy in brick. Construction of the magnificent Gothic **Münster Bad Doberan** (muenster-doberan.de) started in 1280 but the scale of the building meant it wasn't consecrated until 1368. Its treasures include an intricate **high altar** and an **ornate pulpit**.

### THE DRIVE
Leave town driving north on the L12, which curves around to the east for 16km until it meets the B103. Turn north for 3km to Warnemünde.

### 06 WARNEMÜNDE
Genteel Warnemünde is all about promenading, eating fish, sipping cocktails and lazing on its long, wide and startlingly **white beach**. Perfect for the last of these activities is the *Strandkorb*, the iconic German wicker beach chair, complete with its own roof and windbreaks to deflect seaside breezes. Rent one and get cosy on most public beaches.

Walking along **Alter Strom**, the boat-lined main canal, you'll pass a row of quaint cottages housing restaurants.

### THE DRIVE
Drive south on the Werftallee for 10km through Rostock's interesting industrial docklands to the centre.

### 07 ROSTOCK

Rostock was devastated in WWII and later pummelled by socialist architectural 'ideals'. But this large port city still has small but attractive historic enclaves. Perhaps the best feature is the vibrant energy provided by the 11,000 university students.

Central Rostock's pride and joy is the 13th-century **Marienkirche** (marienkirche-rostock.de), the only main Rostock church to have survived WWII unscathed (although restorations are ongoing). Behind the main altar, the church's 12m-high astrological clock was built in 1472 by Hans Düringer.

Red-brick and pastel-coloured buildings on the large **Alter Markt** hark back to the 14th- and 15th-century Hanseatic era.

### THE DRIVE
Drive 22km on the B105. Just before the village of Borg, look for the turn north on the L21 and follow this beautiful coastal road 22km north to Ahrenshoop.

### Photo Opportunity
Lübeck's Holstentor, with the city's iconic church steeples rising up behind.

**Holstentor, Lübeck (p24)**

### 08 AHRENSHOOP
Nature lovers and artists will be captivated by the **Darss-Zingst Peninsula**. This far-flung splinter of land has a seaside that is raw and bracing, with trees growing sideways away from the constant winds. The artists' village of Ahrenshoop is a great place to wander. It has some of the region's most strikingly painted reed-thatched houses.

#### THE DRIVE
Drive 0km northeast on the L21, then turn due north for 7km to Prerow, right on the coast.

### 09 PREROW
The tiny town of Prerow is renowned for its model-ship-filled seafarers' church and lighthouse. Look for charming 'captains' houses' – reed-thatched dwellings with colourfully painted doors depicting sunflowers, fish and other regional motifs. Also common are *Zeesenboote* (drag-net fishing boats) with striking brown sails.

#### THE DRIVE
Take the L21 and L23 44km south via Löbnitz to the A20. Now you get to open up the car while heading east for 31km to exit 25, where you'll take the B109 25km east to Greifswald.

### 10 GREIFSWALD
The skyline of this compact former Hanseatic city is defined by three churches: the 'Langer Nikolas' (Long Nicholas), 'Dicke Marie' (Fat Mary) and 'Kleine Jakob' (Small Jacob). Don't miss climbing the tower of the first, 14th-century **Dom St Nikolai** (dom-greifswald.de), for sweeping views.

The richly ornamented buildings ringing the **Markt** hint at Greifswald's stature in the Middle Ages. The **Rathaus**, at the western end, started life as 14th-century shops. Among the red-brick gabled houses on the eastern side, the **Coffee House** (No 11) is gorgeous and a good example of a combined living-and-storage house owned by Hanseatic merchants.

#### THE DRIVE
It's an easy 36km northwest on the B105 to Stralsund. Watch for the huge church spires as they appear on the horizon.

### Detour
**Peenemünde**
Start: ⑩ Greifswald

Amid the sandy dunes and bleak expanses of Usedom Island, the notorious village of Peenemünde is at the end of a scenic 52km drive via the B109 and B111.

It was here, on the island's western tip, that Wernher von Braun developed the V2 rocket, first launched in October 1942. It flew 90km high and a distance of 200km before plunging into the Baltic – the first time in history that a flying object exited the earth's atmosphere. Displays at the **Historisch-Technisches Museum** (Historical & Technological Museum; peenemuende.de) – some in surviving buildings – do a good job of showing how the rockets were developed and the destruction they caused.

## 11 STRALSUND

Stralsund was once the second most important member of the Hanseatic League after Lübeck, and its square gables interspersed with Gothic turrets, ornate portals and vaulted arches make it one of the leading examples of *Backsteingotik* (classic red-brick Gothic gabled architecture) in northern Germany.

This vibrant city's historic cobbled streets and many attractions make it an unmissable stop. The main square, **Alter Markt**, is a hub of its architectural treasures. The soaring 1270 **Nikolaikirche** (Church of St Nicholas; hst-nikolai.de) is a masterpiece of medieval architecture. Its interior is colourful and filled with art treasures.

Seven copper turrets and six triangular gables grace the red-brick Gothic facade of the splendid 1370 **Rathaus**.

In an arctic-white wavelike building that leaps out from the surrounding red-brick warehouses, the state-of-the-art **Ozeaneum** (ozeaneum.de) takes you into an underwater world of creatures from the Baltic and North Seas and the Atlantic Ocean.

Stroll the nearby harbour area for lots of stands selling smoked fish.

### THE DRIVE
Soar over the water on the bridge to Rügen Island on the B96. Once on the island (7km from Stralsund) turn southeast on the L29 and drive through a canopy of trees. Pass through villages for 36km to the B196, where another 10km southeast brings you to Göhren.

Binz

## 12 GÖHREN

Göhren's stunning 7km-long **beach** – divided into the sleepier Südstrand and the more developed Nordstrand – lives up to its hype as Rügen's best resort beach.

Göhren is the eastern terminus of the **Rügensche Bäderbahn** (RBB; ruegensche-baederbahn.de) steam train that chuffs between Putbus and Göhren. En route, it stops in Binz, Jagdschloss Granitz, Sellin and Baabe. Much of the narrow track passes through sun-dappled forest. Its nickname is the ironic 'Rasender Roland' (Rushing Roland).

### THE DRIVE
Take the B196 northwest for a mere 12km to the L29, then turn east for the final 3km to the Jagdschloss Granitz car park.

## 13 JAGDSCHLOSS GRANITZ

A grandiose hunting palace built in 1723 on top of the 107m-high Tempelberg, **Jagdschloss Granitz** (mv-schloesser.de/location/schloss-granitz) was significantly enlarged and altered by Wilhelm Malte I in 1837. The results will remind you of salt and pepper shakers or a phallic fantasy, depending on your outlook. Malte's flights of fancy also gave Rügen the grandiose **Putbus**.

The RBB steam train stops at Jagdschloss and Garftitz, which serve the palace. Get off at one, enjoy some lovely hiking and reboard at the other for a trip to either Göhren or Binz (where you might have left your car). The palace parking itself is 2km from the complex.

### THE DRIVE
It's only 2km northwest on the L29 to the beachy pleasures of Binz.

## 14 BINZ

Rügen's largest and most-celebrated seaside resort, Binz is an alluring confection of ornate, white Victorian-era villas, white sand and blue water. Its roads are signposted in Gothic script and lined with coastal pines and chestnut trees. Even if all the signs of 21st-century capitalism abound, especially along jam-packed Hauptstrasse, you can still feel the pull of history amid the modern-day crowds.

A highlight of Binz is simply strolling its 4km-long north–south **Strandpromenade**, lined with elegant villas. At the southern end of the built-up area, you'll find the palatial **Kurhaus**, a lovely-looking 1908 building containing a luxury hotel. In front of it is the long pier. Strandpromenade continues further south from here, and becomes markedly less busy. Join the mobs and stop frequently for ice creams.

---

### The Hanseatic League

The legacy of the Hanseatic League lives on in many of the towns and cities on this route, including Lübeck, Wismar, Stralsund, Greifswald and more. Its origins go back to various guilds and associations established from about the mid-12th century by out-of-town merchants to protect their interests. After Hamburg and Lübeck signed an agreement in 1241 to protect their ships and trading routes, they were joined in their league by Lüneburg, Kiel and a string of Baltic Sea cities east to Greifswald. By 1356 this had grown into the Hanseatic League, encompassing half a dozen other large alliances of cities, with Lübeck playing the lead role.

At its zenith, the league had about 200 member cities. It earned a say in the choice of Danish kings after fighting two wars against the Danes between 1361 and 1369. The resulting Treaty of Stralsund in 1370 turned it into northern Europe's most powerful economic and political entity. Some 70 inland and coastal cities – mostly German – formed the core of the Hanseatic League, but another 130 beyond the Reich maintained a loose association, making it truly international. During a period of endless feudal squabbles in Germany, it was a bastion of political and social stability.

By the 15th century, however, competition from Dutch and English shipping companies, internal disputes and a shift in the centre of world trade from the North and Baltic Seas to the Atlantic had caused decline. The ruin and chaos of the Thirty Years' War in the 17th century delivered the final blow, although Hamburg, Bremen and Lübeck retained the 'Hanse City' title. Since reunification, however, well over a dozen cities have decided to adopt the title once again.

# 02
# Design for Life: Bauhaus to VW

**BEST FOR FAMILIES**
Wolfsburg's fun museums delight young and old.

| DURATION | DISTANCE | GREAT FOR |
|---|---|---|
| 2–4 days | 487km / 304 miles | History & families |

| BEST TIME TO GO | Long days and clear skies from May to September mean bonus hours. |
|---|---|

AutoMuseum, Wolfsburg (p32)

Fans of modern architecture, design and technology will find this easy, engaging trip hard to resist. You'll take in the history of the Bauhaus movement in Dessau-Rosslau, where it all took off, get a taste of German Art Deco and quirky Austrian architect Hundertwasser's off-the-wall ideas in Magdeburg, explore the world's first modern factory in Alfeld, and delve into German automotive genius, firsthand, in Wolfsburg.

### Link Your Trip

**05 Central Germany's Castles & Palaces**

Fancy some medieval with your modern? From Weimar, take our castles and palaces trip, too.

**09 North Sea Coast**

If you do like to be beside the seaside, follow the autobahn for 130km northwest from Hanover to Bremen for this nautical jaunt.

### 01 WEIMAR

Weimar is best known as the stomping ground for cultural heavyweights Goethe and Schiller, and its post-WWI dalliance with international fame as the place where the constitution of the German Reich (the Weimar Republic) was drafted. Weimar is teeming with historical sights and museums, and is home to the **Bauhaus Museum** (klassik-stiftung.de), which is why you're here. Although the movement did most of its work from Dessau-Rosslau, it was founded here by Walter Gropius in 1919. The tiny **Haus am Horn** (hausamhorn.de) is the only remaining Bauhaus structure in Weimar,

### THE DRIVE
Follow the B184 through farms and rapeseed fields for 63km, into Magdeburg.

### Detour
**Wörlitz Park & Schloss Wörlitz**
Start: 02 Dessau-Rosslau

The 112-hectare **Wörlitz Park & Schloss Wörlitz** (woerlitz-information.de) is the pinnacle of Prince Leopold III's so-named Gartenreich Dessau-Wörlitz (Garden Realm), one of the finest garden ensembles in Germany. A visit, to contemplate Bauhaus in contrast to the culture from which it emerged, is highly recommended. Allow at least a half-day including travel time to appreciate the beauty on display. To get here from Dessau-Rosslau, take the B185 east until the junction with the L133. Follow the L133 for 14.5km until you reach the park.

There are five other parks belonging to the Gartenreich Dessau-Wörlitz: Oranienbaum, Luisium, Georgium, Mosigkau and Grosskühnau. Scattered over 142 sq km, each comes with its own palace and other buildings, in styles ranging from neoclassical to neo-Gothic, and reflects the vision of Prince Leopold III Friedrich Franz von Anhalt-Dessau (1740–1817). A highly educated man, he travelled to the Netherlands, Italy, France and Switzerland, gaining inspiration to apply the philosophy of the Enlightenment to the design of a landscape that would create a harmony of nature, architecture and art.

The gardens were added to UNESCO's World Heritage list in 2000 and are protected under the Biosphärenreservat Mittelelbe (mittelelbe.com). All parks are free and can be roamed during daylight hours, but the palaces charge admission and have their own opening hours.

but the fascinating Art Nouveau **Haus Hohe Pappeln** (klassik-stiftung.de) predates the movement and is considered a pioneer of modernity.

### THE DRIVE
Take the B7 for 7.5km east to the village of Umpferstedt, where you'll pick up the B87, heading north. Follow the B87 for 50km as it winds through fields and forests to the pretty Saale River township of Naumburg: a nice place to stop. Take the B180 east for 14km to the A9 autobahn for the remaining 90km north into **Dessau-Rosslau**.

### 02 DESSAU-ROSSLAU
Welcome to the hub of Bauhaus, the most influential design school of the 20th century, which gave us the mantras 'less is more' and 'form follows function'. Nowhere else will you find a greater concentration of structures from Bauhaus' most creative period, 1925 to 1932. If you're a student of architecture or design, you might not want to leave. Pick up a tour at the epicentre of activity, the **Bauhausgebäude** (Bauhaus Building; bauhaus-dessau.de), erected in 1925–26 as the school of Bauhaus art, design and architecture. Next, check out the **Meisterhäuser** (Masters' Houses; bauhaus-dessau.de) where the likes of Kandinsky and Gropius once lived. Proceed to the 300-plus homes of the **Törten Estate**, prototype of the first-ever housing estate. To complete the experience, why not spend the night?

### 03 MAGDEBURG

Few people could deny that Magdeburg is aesthetically challenged, thanks to WWII bombs and socialist city planners in love with sparse boulevards and prefab concrete apartment blocks (the so-called Plattenbauten). Yet this is one of the country's oldest cities, founded some 1200 years ago, and its imposing **Dom** (magdeburger dom.de) is the first Gothic cathedral on German soil. The reason you're here, however, is the love-it-or-hate-it, whimsical **Grüne Zitadelle** (Green Citadel; gruene-zitadelle.de), the last building of eccentric artist-architect Friedensreich Hundertwasser. For a little more architectural contrast, stop to admire the ornately detailed dark-green walls of **Die Saison** (herrenkrug.de), or dine alfresco and admire the hotel's handsome Art Deco facade and immaculate gardens.

#### THE DRIVE
Follow the B71 north for 10km, then pick up the A2 autobahn at exit 69 Magdeburg-Kannenstieg. It's 69km of autobahn action until exit 58 Kreuz Wolfsburg/Königslutter, before heading north for 15km on the A39 into Wolfsburg.

### 04 WOLFSBURG

Volkswagen is the world's second-largest vehicle manufacturer, and its global headquarters employ about 40% of Wolfsburg's residents: you can't miss the massive VW emblem on the side of the textbook post-war factory building. Designed by Ferdinand Porsche under Hitler's orders, the Volkswagen Beetle (or 'People's Car') influenced the auto-mobile industry in much the same way as the Bauhaus movement influenced architecture. Of Wolfsburg's numerous shiny state-of-the-art museums, loved by adults and kids alike, you'll want to check out Volkswagen's own **AutoMuseum** (automuseum-volkswagen.de), or the big draw for rev-heads, **Autostadt** (Car City; autostadt.de), a celebration of all things automobile spread across 25 hectares. To see where design and science meet, head straight to the informative and engaging **Phaeno** (phaeno.de), or swap your smarts for the arty side of modern design at the **Kunstmuseum** (Art Museum; kunstmuseum-wolfsburg.de).

#### THE DRIVE
Follow the A39 south for 76km to exit 65 Bockenem. Take the B243 north to the tiny village of Nette, then scoot west on the L493 for 6km to another tiny village, Bodenburg. Drive the less than 1km across town to pick up the L490, which winds through picturesque hills and fields for 17km to the town of Alfeld. Your next stop, Fagus Werk, is clearly signposted.

### 05 ALFELD

Designed and built by Bauhaus founder Walter Gropius in 1911, the **Fagus Werk** (Fagus Factory; fagus-werk.com) has been producing shoe lasts – the basic moulds around which shoes are made – for over a century. It's regarded as the first building in the world to conform to the modern architectural style and is the last Bauhaus stop on your pilgrimage. Given UNESCO World Heritage status in 2011, sections of the building have been turned into a gallery which focuses on Gropius' life, the Bauhaus movement, the history of the Fagus company and footwear in general. Guided factory tours are recommended.

#### THE DRIVE
The B3 runs north for 45km where it merges with the B6 and proceeds for 5km into the heart of Hanover.

### 06 HANOVER

Capital of the state of Lower Saxony, Hanover has a wealth of cultural attractions, pretty parks and plenty of top-notch nosh. Few realise that from 1714, monarchs from the house of Hanover also ruled the entire British Empire, for over a century. In a cruel irony, extensive Allied bombing in 1943 wiped out much of Hanover's rich architectural and cultural heritage. But there are a few highlights to round out your trip. The **Neues Rathaus**, completed in 1913, features a curved lift – the only one of its kind in the world – that travels 98m to four observation platforms offering panoramic views. For something completely different architecturally, the 1979 **Sprengel Museum** (sprengelmuseum.com) houses one of Germany's finest art collections. Complete your visit with a stroll through the grandiose, baroque **Herrenhäuser Gärten** (herrenhaeuser-gaerten.de), the city's pride and joy.

**Photo Opportunity**
Design-heads' Holy Grail: Bauhausgebäude signage.

# 03

## Lakes & Treasures of Mecklenburg–Western Pomerania

**BEST FOR FAMILIES**

Exploring Schwerin's lakes and gardens on a family bike ride.

| DURATION | DISTANCE | GREAT FOR |
|---|---|---|
| 2–3 days | 387km / 240 miles | History, nature & families |

| BEST TIME TO GO | May to October, the beautiful forests and lakes are at their best. |
|---|---|

Biking, Schwerin

During the 15th century, the dukes of Mecklenburg–Western Pomerania built palaces across the lake-strewn plains of Germany's north so they could luxuriate in their wealth. Get a taste of their coddled lives, while you also taste the hearty fare of the north at the many excellent restaurants and cafes. Walk it off in the ancient and fabled beech forests of Müritz National Park.

### Link Your Trip

**01 Along the Baltic Coast**
This trip ends in Greifswald where you can join the coastal trip.

**10 German Fairy Tale Road**
From Lüneburg it's only 141km on the A39 and A1 to Bremen in the west, where you can plunge into the world of the Brothers Grimm.

**01** ### LÜNEBURG
An off-kilter church steeple, buildings leaning on each other and houses with swollen 'beer-belly' facades: in parts it looks like the charming town of Lüneburg has drunk too much of the pilsner lager it used to brew. Of course, the city's wobbly angles and uneven pavements have a more prosaic cause: shifting ground and subsidence due to salt mining has caused many buildings to tilt sideways.

The medieval **Rathaus** (Town Hall) on the **Markt** has a spectacular baroque facade, added in 1720

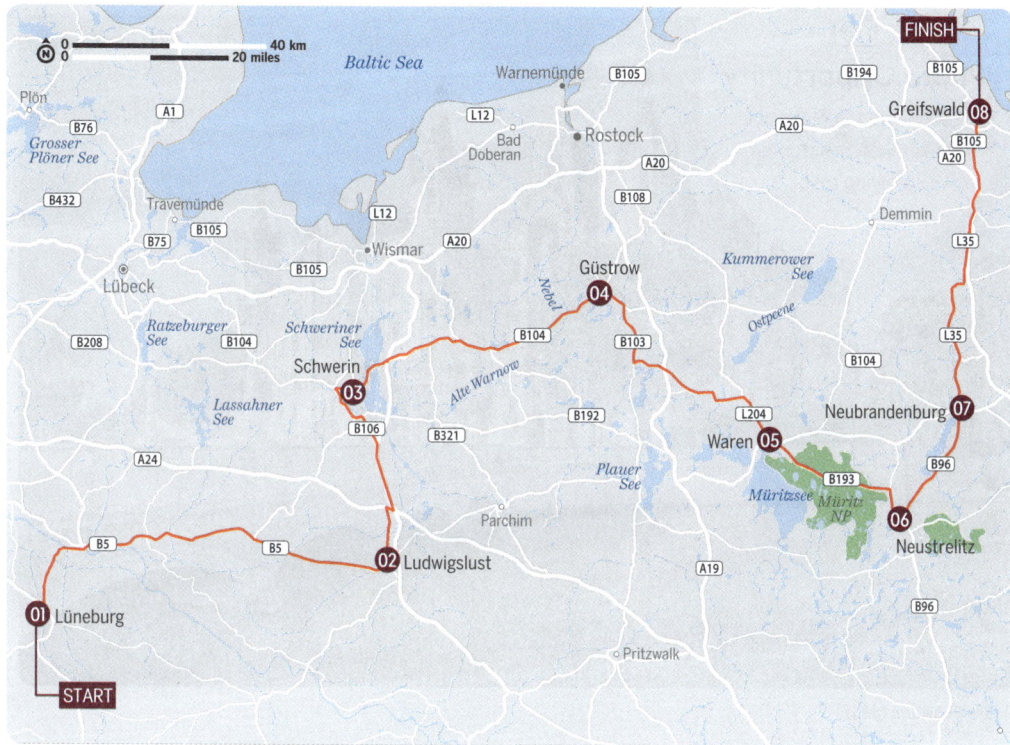

and decorated with coats of arms and three tiers of statues. The top row represents (from left to right) Strength, Trade, Peace (the one with the staff), Justice and Moderation.

The cobbled, slightly wobbly street and square **Am Sande** is full of red-brick buildings with typically Hanseatic stepped gables.

### THE DRIVE
Take the B5 north and east 89km to Ludwigslust. At 20km watch for the crossing of the historic Elbe River, which flows towards Hamburg.

## 02 LUDWIGSLUST
Such was the allure of the grand palace, **Schloss Ludwigslust** (schloss-ludwigslust.de), that when the ducal seat moved 36km north to Schwerin in 1837, some family members continued living here until 1945. Now part of the Schwerin State Museum, its high point is the stately, gilt-columned, high-ceilinged Golden Hall.

A planned baroque town, Ludwigslust showcases a neat, orderly layout that is an attraction in itself.

### THE DRIVE
Go straight north for 38km on the B106. As you near Schwerin, you'll start to see some of the lakes that make the district famous, like the Ostorfer See, Fauler See and Schweriner See.

## 03 SCHWERIN
Picturesquely sited around seven lakes (possibly more, depending how you tally them), Schwerin is the unofficial capital of the lakes district. The centrepiece of this engaging city is its **Schloss** (schloss-schwerin.de), a castle built in the 14th century during the city's six centuries as the former seat of the Grand Duchy of Mecklenburg. It's an appealing mishmash of architectural styles and is crowned by a gleaming golden dome. Nowadays the Schloss earns its keep as the state's parliament building. Crossing the causeway south from the palace-surrounding **Burggarten** brings you to the baroque **Schlossgarten** (Palace Garden), intersected by several canals.

Schwerin has an upbeat, vibrant energy on its restored streets that befits its role as the capital of Mecklenburg–Western

### Photo Opportunity
Schwerin's Schloss at dawn, with the stones glowing rose.

**Schloss Schwerin (p35)**

Pomerania. Cafes, interesting shops and flashes of its regal past make wandering the **Altstadt** (old town) a delight. The bustling **Markt** is home to the Rathaus and the colonnaded neoclassical Neues Gebäude (1780–83).

Schwerin's central lake, the **Pfaffentiech**, was created by a dam in the 12th century. Through the centuries it was surrounded by some of the city's most elegant buildings. At the southwest corner, the vividly orange **Arsenal** dates from 1840. You can cross the waters on a small **ferry**.

**THE DRIVE**
Drive directly east for 63km on the B104. As you go, the land becomes increasingly moist, with rivers and tiny lakes appearing in profusion.

**04 GÜSTROW**
This charming town is over 775 years old and is a great place to explore on foot. The fabulous Renaissance 16th-century **Schloss Güstrow** (schloss-guestrow.de) is home to a historical museum, luxe rooms and formal **gardens**.

Built between 1226 and 1335, the richly ornamented Gothic **Güstrow Dom** (dom-guestrow.de) is an old-town highlight.

Famed 20th-century sculptor Ernst Barlach spent most of his working life in Güstrow. You can view his deeply felt, humanist works in the **Gertrudenkapelle** and at the **Atelierhaus** (barlach-museen.de).

**THE DRIVE**
Drive due south for 20km on the B103. At Krakow-am-See (and its large lake) turn southeast for 14km on the L204, then continue east for another 14km on the Kastanienallee to the B108, which you take southeast to Waren.

**05 WAREN**
Right on the sparkling blue waters of **Lake Müritz**, Waren is a lovely village and one of the more popular in the lakes region. You can stroll streets lined with half-timbered buildings, poke in and out of churches and best of all, relax at a waterfront cafe while you watch small sailboats darting past. Large-scale renovation schemes have restored much of the 16th-century feel to the town. Should the waters beckon, there are several places where you can rent a kayak or small boat to

explore the chain of lakes that includes the **Tiefwarensee** and the **Kölpinsee**.

 **THE DRIVE**
Leave Waren on Kargower Weg and plunge right into the heart of the Müritz National Park. Drive for 32km following the signs for Neustrelitz via Kratzeburg, then turn south for 10km on the B193.

## 06 NEUSTRELITZ

Situated on the Zierker See within the national park, the pretty, planned baroque town of Neustrelitz centres on its circular **Markt**, from which streets radiate like the spokes of a wheel.

The town's Schloss fell victim to WWII damage, but its beautiful **Schlossgarten** retains its 18th-century orangery (with a restaurant open Tuesday to Sunday May to September), and hosts the **Schlossgartenfestspiele**, a series of classical music and other concerts in summer.

The **national park office** (mueritz-nationalpark.de) is a good stop as it has a lot of information on the lakes, forests and park in English. Fish plucked fresh from the lake is the highlight at simple restaurants along the shore, near the centre.

 **THE DRIVE**
For more than half your 31km drive on the B96 to Neubrandenburg, you'll be passing by a beautiful lake, the Tollensesee.

## 07 NEUBRANDENBURG

Neubrandenburg bills itself as 'the city of four gates on the Tollensesee Lake', and you'll see why during this enjoyable stop. A largely intact medieval **wall**, with those gates, encircles the city, which was founded in 1248. Made of stone,

the wall is 2.3km in circumference and averages 7.5m in height. To navigate it, consider the wall as the rim of a clock face, with the train station at 12 o'clock.

The **Friedländer Tor** (two o'clock), begun in 1300 and completed in 1450, was the first gate. **Treptower Tor** (nine o'clock) is the largest and contains an archaeological collection. At the southern end of the city is the gaudy **Stargarder Tor** (six o'clock). The simple brick **Neues Tor** (three o'clock) fronts the east side of the Altstadt. Southwest of the train station is the city's former dungeon, the **Fangelturm** (11 o'clock). You'll recognise it by its pointy tower.

Wedged into the stone circumference are the 27 sweet half-timbered houses, the remains of the original sentry posts. Most of the surviving homes are now craft shops, galleries and cafes.

 **THE DRIVE**
Fertile fields keep the view from your car green as you go 65km straight north on the L35 to Greifswald.

## 08 GREIFSWALD

The old university town of Greifswald, south of Stralsund, was largely unscathed by WWII thanks to a courageous German colonel who surrendered to Soviet troops (a move usually punishable by execution).

This former Hanseatic city is small and easy to explore on foot. Start at the **Markt** and be sure to see its three famous churches: the 'Langer Nikolas' (Long Nicholas), 'Dicke Marie' (Fat Mary) and the 'Kleine Jakob' (Small Jacob).

Trade the fresh water encountered on this drive for the salt variety with a visit to Greifswald's pretty harbour in the charming district of **Wieck**, reached by a Dutch-style wooden drawbridge; its medieval city walls have been turned into a wide, tree-shaded promenade. If forsaking the car, it's easily reached via a 5km foot/bike path. More paths follow the pretty and sinuous waterfront.

---

### Müritz National Park

Müritz is commonly known as the land of a thousand lakes. While that's an exaggeration, there are well over 100 lakes here, as well as countless ponds, streams and rivers in this beautiful area midway between Berlin and Rostock.

The serene **Müritz National Park** (mueritz-nationalpark.de) consists of bog and wetlands, and is home to a wide range of waterfowl, including ospreys, white-tailed eagles and cranes. Its two main sections sprawl over 300 sq km to the east and (mainly) west of Neustrelitz, where the park's waterway begins on the Zierker See. Boardwalks and other features let you get close to nature.

The country roads between Waren and Neustrelitz cut through the heart of the park and offer plenty of places to stop and admire the UNESCO-recognised **beech forests**.

# 04
# Highlights of Saxony

**BEST FOR HISTORY**

The silhouette of the magnificently rebuilt Altstadt in Dresden.

| DURATION | DISTANCE | GREAT FOR |
|---|---|---|
| 5-7 days | 241km / 134 miles | History & nature |

| BEST TIME TO GO | April to October for warmer hiking weather. |
|---|---|

Altstadt, Dresden (p42)

On this unforgettable journey through the state of Saxony, you'll see castles and fortresses, one of Germany's great rivers, impossibly shaped sandstone mountains, and several magical baroque cities and palaces along the way. These extraordinary landscapes then give way to magnificent Dresden, the 'Florence of the North', then to charming cool-kid Leipzig, one-time home to Bach and Wagner but long touted as the 'New Berlin'.

### Link Your Trip

**03 Lakes & Treasures of Mecklenburg-Western Pomerania**

From Leipzig, take the A14 and then the B71 northwest for 300km to Lüneburg for this verdant slice of northeastern Germany.

**06 Berlin & the Jewels of Eastern Brandenburg**

From Dresden, take the A13 north for the 103km drive to Lübbenau to discover this fascinating and multifaceted region.

### 01 GÖRLITZ

This border town (half of which, on the other side of the Neisse River, became Polish territory after WWII), is an utter beauty and easily one of Saxony's most charming cities. Having miraculously survived the war intact, Görlitz has been used on numerous occasions as the backdrop to several Hollywood movies, and one look at its skyline of medieval towers and baroque churches will tell you why. The **Reichenbacher Turm** (goerlitzer-sammlungen.de) and the interesting **Barockhaus** (goerlitzer-sammlungen.de) are the two most obvious sights, but nearly all visitors simply enjoy strolling

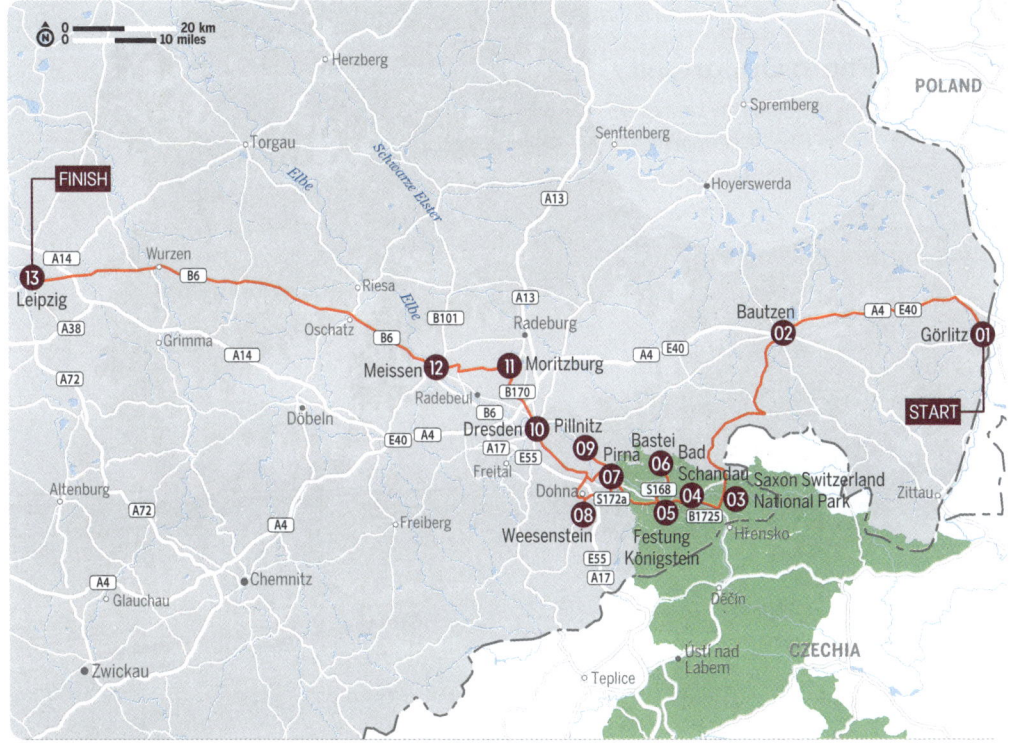

around. In the last decade Görlitz has grown enormously as a weekend destination and consequently has some excellent restaurants and accommodation options.

### 🚗 THE DRIVE
It's an easy 50km drive due west out of Görlitz along the A4/E40 directly to Bautzen.

### 02 BAUTZEN
Quirky Bautzen has an attractive cobblestone old town surrounding a fairy tale castle and attracts visitors for three main, rather diverse reasons. It's home to the Sorbian people, an ethnic minority within Germany that has its own Slavic language and very distinct cultural identity – best explored at the **Sorbisches Museum** (sorbisches-museum.de). It's also where you'll find Germany's most famous brand of mustard (and on top of numerous mustard shops, there's also an all-mustard restaurant to try). Finally, Bautzen has two prisons – one of them still operational today. The other, which is now closed but previously hosted political prisoners under the Nazi and communist governments, is the focus of a compelling **Gedenkstätte** (gedenkstaette-bautzen.de), or memorial museum.

### 🚗 THE DRIVE
Take the picturesque S154 through Neustadt towards the gorgeous scenery of the Saxon Switzerland National Park.

### 03 SAXON SWITZERLAND NATIONAL PARK
Saxony may only have one national park, but Saxon Switzerland is a real stunner. There is an enormous number of hiking and climbing opportunities here, including some 700 peaks to climb and 400 sq km of hiking routes. The entire place is simply stunning, with ethereal sandstone formations that look quite unlike anything else in Europe. It's best to park outside the park itself then take public transport into it, in particular the solar-powered **Kirnitzschtalbahn** (ovps.de) which runs from Bad Schandau to Beutenfall along the Kirnitzsch River.

### 🚗 THE DRIVE
From the national park, take the B172 from Schmilka to Bad Schandau, a gorgeous 8km drive that runs along the banks of the Elbe with mountains visible on both sides.

BEST ROAD TRIPS: GERMANY, AUSTRIA & SWITZERLAND   39

### 04 BAD SCHANDAU

The charming 'capital' of Saxon Switzerland, this friendly little town is a good place to bed down for the night after a day of walking in the national park. There's a wonderful early 20th-century lift, the **Personenaufzug**, which takes you to the town's highest point for some breathtaking views. Hikers should not miss the glorious trek to the **Schrammsteinaussicht**, a moderate-to-strenuous trail that leads to a fantastic viewpoint of the rocks, the Elbe Valley and national park beyond. The first 20 minutes up the steep **Obrigensteig** are tough but then the trail levels out and leads through fabulous rock formations. The final 'ascent' is straight up the rocks via a one-way network of steel stairs and ladders.

 **THE DRIVE**
Leaving Bad Schandau, cross the Elbe at the bridge outside of town and continue along the B172 to Königstein. This charming small town is a good spot to stop for breakfast or lunch before continuing up to the famous Königstein Fortress high above the town. Park in the car park and walk five minutes to the fortress entrance.

### 05 FESTUNG KÖNIGSTEIN

**Festung Königstein** (festung-koenigstein.de) is the largest intact fortress in Germany, and so imposing and formidable that no one in history has ever even bothered to attack it, let alone managed to conquer it. Begun in the 13th century, it was repeatedly enlarged and is now a veritable textbook in military architecture, with 30 buildings spread across 9.5 hectares. Inside, the main highlight is the **In Lapide Regis**, a superb permanent exhibition that tells the dramatic story of the fortress in an engaging and interactive way.

 **THE DRIVE**
Drive back down into the valley along the S168 and in a couple of kilometres you'll come to Rathen. Park in the car park here and take the ferry across the Elbe.

### 06 BASTEI

The resort town of Rathen, in the northwestern corner of the national park, is the access point for the Bastei, the most famous rock formations in the Elbe Valley, and also the most popular spot in the park to visit. It's an easy and gentle hike up to the magnificent **Felsenburg Neurathen**, a partly reconstructed medieval castle in the Bastei, from which there are numerous lookouts and viewpoints, including a stunning panorama over the Elbe hundreds of metres below. The much-photographed Basteibrücke, a sandstone bridge built in 1851, leads through the rocks, though this is the busiest part of the park. Try taking the 5km loop back to Rathen to escape the crowds.

 **THE DRIVE**
After returning to Rathen, where there are numerous spots for a meal, cross the Elbe again to get back to your car, then take the S168 to Pirna. It's a short drive through some lovely countryside.

### 07 PIRNA

Pirna is a charming town on the Elbe, famous as Canaletto's home during his years in Saxony, and a friendly and easy-going place today. The big attraction in town is the excellent **DDR Museum** (ddr-museum-pirna.de), in a former army barracks on the outskirts of town. You can wander around a fully furnished East German apartment, sit in a classroom with GDR president Walter Ulbricht glowering at you, or find out how much a Junge Pioniere youth organisation uniform cost.

 **THE DRIVE**
It's just 10km along the B172a to Weesenstein, and a lovely drive that wends its way between valleys along the river.

### 08 WEESENSTEIN

With its gorgeous setting towering above the valley, **Schloss Weesenstein** (schloss-weesenstein.de) has an unforgettable setting and looks as fairy tale perfect as can be. The castle itself is an amazing alchemy of styles, blending medieval roots with Renaissance and baroque embellishments. This resulted in an architectural curiosity where the banquet halls ended up beneath the roof, the horse stables on the 5th floor and the residential quarters in the cellar. There's lots to see inside, with an entire wing of the castle still filled with furniture and an exhibition on life here over the centuries. There's also a wonderful formal garden to explore.

 **THE DRIVE**
Take the B172a then cross the Elbe at Pirna and follow the signs to Pillnitz. The drive should take around 15 minutes and the views while crossing the river are superb.

### 09 PILLNITZ

Right on the banks of the Elbe, **Schloss & Park Pillnitz** (schlosspillnitz.de) is a delightful baroque pleasure palace festooned with fanciful Chinese flourishes. This is where

Viewpoint, Felsenburg Neurathen

## Dresden & WWII

Between 13 and 15 February 1945, British and US planes unleashed 3900 tonnes of explosives on Dresden in four huge air raids. Bombs and incendiary shells whipped up a mammoth firestorm, and ashes rained down on villages 35km away. Historians still argue over whether or not this constituted a war crime committed by the Allies on an innocent civilian population. Some claim that with the Red Army at the gates of Berlin, the war was effectively won, and the Allies gained little military advantage from the destruction of Dresden. Others have said that as the last urban centre in the east of the country left intact, Dresden could have provided shelter for German troops returning from the east and was a viable target. What's undeniable though, is that when the blazes had died down and the dust settled, tens of thousands of Dresdners had lost their lives and 20 sq km of this once-elegant baroque city lay in smouldering ruins.

### THE DRIVE
Take the Pillnitzer Landstrasse from the palace towards Dresden. It's a half-hour, 14km journey that in parts runs along the Elbe's edge. Cross the river at Loschwitz and follow signs for Dresden's Altstadt.

### 10 DRESDEN
There are few city silhouettes more striking than Dresden's. The classic view from the Elbe's northern bank takes in spires, towers and domes belonging to palaces, churches and stately buildings, and indeed it's hard to believe that the city was all but wiped off the map by Allied air raids in 1945. There's an enormous amount to see in the relatively small area that makes up Dresden's **Altstadt** (old town). First on the list should be the **Zwinger** (der-dresdner-zwinger.de), the incredible pleasure palace of the Saxon electors, which now contains three superb museums. Next up, visit the **Residenzschloss** (skd.museum), the seat of power of the Saxon electors and now the setting for several impressive museums, the most important of which is the **Historisches Grünes Gewölbe** (Historic Green Vault; skd.museum), which displays some 3000 precious items on shelves and tables (without glass protection) in a series of increasingly lavish rooms. Finally, be sure not to miss the famous **Frauenkirche** (frauenkirche-dresden.de), which graced the Dresden skyline for two centuries before collapsing after the February 1945 bombings. It was rebuilt from a pile of rubble between 1994 and 2005, and is now Dresden's most enduring symbol.

the Saxon rulers once lived it up during long, hot Dresden summers. Explore the wonderful formal gardens, then learn about the history of the palace and life at court in the Schloss museum inside the palace itself. Two other buildings, the **Wasserpalais** and the **Bergpalais**, house the **Kunstgewerbemuseum**, which is filled with various valuables from the Saxon court, including Augustus the Strong's throne.

### THE DRIVE
Take the B170 for 16km to reach Moritzburg. It's a picturesque drive through some charming countryside. Park in the car park in the centre of the village and you'll see the castle in the distance ahead of you.

### 11 MORITZBURG
**Schloss Moritzburg** (schloss-moritzburg.de;) is the third of the famous palaces surrounding Dresden, but in many ways it's the most impressive, set in the middle of an enormous lake that doubles as a moat, and standing magnificently overlooking a huge park. It was the preferred hunting palace of the Saxon rulers, and its interiors are dominated by hundreds of framed antlers, which are quite a sight to behold in the sumptuous state rooms. Prized trophies include the antlers of an extinct giant stag and bizarrely misshapen ones in the **Hall of Monstrosities**. Considerably prettier is the legendary **Federzimmer** (Feather Room) downstairs, whose centrepiece is a bed made from over a million colourful duck, pheasant and peacock feathers. A walk through the gorgeous formal gardens and then through the wilder, forested park around the ornamental lake will return you to the car park.

### THE DRIVE
It's an easy 16km drive to Meissen along Köhlerstrasse.

### 12 MEISSEN
Straddling the Elbe around 25km upstream from Dresden, Meissen is the cradle of European porcelain manufacturing and still hitches its tourism appeal to the world-famous china first cooked up in its imposing castle in 1710. But even those left unmoved by August the

**Leipzig**

Strong's 'white gold' will find the impressive position of the town, dominated by its soaring Gothic cathedral, impressive fairy tale castle and wonderful Elbe valley views, quite compelling. Most visitors will want to head straight up the hillside to glorious **Albrechtsburg** (albrechtsburg-meissen.de), Meissen's enormous castle. After a stroll through the delightful old town, end the day with a visit to the superb **Erlebniswelt Haus Meissen** (erlebniswelt-meissen.com), the place to witness the astonishing artistry that makes Meissen porcelain unique.

### THE DRIVE
Head out of Meissen and take the B6, a pleasant alternative to the motorway, directly to Leipzig. The drive is 88km and takes 1½ hours.

### 13 LEIPZIG
The final destination on this trip is Leipzig, a fascinating combination of cultural powerhouse and contemporary creative hothouse. Head to the storied Altstadt to explore the city's dramatic past, from the choir once led by Bach, which still goes strong at the **Thomaskirche** (thomaskirche.org), to the chilling **Stasi Museum** (runde-ecke-leipzig.de) and the first-class **Zeitgeschichtliches Forum** (Forum of Contemporary History; hdg.de/leipzig), which gives a detailed account of the creation and collapse of East Germany. Another museum not to miss is the excellent **Museum der Bildenden Künste** (Museum of Fine Arts; mdbk.de), a first-class art collection in an amazing building. Visit the famous **Oper Leipzig** (oper-leipzig.de) or see the **Thomanerchor** (thomaskirche.org) perform, before discovering Leipzig's relaxed nightlife and contemporary art and music scenes in the student-creative neighbourhoods of the Südvorstadt and Plagwitz. Stroll down Karli, the main street of the Südvorstadt, or Karl-Heine-Strasse, Plagwitz' main thoroughfare, both of which are packed with bars, restaurants, cafes and clubs. Finally, don't miss the amazing **Völkerschlachtdenkmal** (Monument to the Battle of the Nations; stadtgeschichtliches-museum-leipzig.de), the mother of all war monuments.

# 05
# Central Germany's Castles & Palaces

**BEST FOR FOODIES**

Dine in classic style at Weimar's romantic AnnA.

| DURATION | DISTANCE | GREAT FOR |
|---|---|---|
| 3–5 days | 305km / 224 miles | History & nature |

| BEST TIME TO GO | May to September has crisp, clear skies and luminous rapeseed fields. |
|---|---|

Schloss Neuenburg, Freyburg

Journey into the historical and geographical heartland of Germany, where cultural titans Goethe and Schiller once deliberated. You'll pass through ancient forests and villages, alongside sparkling rivers and working farms to visit spectacular castles and palaces in medieval, Renaissance, baroque and rococo styles. The magnificent Wartburg castle, inspiration for Ludwig II's famous Neuschwanstein, is one of Germany's finest.

## Link Your Trip

**02 Design for Life: Bauhaus to VW**
Have some Bauhaus with your baroque, on this exploration of modern German design and architecture that begins in Weimar.

**10 German Fairy Tale Road**
Delve into the world of the Brothers Grimm in Kassel, heading north or south along Germany's beloved Fairy Tale Road.

## 01 LEIPZIG

Leipzig could well be Germany's 'it' city, a playground for nomadic young creatives displaced by the fast-gentrifying German capital, but it's also a city of enormous history, set solidly in the sights of music lovers due to an intrinsic connection to the lives and works of Bach, Mendelssohn and Wagner. There's much to see and do here. At the very least, you'll want to check out the enormous art collection of Museum der Bildenden Künste in its modernist glass cube home (for a little architectural contrast), and get an overview of this rapidly changing city in the **Stadtgeschichtliches Museum** (City History Museum; stadtgeschichtliches-museum-leipzig.de), housed in Leipzig's beautiful Renaissance town hall.

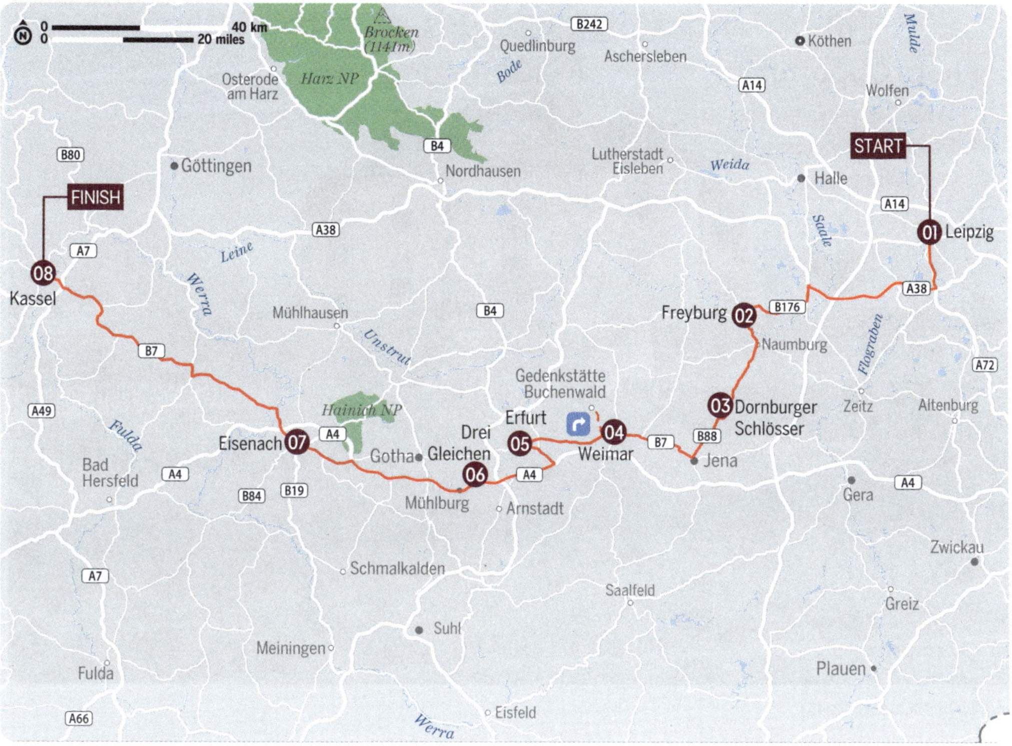

### 🚗 THE DRIVE
Take the B2 south out of Leipzig until you reach the A38 at exit 31, for some 33km of autobahn action west to exit 26. Head south on the B91 until the junction with the B176 outside Burgwerben. Follow the B176 west for 17km until you reach a roundabout: head straight through then turn left on Merseburger Strasse into Freyburg.

### 02 FREYBURG
With its cobblestone streets and medieval castle clinging to vine-covered slopes, Freyburg puts the 'r' in rustic. Sparkling-wine production has been the town's focus since the mid-19th century. Pop into **Rotkäppchen Sektkellerei** (rotkaeppchen.de) to toast the start of your trip with a glass of Germany's best-known home-grown bubbles, then head to the imposing medieval **Schloss Neuenburg** (schloss-neuenburg.de), on the hill above town. There's an excellent museum, a rare Romanesque two-storey chapel and a free-standing tower, the Dicker Wilhelm, with splendid views over the Saale River valley. It's possible to spend the night in one of two charming apartments within the castle walls: book ahead if this tickles your fancy.

### 🚗 THE DRIVE
Take the B180 south for 11km to the pretty town of Naumburg. Pick up the B88 for 15km until it meets the Saale River at Camburg. Cross the bridge and follow the scenic L1059 for 9km until you reach a tiny hamlet belonging to Saaleplatte village, where you'll drop south along Wilsdorfer Strasser for 5km to Dornburg.

### 03 DORNBURGER SCHLÖSSER
There are few places in the world where you can get a snapshot of three distinct historical periods, side by side. The **Dornburger Schlösser** (dornburg-schloesser.de) is one – a hillside trilogy of superbly restored palaces in medieval,

### Photo Opportunity
The Saale River valley from Dornburger Schlösser's clifftop perch.

**Dornburger Schlösser (p45)**

Renaissance and rococo styles, with stunning views and immaculate gardens. The **Altes Schloss**, the oldest, blends Romanesque, late-Gothic and baroque elements but can only be viewed from the outside. You can enter both the 1539 **Renaissance Palace** (where Goethe once stayed) and the gorgeous **Rococo Palace**. It's free to stroll around the magnificent gardens, to enjoy the wonderful views and admire the palaces from the outside.

#### THE DRIVE
Head south on the B88 for 12km through the picturesque Saale valley. The road hugs the river, even meeting for a brief kiss here and there, until it reaches the outskirts of Jena, where you'll pick up the B7 heading west. Follow it for 21km until you reach Weimar.

### 04 WEIMAR
A pantheon of intellectual and creative giants lived and worked in Weimar: historical epicentre of the German Enlightenment. Goethe, Schiller, Bach, Nietzsche and Kandinsky are all memorialised throughout town. History buffs may want to linger here a few days. The **Herzogin Anna Amalia Bibliothek** (klassik-stiftung.de) displays precious tomes in its magnificent Rokokosaal (Rococo Hall), including some once used by several of the aforementioned creators, whose busts and paintings still keep watch over the collection. About 4km south of town, baroque **Schloss Belvedere** (klassik-stiftung.de) is set among manicured grounds and has a museum of artefacts from the 17th and 18th centuries. Complete your visit with a comprehensive overview of Weimar's beloved genius at the **Goethe-Nationalmuseum** (klassik-stiftung.de).

#### THE DRIVE
Take the B7 west through fields of rapeseed and wind turbines for 22km, directly into Erfurt.

#### Detour
**Gedenkstätte Buchenwald**
Start: 04 Weimar

A visit to the sombre **Gedenkstätte Buchenwald** (buchenwald.de) memorial, in the former concentration camp 10km northwest of Weimar, might be the most memorable of your trip. Drive north out of town along Ettersburger Strasse to Blutstrasse and head west. You'll first pass the striking memorial to your left: be sure to approach the massive hillside monument to fully appreciate it. Publications from the museum store explain the symbolic significance of its many elements. Follow the road for 1km into the camp towards the visitor centre, then wander around the numerous intact structures to deepen your understanding of the horrors that played out here. Between 1937 and 1945, hidden from Weimarers and surrounding villagers, some 56,500 of the 250,000 men, women and children who were incarcerated here lost their lives.

### 05 ERFURT
Thuringia's capital is a scene-stealing mix of sweeping squares, cobblestone alleyways, perky church towers, idyllic river scenery and pan-generational architecture. It's a great place to stop for a meal or two and makes a good base if you decide to explore the area over a few days. Perched on the only hill above town, Erfurt's **Zitadelle Petersberg** ranks among Europe's largest and best-preserved baroque fortresses. It sits above a honeycomb of tunnels, which can be explored on guided tours. It's free to roam the external grounds and enjoy the fabulous views.

#### THE DRIVE
Head south on the L1052 for 9km. Pick up the A4 autobahn at exit 47a Erfurt-Ost, heading west in the direction of Frankfurt. Stay on the A4 until you reach exit 43 Wandersleben, then head south into the pretty village of Mühlburg. You'll be able to see Burg Gleichen to the north.

### 06 DREI GLEICHEN
Allow a few hours to enjoy this fascinating medieval stop comprising three similar hilltop castles, collectively known as Drei Gleichen, each within eyesight of the other. North of the autobahn, **Burg Gleichen** (drei-gleichen.de) makes a rewarding visit for castle fans, but it's a 30-minute uphill climb from the car park to the ruins. Of the three castles, **Mühlburg** (drei-gleichen.de) is the oldest and closest, dating to around 704. Its moat walls, drawbridge and 22m-high castle tower are intact. **Veste Wachsenburg** (wachsenburg.com), 10km south of the A4, is fully preserved, housing a hotel, restaurant and museum; it's possible to drive right up to the castle gate.

#### THE DRIVE
Take the A4 autobahn west towards Frankfurt for 36km, to exit 40a Eisenach Ost. From here, follow the signs for Eisenach/Wartburg for another 10km.

### 07 EISENACH
Hilly Eisenach, on the edge of the Thuringian forest, is best known for its UNESCO World Heritage castle **Wartburg** (wartburg-eisenach.de), where Martin Luther hid while his controversial theses brought about the Reformation. This huge, medieval fortress is magnificently preserved, offering much by way of its permanent and visiting exhibitions, intact structure and breathtaking views over little Eisenach, the forest and beyond. Allow at least two hours: one for the guided tour,

the rest for the museum and the views. If you love classical music, you'll also want to take a look at **Bachhaus** (bachhaus.de) and the **Reuter-Wagner Museum**, while rev-heads won't want to miss **Automobile Welt Eisenach** (awe-stiftung.de).

#### THE DRIVE
Head north on Mühlhäuser Strasse for 2km, then pick up the B19 heading west. Follow the B19 north for 5km until the start of the B7. Follow the B7 northwest as it winds through forests, farmlands and pretty villages for 75km towards Kassel.

### 08 KASSEL
Although WWII bombing and postwar reconstruction left Kassel looking undeniably utilitarian, you'd hardly know it today. This culture-rich city on the Fulda River boasts some impressive attractions. The palatial **Schloss Wilhelmshöhe** (museum-kassel.de) contains a premier baroque art collection – time your visit to coincide with the Wednesday and Sunday operation of the spectacular **Herkules** (museum-kassel.de) fountain. Both are within **Bergpark Wilhelmshöhe** (museum-kassel.de), as is the smaller, equally adored **Löwenburg** (Lion Castle; museum-kassel.de) Round out your visit with some fun and fantasy in Kassel's fairy tale **Grimmwelt** (grimmwelt.de), paying homage to the Brothers Grimm. Or make a 10km side trip to **Schloss Wilhelmsthal** (museum-kassel.de), in Calden; almost due north of Wilhelmshöhe, it's one of Germany's finest rococo palaces.

# 06

# Berlin & the Jewels of Eastern Brandenburg

**BEST FOR HISTORY**

The heart-wrenching memorial exhibit at Sachsenhausen concentration camp.

Sachsenhausen (p51)

| DURATION | DISTANCE | GREAT FOR |
|---|---|---|
| 4 days | 366km / 250 miles | History & nature |

| BEST TIME TO GO | Any time is possible, but April to October has better weather. |
|---|---|

This trip gets your head spinning in scintillating Berlin, then slows you back down on a leisurely tour around sparsely populated eastern Brandenburg. You'll meet the Sorbs, a traditional Slavic people at home in the Spreewald, a rivulet-laced fairy tale forest. You'll visit gardens created by an eccentric prince, soul-stirring monasteries, a technological marvel and socialist model cities. WWII comes hauntingly alive in a concentration camp and on the largest battlefield on German soil.

## Link Your Trip

**03 Lakes & Treasures of Mecklenburg–Western Pomerania**

From Berlin, head north on the B96 for 120km to pick up this route in Neustrelitz, through the heart of one of Germany's oldest provinces.

**04 Highlights of Saxony**

From Lübbenau, head 100km south on the A13 to jewel-like Dresden and on to whimsical sandstone formations.

### 01 BERLIN

Your adventure starts in the German capital, an intoxicating cocktail of culture, history, off-beat experiences and nightlife. Tick off sightseeing blockbusters, then devote time to exploring the city's grand museum landscape. A good bet are the five treasure chests on Museum Island, which showcase 6000 years of art and cultural history, including the ethereal 3300-year-old bust of Egyptian Queen Nefertiti at the **Neues Museum** (New Museum; smb.museum), and the radiantly

blue Babylonian Ishtar Gate at the **Pergamonmuseum** (smb. museum). To come to grips with Berlin's division during the Cold War, there's no better place than the **Gedenkstätte Berliner Mauer** (Berlin Wall Memorial; berliner-mauer-gedenkstaette. de), an indoor-outdoor exhibit along 1.4km of the former barrier. To see the longest remaining Wall vestige, head to the mural-festooned **East Side Gallery** (eastsidegallery-berlin.de).

 **THE DRIVE**
From Berlin, it's a quick one-hour drive to Lübbenau via the A100, A113 and A13, where you leave the autobahn at exit 9.

### 02  LÜBBENAU & THE SPREEWALD

Lübbenau is the main town in the Spreewald, a unique ice-age-formed landscape of jungle-like forest and marshland crisscrossed by some 300 channels fed by the Spree River – a German Everglades, if you will, minus the alligators. About 100km southeast of Berlin, this is the traditional homeland of the Sorbs, a Slavic tribe whose members maintain their age-old customs, costumes and language (all signs are bilingual).

Until the first road was built in 1936, Spreewald villages were accessible only by flat-bottomed punt boats. Today, exploring the UNESCO biosphere reserve in a Kahn piloted by a ferryman in traditional garb is a Spreewald must-do. Trips last from one hour to all day and depart from various spots, including the **Grosser Hafen** (grosser-kahnhafen.de). A particularly nice one goes to the Sorb village of Lehde, whose **Freilandmuseum** (Open-Air Museum Lehde; museum-osl.de) gives you a good sense of what rural life in the Spreewald was like a century ago. DIY types can also rent a canoe or kayak, including from **Bootsverleih Richter** (bootsverleih-richter.de).

**THE DRIVE**
The A15 takes you from Lübbenau to Cottbus in 30 minutes. For the scenic drive through Sorb heartland, head south on the L49, turn left on Radduscher Bahnhofstrasse (L51) and follow it via Burg for about 28km to Cottbus.

### 03  COTTBUS

Cottbus has a handsomely restored historic centre but its star attraction is **Park & Schloss Branitz** (puecklermuseum.de) on the southeastern edge of town. The sprawling park-and-palace ensemble was dreamed up by Prince Hermann von Pückler-Muskau, a kooky 19th-century aristocrat, writer, ladies' man and renowned garden architect. For over 20 years, he feverishly turned his ancestral family estate into an Arcadian English-style landscape park by shaping hills, digging canals and lakes, and building earthen pyramids, one of which serves as his tomb. Exhibits in the Schloss (by Gottfried Semper, of Dresden opera house fame) and outer buildings tell the story of the man and his ultimate pet project.

**THE DRIVE**
The 60km-ride to Neuzelle (which has a feel-good eating option) takes you northeast on the B168 past the Peitzer Teiche, a huge network of carp-farming ponds, and through the southern reaches of the romantic Schlaube Valley Nature Park, a hikers' and cyclists' paradise. At Schenkendobern turn north onto the B112.

### 04 NEUZELLE

Having hit the three-quarters-of-a-millennium mark in 2018, the Cistercian **Stift Neuzelle** (Neuzelle Abbey; stift-neuzelle.de) wears the moniker 'Brandenburg's baroque miracle' with pride. Gothic at its core, it received a baroque makeover in the 18th century that included the addition of exuberant gardens with water features, terraced hillsides and an orangery. A museum presents scenes from the **Passion of Christ** composed of 250-year-old vividly painted, life-sized cut-out figures dramatically arranged in a 'heavenly theatre'. Make your pilgrimage to the Neuzeller Kloster **brewery** to try its *Bock*, porter, pilsner or 'anti-ageing' beer.

 **THE DRIVE**
Follow the B112 north for 36km to Frankfurt (Oder), perhaps stopping briefly in Eisenhüttenstadt, a once-thriving East German 'socialist model city'.

### 05 FRANKFURT (ODER)

Germany's 'other' Frankfurt sits on the Oder River right on the Polish border. WWII bombs and socialist reconstruction wiped out most vestiges of its one-time grandeur as a medieval trading centre and university town. Still, the scenic river setting and unique sightseeing gems invite a quick stopover. The Gothic **Marienkirche** (Church of St Mary; st-marien-ffo.de), for instance, boasts stunning medieval stained-glass windows that were squirrelled away by the Soviets as WWII booty and only returned in 2007. For the world's most comprehensive collection of East German art, drop by the **Museum Junge Kunst** (blmk.de). If it's cheap(er) vodka and cigarettes you're after, walk across the Oder to Słubice, Frankfurt's Polish twin town.

 **THE DRIVE**
Follow the B112 north for 10km to Lebus, then continue west for 18km on the B167 past hillsides and grassland carpeted in wildflowers from spring to autumn.

### 06 GEDENKSTÄTTE SEELOWER HÖHEN

The **Seelow Heights Memorial Exhibit** (gedenkstaette-seelower-hoehen.de) documents one of the last major battles of WWII, which took place on this 48m-high plateau above the Oder River valley in April 1945. Some 100,000 German troops fought tooth and nail – but in vain – to stave off a million Soviet soldiers. After three days of fighting, an estimated 50,000 on both sides had fallen. Imagine the horrors of this brutal battle as you climb to the military cemetery with its striking **memorial**, then pick your way past military vehicles and artillery pieces to the **museum** for the full low-down.

**THE DRIVE**
Follow the B167 northwest for 55km via Neuhardenberg, with its palace turned hotel, and past the Kietzer See birders' paradise. In Niederfinow, turn right on Hebewerkstrasse to arrive at the ship lift.

### 07 NIEDERFINOW

The tiny town of Niederfinow is famous for its spectacular ship lift, the **Schiffshebewerk Niederfinow** (schiffshebewerk-niederfinow.info), which links the Oder River and the Oder-Havel Canal. This remarkable engineering feat was completed in 1934 and measures 60m high, 27m wide and 94m long. Cargo barges sail into a sort of giant bathtub, which is then raised or lowered 36m, water and all. Visitors can enjoy the ride aboard tourist boats operated by **Fahrgastschifffahrt Neumann** (schiffshebewerk-niederfinow.info/neumann). To accommodate larger and multiple barges, an

---

## Gherkin Country

The Spreewald is world-renowned for its pickled cucumbers, cherished by connoisseurs for their low acidity, crunchy texture and delicate spicing. The official name 'Spreewälder Gurke' is even an EU-certified Protected Designation of Origin, just like Champagne and Cognac. Flemish cloth-makers introduced the pickle seeds that thrive in the region's watery and humus-rich soil. Only about 20 companies, each using their own 'secret' family recipe, are allowed to produce the vegetable. Discover more pickle secrets on the 260km-long Gurken-Radweg (Gherkin Cycle Path) or at the Gurkenmuseum in Lehde.

> **Photo Opportunity**
> Capture a traditional Sorb village in Lehde in the Spreewald.

Freilandmuseum, Lehde (p49)

even bigger ship lift is being built adjacent to the historic one. A boat-shaped info centre has details about this ambitious project.

**THE DRIVE**
Head north on Hebewerkstrasse as far as Liepe, then turn left on Brodowiner Strasse and continue for 17km through the Schorfheide-Chorin UNESCO World Biosphere Reserve (Biosphärenreservat), whose woods, ponds and swamps are a haven for storks, cranes, beavers and other critters.

**08 CHORIN**
A romantically ruined abbey, **Kloster Chorin** (kloster-chorin.org) was built by Cistercian monks over six decades starting in 1273, and is widely considered one of the finest red-brick Gothic structures in northern Germany. In summer, the abbey forms an enchanting backdrop for the classical concert series **Choriner Musiksommer** (musiksommer-chorin.de).

**THE DRIVE**
Pick up the A11 in Althüttendorf, drive south to exit 14 and follow the B273 toward Oranienburg, which takes you through the Nature Park Barnim with its many crystal-clear swimming lakes, including the enchanting Liepnitzsee.

**09 ORANIENBURG**
Only 30km north of central Berlin, **Sachsenhausen** (sachsenhausen-sbg.de) was built by prisoners and opened in 1936 as a prototype for other concentration camps. Some 200,000 people passed through its sinister gates, most of them political opponents, Roma, Jews and POWs. By 1945, tens of thousands had died here from hunger, exhaustion, illness, exposure, medical experiments and executions. A tour of the grounds, remaining buildings and exhibits will leave no one untouched. Key stops include the **infirmary barracks**, the **prisoners' kitchen** and the execution area called **Station Z**.

BEST ROAD TRIPS: GERMANY, AUSTRIA & SWITZERLAND

# 07
# Via Regia

**BEST FOR FAMILIES**

Frankfurt's myriad attractions entertain young and old.

PalmenGarten (p57), Frankfurt

| DURATION | DISTANCE | GREAT FOR |
|---|---|---|
| 5–7 days | 875km / 544 miles | History & families |

**BEST TIME TO GO** | Fit more in when days are longest from May to July.

Beginning in Saarbrücken and ending in Görlitz, this spirited west–east romp cuts through the heart of the nation. It juxtaposes Frankfurt's big-city excitement with Fulda's tranquil lanes, gets cultured in Weimar, Dresden and Leipzig, lingers on quiet country highways and roars along autobahns, visiting the key outposts of a road no longer in existence, but once the way of kings.

### Link Your Trip

**08 German Avenues Route**
Link in with this amazing loop that intersects at Dresden and you have central Germany covered.

**12 Romantic Rhine**
Hook up with the Rhine while crossing paths in Mainz for some real river romance.

### 01  SAARBRÜCKEN

Vestiges of Saarbrücken's 18th-century heyday survive in the city's beautiful baroque townhouses and churches. The historic centre around **St Johanner Markt** brims with fine restaurants and cafes. Start with a visit to the **Historisches Museum Saar** (historisches-museum. org), housed in the basement of the **Saarbrücker Schloss**, where you can descend to the castle's massive bastions and casemates. Exhibits look at Saarland from the 1870s, and periods under French and Nazi rule. The Saarland Museum's **Alte Sammlung** (kulturbesitz.de), or 'old collection', displays a millennium of paintings and artefacts from southwest Germany and France's Alsace-Lorraine. Before you hit the road, why not spend a few minutes' quiet contemplation in the dazzling Catholic church, **Basilika St Johann** (pfarrei-st-johann.de), with its gold altars, pulpit, organ case and overhead rayburst design?

**THE DRIVE**
Head south out of town on the A620 for 6km until it becomes the A6 autobahn. Stay on the A6 for 66km until exit 16a Dreieck Kaiserslautern, merging on to the A63 towards Frankfurt. Stay on the A63 for 70km until you reach the outskirts of Mainz, where the road becomes the B40. Keep heading straight for 4km into Mainz.

## 02 MAINZ

Mainz is located at the confluence of the Rhine and Main rivers, its elegance a throwback to its Napoleonic occupation. Strolling along the Rhine and sampling local wines in an **Altstadt** (old town) tavern are as essential as viewing the fabulous Romanesque **Mainzer Dom** (mainzerdom.bistummainz.de), with its octagonal tower; Chagall's ethereal windows in **St-Stephan-Kirche** (bistummainz.de/pfarrei/mainz-st-stephan); or the first printed Bible in the **Gutenberg-Museum Mainz** (gutenberg-museum.de), commemorating the native son who perfected movable type. If you're not claustrophobic, head to the dungeon-like **Heiligtum der Isis und Mater Magna** (roemisches-mainz.de) archaeological site, with its brilliantly illuminated artefacts uncovered in 1999 during the construction of the Römer Passage mall. If you're desperate for more, head to the **Landesmuseum Mainz** (landesmuseum-mainz.de) for outstanding collections of Renaissance and 20th-century German paintings, baroque porcelain and furniture.

**THE DRIVE**
Cross the Rhine on the Theodor Heuss Bridge then pick up the B455 at the roundabout and follow it north for 5km to the junction with the A66 autobahn at exit 6 Weisbaden-Erbenheim. Follow the A66 towards Frankfurt for 30km until exit 21 Frankfurt am Main-Miquelallee.

## 03 FRANKFURT

Beneath the glinting glass, steel and concrete, you'll discover Frankfurt is an unexpectedly traditional city, with its medieval **Altstadt**, village-like neighbourhoods, attractive gardens, riverside paths and wealth of museums. The Main flows from east to west, with the city centre on its northern banks. The **Römerberg**, Frankfurt's ornately gabled central square, with the **Gerechtigkeitsbrunnen** (Fountain of Justice), marks the Altstadt's centre. To its north, shop till you drop along the **Zeil**, linking **An der Hauptwache** and **Konstablerwache** public squares. Must-sees include the photogenic town hall **Römer**, comprising of three step-gabled 15th-century houses; Frankfurt's red-sandstone **Kaiserdom** (Imperial Frankfurt Cathedral; dom-frankfurt.de), dominated by a 95m-high Gothic tower (which you can climb, via 324 steps); and the world-renowned **Städel Museum** (staedelmuseum.de), founded in 1815 and housing outstanding works by Dürer, Rembrandt, Rubens, Renoir, Picasso and Cézanne.

### THE DRIVE
Head south on the B44 for 6.5km to the A3 autobahn at exit 51 Frankfurt Süd. Take the A3 east for 19km until exit 54 Hanau, then follow the B45 for 10km north.

## 04 HANAU

There are two reasons you've stopped by Hanau: first, because brothers Jacob and Wilhelm Grimm were born here, commemorated by a statue located on the **Markt**; and second, for the wonderful **Historisches Museum Schloss Philippsruhe** (museen-hanau.de), located within Philippsruhe Palace. Dating from the early 18th century, this museum has displays on town history, arts and crafts. The parks and gardens are beautiful for a stroll.

### THE DRIVE
Pick up the A66 autobahn at exit 36 Hanau Nord for 48km towards Fulda until exit 47 Steinau an der Strasse.

## 05 STEINAU

Steinau (an der Strasse) has been a stop on the Via Regia for centuries (*an der Strasse* means 'on the road'). At the old-town entrance, you'll see two sandstone pillars commemorating the Via Regia. While you're here, stop by the twinned museums **Brüder Grimm-Haus and Museum Steinau** (brueder-grimm-haus.de), in a house where the Grimm family lived from 1791 to 1796.

### THE DRIVE
Return to the A66 at exit 47 Steinau an der Strasse and follow it for 21km until exit 51 Neuhof-Süd. At the roundabout, veer right onto Hanauer Strasse and follow it through the village of Neuhof for 1.6km until the road forks. Take the left fork and follow Alte Heerstrasse for 7km towards Fulda: you're now driving on an original Via Regia roadway. Turn left at the junction with the K103 then right onto the L3418 until you reach Frankfurter Strasse: follow it for 3km into Fulda.

## 06 FULDA

Founded in 744, photogenic Fulda has a wealth of sumptuous baroque architecture and a delightfully relaxed atmosphere, with plenty of selfie ops and a handful of top spots to pause for a meal or a glass of wine. Fulda's spectacular

### Frankfurt: Then & Now

Around 2000 years ago Frankfurt was a Celtic and Germanic settlement and then a Roman garrison town. Mentioned in historical documents as far back as AD 794, it was an important centre of power in the Holy Roman Empire. With the election of Friedrich I (Barbarossa) in 1152, the city became the customary site of the selection of German kings. In 1372 Frankfurt became a 'Free Imperial City', a status it enjoyed until the Prussian takeover of 1866.

It's hard to believe that about 80% of Frankfurt's medieval city centre was destroyed by WWII Allied bombing raids in March 1944; over 1000 people lost their lives. The area around Römerberg was reconstructed in its original style and, phoenix-like, the city returned to prominence as a thriving contemporary centre of commerce. Frankfurt's first international trade fairs began in the 12th century and continue to attract tens of thousands each year; its airport is the third-busiest in Europe. Frankfurt's first stock exchange began operating in 1585 and is now in the world's top 10. In the 1760s, the Rothschild banking family began their ascent from Frankfurt, and the city is today home to the gleaming HQ of the European Central Bank.

Dom (p56), Fulda

**Photo Opportunity**
Fulda's baroque Dom, crowdless at twilight.

Herzogin Anna Amalia Bibliothek, Weimar

**Stadtschloss** was built (1706–21) as the prince-abbots' residence. Visitors can enter ornate historic rooms and the octagonal Schlossturm (April to October) for great views of the magnificent gardens where locals bronze themselves in summer. Inside the baroque **Dom** (bistum-fulda.de), a cathedral built from 1704 to 1712, you'll find gilded furnishings, statues and the tomb of St Boniface, who died a martyr in 754.

### THE DRIVE
Take the B27 for 5km north to meet the A7 autobahn at exit 91 Fulda Nord. Follow the A7 north for 35km then merge onto the A4 towards Berlin/Dresden at interchange 86 Kirchheimer Dreieck. Follow the A4 for 60km to exit 39 Eisenach West. Take the B19 south for 6km into Eisenach.

### 07 EISENACH
Historically, Eisenach was an important stop on the Via Regia, and its Wartburg castle is one of Germany's most significant medieval sites: it held Martin Luther while his actions brought about the Reformation and was the inspiration for better-known Neuschwanstein, whose creator, Ludwig II, saw it and wanted to build a fortress even more grandiose and impenetrable. Eisenach proudly remembers the birth of Johann Sebastian Bach in the wattle-and-daub home now housing the museum **Bachhaus** (bachhaus.de), and also celebrates its automotive history (the world's first BMW rolled off the assembly line here in 1929): check out **Automobile Welt Eisenach** (awe-stiftung.de) if four wheels and six cylinders kick-start your heart.

### THE DRIVE
Head north on Mühlhäuser Strasse for 2km then turn right on to the L1021 for 6km to the junction with the A4 at exit 40a Eisenach Ost. Head south on the A4 for 9.5km to exit 40b Sättelstädt. Follow the L3007 east for 15km through the small villages of Teutleben and Aspach into Gotha.

### 08 GOTHA
Gotha is no longer Thuringia's wealthiest and most beautiful city, as it was once described, but its focal point remains the enormous **Schloss Friedenstein** (stiftungfriedenstein.de), built by Duke Ernst I of House Saxe-Coburg-Gotha (his descendants reinvented them-

selves as the House of Windsor after WWI and now sit upon the British throne). Inside the palace you'll find the exuberantly stucco-ornamented Festival Hall, a neoclassical wing, a curio cabinet jammed with exotica, the Palace Museum, and stunning Ekhof Theater, one of Europe's oldest baroque theatres. Gotha's **Hauptmarkt** is dominated by the picturesque **Rathaus** (Town Hall), with its colourful Renaissance facade and 35m-tall tower.

**THE DRIVE**
Follow Weimarer Strasse, which becomes Eisenacher Strasse, for 21km east, into Erfurt.

### 09 ERFURT

Founded as a bishopric on the little Gera River in 742, Erfurt was catapulted to prosperity in the Middle Ages when it began producing a precious blue pigment from a woad plant. In 1392 rich merchants founded Erfurt's university, whose most famous graduate was Martin Luther. There's plenty to enjoy here, with the town's history and modernity complementing each other. Head to the **Krämerbrücke** (Merchants' Bridge), a charming 1325 stone bridge flanked by cute half-timbered houses. Erfurt's is the only one of its kind north of the Alps that's still inhabited. Linger a while in the delightful eateries of nearby **Wenigemarkt**, and consider a visit to the **Augustinerkloster** (augustinerkloster.de); this is where Luther lived from 1505 to 1511, was ordained as a monk and read his first Mass. Be sure to stroll about the gorgeous houses on **Fischmarkt** and onwards to the spectacular **Domplatz** and Erfurt's famous **Dom** (Mariendom; dom-erfurt.de).

**THE DRIVE**
Take the B7 22km east, through fields of rapeseed and wind turbines, into Weimar.

### 10 WEIMAR

Historical epicentre of the German Enlightenment, best known as the town where intellectual heavyweights Goethe and Schiller did their thing, Weimar appeals to anyone with a passion for German history and culture. In summer, Weimar's many parks and gardens lend themselves to quiet contemplation of the town's cultural onslaught, or to taking a break from it. Must-sees include the museum at **Stadtschloss Weimar** (klassik-stiftung.de), the UNESCO World Heritage **Herzogin Anna Amalia Bibliothek** (klassik-stiftung.de), and, of course, the Goethe-Nationalmuseum.

**THE DRIVE**
Follow the B7 for 25km east into Jena.

### 11 JENA

Although signs of East German (GDR) aesthetics remain, Jena enjoys a picturesque setting on the Saale River, flanked by limestone hills and blessed with a climate mild enough for orchids and grapevines. Also an old university town (since 1558), Jena has an entirely different feel to Weimar and Erfurt. Close investigation will unearth fun, fringe, Berlin-esque hang-outs and tasty cheap eats. Ascend the **JenTower** (jentower.de) for fabulous views of the surrounding Saale River valley, take a trip into outer space at the **Zeiss Planetarium** (planetarium-jena.de), the world's oldest, or contemplate the life of a literary giant and his little garden in **Schiller's Gartenhaus** (Schiller's Garden House; uni-jena.de).

**THE DRIVE**
Follow the B88 north for 34km through forests and fields, as it chases the sparkling Saale into Naumburg.

---

**TOP TIP:**

## Frankfurt for Kids

Frankfurt is a fun place to linger a little if you've got youngsters in your party: they'll jump at the chance to get out of the car. There are plenty of parks to picnic in and several museums have kid-friendly exhibits. Favourites include the following:

**Senckenberg Museum** (senckenberg.de) Fossils and dinosaurs.

**Frankfurt Zoo** (Zoologischer Garten; zoo-frankfurt.de) Animals galore.

**PalmenGarten** (palmengarten.de) Parkland and fountains.

**Junges Museum** (Young Museum Frankfurt; kindermuseum.frankfurt.de) Specifically designed for children…and to give wise elders a break.

## Goethe: Literary Lion

Johann Wolfgang von Goethe (1749–1832) is the grandaddy of German literature and philosophy. He lived to 82, having written novels, essays, treatises, scientific articles, travelogues, plays and poetry. A consummate politician, Goethe was also a great 'Renaissance man', capable in many disciplines: during his life he served as town planner, architect, social reformer and scientist. Born in Frankfurt am Main and trained as a lawyer, Goethe became the driving force of the 1770s Sturm und Drang (Storm and Stress) literary movement. His work with Friedrich Schiller fostered the theatrical style known as Weimar Classicism. Goethe himself once described his work as 'fragments of a great confession'. His defining play in two parts, Faust, is a lyrical but highly charged retelling of the classic legend of a man selling his soul for knowledge. It's still regularly performed throughout Germany today.

### 12 NAUMBURG

At the confluence of the Saale and Unstrut Rivers, Naumburg has a handsome **Altstadt**, striking Renaissance **Rathaus** and **Marientor** double gateway. Its enormous **Dom** (Cathedral of Sts Peter & Paul; naumburger-dom.de), is a masterpiece of medieval architecture, featuring elements of the Romanesque and early Gothic design. Medieval stained-glass windows are augmented by ruby-red modern panes by Neo Rauch, one of the premier artists of the New Leipzig School. You may also want to pop into the **Nietzsche Haus** (nietzschehaus.de), where the great philosopher spent most of his childhood.

#### THE DRIVE
Head southeast on the B87 for 4km until the intersection with the B180. Continue heading southeast on the B180 for 10km until the junction with the A9 autobahn at exit 21a Naumburg. Head north on the A9 for 32km until exit 17 Leipzig West. Head east on the B181 for 13km into Leipzig.

### 13 LEIPZIG

Leipzig's love affair with music stems from its connection to the lives and work of Bach, Mendelssohn and Wagner. Today, one of the world's top classical orchestras, the Gewandhausorchester, and the 800-year-old Thomanerchor boys' choir continue to delight audiences here. Along this theme, the **Bach-Museum** (bachmuseumleipzig.de) lets you treat your ears to any composition Bach wrote, while **Mendelssohn-Haus** (mendelssohn-stiftung.de) teaches you about Mendelssohn in the Biedermeier-furnished apartment where this remarkable musical prodigy lived until his sudden death, aged 38. At the fabulous **Museum für Musikinstrumente** (mfm.uni-leipzig.de), housed inside the complex of the **Museen im Grassi** (grassimuseum.de), you can discover music from five centuries through an interactive sound laboratory.

#### THE DRIVE
Take Torgauer Strasse northeast for 4.5km to the intersection with the A14 autobahn at exit 25 Leipzig Nordost. Head southeast on the A14 for 75km to the A4 interchange 76 Autobahn Dreieck Nossen. Merge here onto the A4 and head east for 20km to exit 78 Dresden Altstadt.

#### Detour
**Halle**
Start: 13 Leipzig
Best known as the birthplace of Georg Friedrich Händel – learn all about him in the **Händel-Haus** (handel-house.com) – Halle is one of Germany's oldest cities, having celebrated its 1200th birthday in 2006. But the main reason to visit is to check out two impressive museums. The **Landesmuseum für Vorgeschichte** (State Museum of Pre-History; da-lsa.de) houses a phenomenal collection of major archaeological finds, one of the most significant in Europe. Permanent exhibits shed light on the early to late Stone Age and early Bronze Age, and include the oldest known fingerprint, the graves of Eulau and the Nebra Sky Disc. Art lovers will make a beeline to **Kunstmuseum Moritzburg** (Moritzburg Art Gallery; kunstmuseum-moritzburg.de), where the late-Gothic Moritzburg castle is a fantastic setting for a superb permanent collection, from the classics to the modern. When you're done, there are fine places to wine and dine. Halle is 40km northwest from Leipzig on the A14.

Zwinger, Dresden

### 14 DRESDEN

Dresden's cultural heyday came under the 18th-century reign of Augustus the Strong, who supervised many of Dresden's iconic buildings. These include the **Zwinger** (der-dresdner-zwinger.de), inspired by the palace at Versailles, which today houses three superb museums within its baroque walls, and the **Frauenkirche** (frauenkirche-dresden.de), Dresden's most beloved symbol, rebuilt from a pile of rubble between 1994 and 2005. The original graced the skyline for two centuries until the devastating 1945 Allied firestorm of WWII levelled the church and most of the city. For something completely different, the **Deutsches Hygiene-Museum** (German Hygiene Museum; dhmd.de) is, in fact, all about human beings. Living and dying, eating and drinking, sex and beauty are all addressed. There's a Children's Museum in the basement. If the kids have made it this far, why not head to the **Zoo** (zoo-dresden.de)?

🅿 **THE DRIVE**
Pick up the A4 autobahn at exit 78 Dresden Altstadt and follow it east for 102km to exit 94 Görlitz.

### 15 GÖRLITZ

Congratulations, you made it. Görlitz, Germany's most eastern city, is a dreamy coalescence of fabulous architecture, cobbled streets and an intriguing history. Having miraculously escaped destruction during WWII, Görlitz offers the visitor nearly 4200 heritage buildings in styles from the Renaissance to 19th century. Be sure to pop in to the Barockhaus, which will fascinate anyone with a taste for the odd with its curiously broad exhibits. For a history of the area, visit the **Schlesisches Museum zu Görlitz** (schlesisches-museum.de), and drop by **Untermarkt** to see the **Rathaus** and **Peterskirche**, with its remarkable Sun Organ.

# 08
# German Avenues Route

**BEST FOR HISTORY**

Few places pack as much punch as Eisenach's Wartburg.

| DURATION | DISTANCE | GREAT FOR |
|---|---|---|
| 5–7 days | 1050km / 652 miles | History & nature |

| BEST TIME TO GO | Visit from May to July for fewer crowds and the best weather. |
|---|---|

Wartburg, Eisenach (p66)

On this magic loop through the diverse natural beauty of the ancient states of Saxony-Anhalt, Lower Saxony, Thuringia and Saxony, you'll fall in love with the eye-catching villages of Quedlinburg and Goslar, perhaps take a steam train to the top of a mountain, see where Bach was born and Goethe died, keep watch from the Wartburg and ponder the histories written upon the culture-laden cities of Erfurt, Weimar, Dresden and Leipzig.

## Link Your Trip

**04 Highlights of Saxony**
Pick up this scenic jaunt in Dresden to immerse yourself in Saxony's rich history and diverse architecture.

**10 German Fairy Tale Road**
From Schmalkalden, head southwest for 110km to Steinau to link up with this whimsical journey.

### 01 DESSAU-ROSSLAU

The former East German (GDR) town of Dessau-Rosslau, 130km south of Berlin, is best known for being the birthplace of the Bauhaus movement, but is also famed for the **Gartenreich Dessau-Wörlitz**, one of the finest garden ensembles in Germany. Begin at the main Bauhaus sites: the **Bauhausgebäude** (Bauhaus Building; bauhaus-dessau.de), erected in 1925–26 as a school of Bauhaus art, design and architecture, and the three **Meisterhäuser** (Masters' Houses; bauhaus-dessau.de) where Bauhaus' leading lights lived. Juxtapose these with the 112-hectare **Wörlitz Park & Schloss Wörlitz**

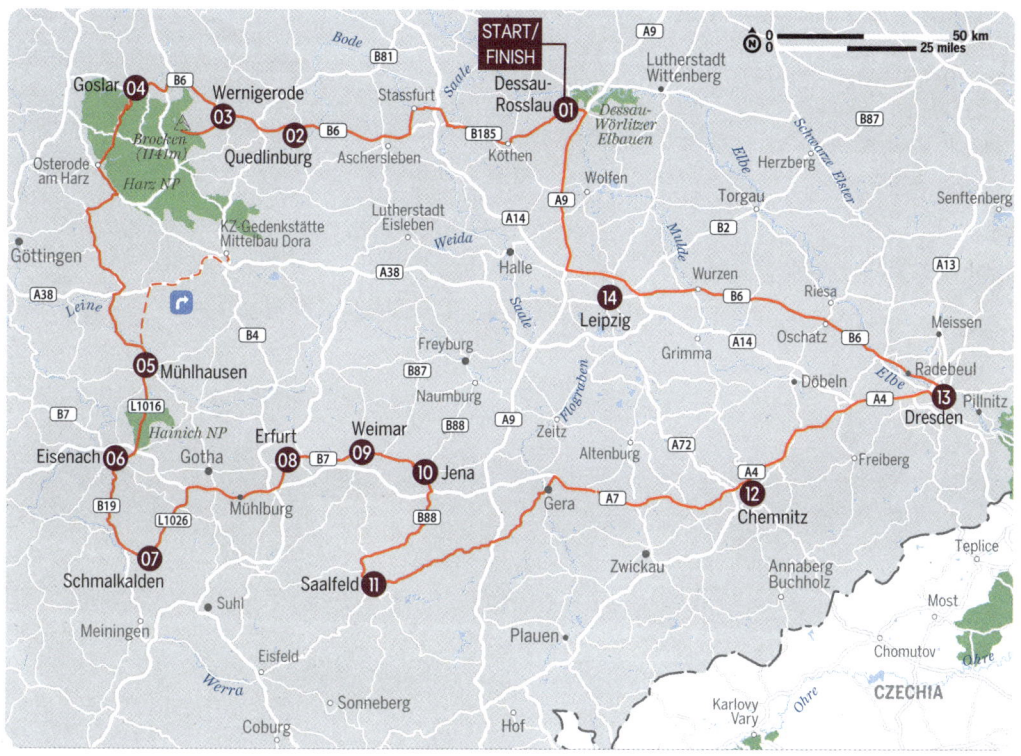

(woerlitz-information.de), the pinnacle of the Garden Realm, which is 20km east of town on the L133. Return to Dessau-Rosslau and head southwest on the B185 for 11km, for a peek at petite **Schloss & Park Mosigkau** (gartenreich.com), a 'miniature Sanssouci'.

### THE DRIVE
From Schloss & Park Mosigkau, take the B185 for 15km to the pretty village of Köthen, where Bach composed his Brandenburg Concertos and The Well-Tempered Clavier. Continue on the B185 for 45km to the junction with the B6. Follow the B6 for 20km, to Quedlinburg.

### 02 QUEDLINBURG
Situated on a fertile plain at the northern cusp of the Harz Mountains, little Quedlinburg, a UNESCO World Heritage town, is one of the loveliest in the region. Learn about its centuries-old Fachwerk (half-timbered) houses (there are 1400 or so) in the **Fachwerkmuseum im Ständerbau**. Wander freely around its enchanting cobblestone streets and spectacular medieval marketplace, where you'll find a wonderful mix of original options for wining, dining and resting your head. Also on the hill is the Schloss Quedlinburg, a Renaissance palace containing the **Schlossmuseum**, with a fascinating collection of Ottonian relics and a focus on the development of the region, the monastery and the town; the museum is closed for major renovations; check at the tourist office for the latest estimate for its reopening. The **Lyonel Feininger Galerie** (feininger-galerie.de) exhibits the work of influential Bauhaus artist Lyonel Feininger (1871–1956). Feininger was born in New York and came to Germany at the age of 16, later fleeing the Nazis and returning to the US in 1937. Timing your visit for a weekday will make all the difference: Quedlinburg is a popular weekend destination.

### THE DRIVE
Head west on Westerhäuser Strasse (which becomes the B27) through another lovely village – Blankenburg – to the junction with the B81. Follow the B81 for 4km north: you'll see Blankenburg's handsome castle to your right. Turn left on the L85 and head west for 11.5km into Wernigerode.

## Harz Mountain Railways

Fans of old-time trains will be eager to get out from behind the wheel and into a *Wagen* on any of the three narrow-gauge railways, a legacy of the GDR, that cross the Harz. This 140km integrated network is the largest in Europe, serving steam and diesel locomotives, and tackling gradients of up to 40% and curves as tight as 60m in radius.

The **Harzquerbahn** runs 60km on a north–south route between Wernigerode and Nordhausen. The serpentine 14km between Wernigerode and Drei Annen Hohne includes 72 bends; you'll get dropped off on the edge of Harz National Park.

From the junction at Drei Annen Hohne, the **Brockenbahn** begins the steep climb to Schierke and the Brocken. Trains to the Brocken (via Drei Annen Hohne) can be picked up from Wernigerode and Nordhausen; single/return tickets cost €29/45 from all stations. Many visitors take the train to Schierke and then follow a trail on foot to the Brocken summit (1141m).

The third service is the **Selketalbahn**, which begins in Quedlinburg and runs to Eisfelder Talmühle or Hasselfelde. At Eisfelder Tal, you can change trains for other lines. The picturesque Selketalbahn crosses the plain to Gernrode and follows Wellbach, a creek with a couple of good swimming holes, through deciduous forest to Mägdesprung, before joining the Selke Valley and climbing past Alexisbad to high plains around Friedrichshöhe, Stiege and beyond.

Check in with the folks at **Harzer Schmalspurbahnen** (hsb-wr.de) for fares and timetables.

## 03 WERNIGERODE

The winding streets of Wernigerode's attractive **Altstadt** (old town) are flanked by pretty half-timbered houses. This is the northern terminus of the steam-powered narrow-gauge heritage Harzquerbahn railway; the line to the summit of the Brocken also starts here. Dominating Wernigerode's town square, the spectacular towered **Rathaus** (town hall) began life as a theatre around 1277; it was given its mostly late-Gothic features in the 16th century. Take a stroll along **Breite Strasse**, essentially Wernigerode's main street, for both architectural and gastronomic reasons. A visit to the **Harzmuseum** (harzmuseum.de) will top up your knowledge on local geology, history and architecture. Round out a magical day with a castle visit to **Schloss Wernigerode** (schloss-wernigerode.de), originally built in the 12th century but enlarged over the years to reflect late-Gothic and Renaissance tastes. You'll need to leave your car below; it's a 1.5km walk if you fancy it, but the easiest way to get there is by Bimmelbahn wagon from Marktstrasse.

### THE DRIVE
Head north on the B244 for 4km to the junction with the B6. Follow the B6 for 32km, over undulating hills, by meadows of golden rapeseed and the odd wind turbine, and through picturesque villages into Goslar.

## 04 GOSLAR

Gorgeous Goslar's beautiful medieval **Altstadt** attracts visitors by the busload. Founded by Heinrich I in 922, the town was important in its early days for silver mining. One of the nicest things to do here is wander through the historic streets around the **Markt**. Opposite the **Rathaus** is the **Glockenspiel**, a chiming clock depicting four scenes of mining in the area. It plays at 9am, noon, 3pm and 6pm. A visit to the **Goslarer Museum** offers a good overview of local history. The town's pride and joy is its reconstructed 11th-century Romanesque imperial palace, the **Kaiserpfalz**, seat of Saxon kings from 1005 to 1219. After centuries of decay, the building was resurrected in the 19th century and adorned with interior frescos of idealised historical scenes. About 3km south on Rammelsberger Strasse is the **Rammelsberg Museum & Besucherbergwerk** (Rammelsberg Museum & Visitors' Mine; rammelsberg.de), the shafts and buildings of a 1000-year-old mine that are now a must-see UNESCO World Heritage site and museum.

### THE DRIVE
Allow at least two hours for this scenic Harz Mountains section. Take the B241 as it twists and turns for 31km to the junction of the B243, just through the village of Osterode am Harz. Continue south on the forested B243 for 30km: you'll cross the border of Lower Saxony into Thuringia, from where it's 49km of country roads, heading south on the L1014 and L1015 to Mühlhausen.

## 05 MÜHLHAUSEN

Mühlhausen flaunts medieval charisma. Encircled by nearly intact fortifications, its historic centre is a warren of cobbled alleyways linking proud churches and half-timbered houses. Admire its beauty from the 330m section of the **Am Frauentor** (Town Fortification), accessible through Inneres Frauentor, and the viewing platform in the **Rabenturm** (Raven's Tower). Originally the 12th-century fortification ran for 2.8km around the town, and a remarkable 2km remain. In the early 16th century, the town became a focal point of the Reformation and a launch pad for the Peasants' War of 1525, led by local preacher Thomas Müntzer. With reunification, Mühlhausen became united Germany's most central town, located a mere 5km north of the country's geographical centre in Niederdorla. Mühlhausen's **Rathaus** is an architecturally intriguing hotchpotch of Gothic, Renaissance and baroque styles. Inside, pay special attention to the **Great Hall** and the **Councillors' Chamber**.

### THE DRIVE
Follow the L1016 south for 35km to Eisenach.

### Detour
**KZ-Gedenkstätte Mittelbau Dora**
Start:  Mühlhausen

During the final stages of WWII, when Hitler's grand plan turned to conducting war from underground bunkers, Mittelbau Dora was established as a satellite of the Buchenwald concentration camp after British bombers destroyed missile plants in Peenemünde. At least 20,000 prisoners were worked to their deaths here. After years of decay under the GDR, the **memorial site** (buchenwald.de) today gives an insight into the horrors that unfolded here, and includes a modern museum that explains the background of the camp and the experiences of the prisoners.

From late 1943, thousands of mostly Russian, French and Polish POWs (many of whom had survived Auschwitz) toiled under horrific

Quedlinburg

### Quedlinburg's Historic Buildings

With so many historic buildings, Quedlinburg is one town in which it's nice just to stroll the streets and soak up the atmosphere. The **Rathaus** (1320) dominates the **Markt**, and in front of this is a **Roland** statue from 1426. Just behind the Rathaus is the **Marktkirche St Benedikti** (1233), and nearby is the **Gildehaus zur Rose** (1612) at Breite Strasse 39. Running off Markt is the tiny **Schuhhof**, a shoemakers' courtyard, with shutters and stable-like 'gossip doors'. **Alter Klopstock** (1580), which is found at Stieg 28, has scrolled beams typical of Quedlinburg's 16th-century half-timbered houses.

From Stieg 28 (just north of Schuhhof), it's a short walk north along Pölle to **Zwischen den Städten**, a historic bridge connecting the old town and Neustadt, which developed alongside the town wall around 1200 when peasants fled a feudal power struggle on the land. Behind the Renaissance facade, tower and stone gables of the **Hagensches Freihaus** (1558) is the Wyndham Garden Quedlinburger Stadtschloss. Many houses in this part of town have high archways and courtyards dotted with pigeon towers. A couple of other places of special note are the **Hotel zur Goldenen Sonne** building (1671) at Steinweg 11 and **Zur Börse** (1683) at No 23.

conditions. They dug a 20km labyrinth of tunnels in the chalk hills north of Nordhausen, within which were built the V1 and V2 rockets that rained destruction on London, Antwerp and other cities during the war's final stages. The US Army reached the gates in April 1945, cared for survivors and removed all missile equipment before turning the area over to Russia.

Visitors are free to roam the grounds, crematorium and museum. The tunnels (roughly the diameter of an aircraft hangar) are only accessible on free 90-minute guided tours, running at 11am and 2pm Tuesday to Friday and at 11am, 1pm and 3pm on weekends. Within the dank walls you can see partially assembled rockets that have lain untouched for decades.

To get here, head north for 29km on the L1015 until you reach the A38 at exit 6 Leinefelde-Worbis, then follow it east for 26km to exit 10 Werther. Follow Kassleler Landstrasse and Strasse der Opfer des Faschismus for 8km until you reach a railway crossing. Turn left and follow the road into the memorial site.

Erfurt

### 06 EISENACH

The modest appearance of hilly Eisenach, a small town on the edge of the Thuringian Forest, belies its association with two German heavyweights: Johann Sebastian Bach and Martin Luther. Luther went to school here and later returned to protective custody in the **Wartburg** (wartburg-eisenach. de), now itself protected by UNESCO World Heritage status. When it comes to medieval castles and their importance in German history, you've hit the mother lode: allow at least two hours for exploration with your camera batteries fully charged. A century after Luther's incarceration, Bach, the grandest of all baroque musicians, was born in the **Bachhaus** (bachhaus.de), a wattle-and-daub home, now one of Germany's best biographical museums. Admission includes a 20-minute concert played on antique instruments. Music-lovers will also appreciate the **Reuter-Wagner Museum**, honouring composer Richard Wagner in a villa once owned by writer Fritz Reuter. Eisenach also has a century-old automotive tradition – the world's first BMW rolled off the local assembly line in 1929. Since you're on a road trip why not check out **Automobile Welt Eisenach** (awe-stiftung.de) as well?

#### THE DRIVE

Take the B19 south for 37km, admiring the tree-lined avenues, thick forests and lush fields, passing through the occasional sleepy village here and there, then take the L1026 east for 7km into Schmalkalden.

### 07 SCHMALKALDEN

As you drive into town, you'll pass the unmissable **Viba Nougat Welt** (viba-sweets.de) where you'd be forgiven for being seduced into a sweet-toothed visit, but be sure to press on into Schmalkalden's **Altmarkt** as well, where in 1531 the Protestant princes established the Schmalkaldic League to counter the central powers of Catholic emperor Charles V, thus thrusting the little town into the heart of the Reformation. The town's handsome **Rathaus** (1419) once functioned as the meeting place of the Schmalkaldic League. The incongruous towers of the late-Gothic **Stadtkirche St Georg** (1437–1509) overlook the square. You can almost hear the

groans and creaks of its half-timbered houses, crowned by the hilltop, late-Renaissance **Schloss Wilhelmsburg** (museumwilhelmsburg.de). Conceived by Landgrave Wilhelm IV of Hessen as a hunting lodge and summer residence in the 1580s, it has largely kept its original design, with lavish murals and stucco decorating most rooms.

**THE DRIVE**
Head north on the L1026, as it skirts the dense Thuringian Forest, with stretches of road fully covered by ancient trees and epitomising the Avenues Route. After 22km you'll reach the village of Friedrichroda, with its pretty castle and mysterious caves, but tarry not. A further 8km north brings you to the A4 autobahn at exit 41b Gotha-Boxberg. Head east for 45km to exit 46 Erfurt West. From here, take the L3004 north for 11km into Erfurt.

**08 ERFURT**
Thuringia's attractive capital has seen much since being founded in 742 by St Boniface as a bishopric on the Gera River. Known for its churches, steeples and synagogues, today's Erfurt is a vibrant city with an appearance that honours its medieval roots, while adding classy, contemporary flourishes. An overnight stay is recommended. Erfurt has a number of lovely squares to stroll between. Be sure to visit Domplatz and the monumentous **Erfurter Dom** (Mariendom; dom-erfurt.de); **Anger**, a transport and shopping hub where old meets new; **Wenigemarkt**, the perfect place for a casual meal; and **Fischmarkt**, Erfurt's central square, where you'll find the neo-Gothic **Rathaus** and a collection of spectacular historical buildings. Museums abound, including the worthwhile **Angermuseum** (angermuseum.de), with its strong collection of medieval art, and the fascinating **Alte Synagoge** (juedisches-leben.erfurt.de), one of Europe's oldest Jewish houses of worship.

**THE DRIVE**
Take the B7 for 22km east, through fields of rapeseed and wind turbines, into Weimar.

**09 WEIMAR**
Few German cities of Weimar's size can boast such a wealth of culture and history. Weimar's main claim to fame is that literary and philosophical titans Goethe and Schiller spent the bulk of their days here. If you're interested in these big daddies of German culture, you've come to the right place. You can't get much more authentic than **Goethe Gartenhaus** (klassik-stiftung.de), where the great man lived between 1776 and 1782. Learn all about him in the **Goethe-Nationalmuseum** (klassik-stiftung.de), then take a peek at the **Nietzsche Archiv** (klassik-stiftung.de), where philosopher Friedrich Nietzsche spent his final years in illness. Perhaps the most spectacular and thought-provoking site is the UNESCO World Heritage **Herzogin Anna Amalia Bibliothek** (klassik-stiftung.de), which has been beautifully reconstructed after a fire in 2004 destroyed much of the building and its priceless contents. Some of the most precious tomes are housed in the magnificent **Rokokosaal** (Rococo Hall).

**THE DRIVE**
Follow the B7 for 25km east into Jena.

**TOP TIP:**
**WeimarCard**

Pick up a great-value **WeimarCard** from the **tourist office** (weimar.de) for free admission to most museums, discounted tours, free iGuides and free travel on local buses if you want to let someone else do the driving for a while.

## 10 JENA

Unlike its neighbours Erfurt and Weimar, Jena owes its beauty more to the Saale River and the surrounding limestone hills than to a wealth of architectural and heritage sites. That said, Jena too has an age-old history as well as a fun, modern vibe, courtesy of the 19,000 strong student body. The birthplace of precision optics – pioneered here by Carl Zeiss, Ernst Abbe and Otto Schott – it is Jena's pedigree as a city of science that sets it apart from other Thuringian towns. Today, several museums attest to this legacy, including the **Stadtmuseum & Kunstsammlung Jena** (City Museum & Art Collection; stadtmuseum-jena.de), where you can learn how the city evolved into a centre of philosophy and science, and the public **Zeiss Planetarium** (planetarium-jena.de), the world's oldest. Goethe himself planted the ginkgo tree in the wonderful **Botanischer Garten** (spezbot.uni-jena.de/botanischer-garten), which boasts more than 12,000 plants from every climatic zone on earth.

### WHY I LOVE THIS TRIP

**Marc Di Duca**, writer

This trip showcases Germany's evolution from medieval times to the industrialised, environmentally aware nation that's celebrated today. From just over an hour outside Berlin you can pick up this fantastic time warp around one of the longest-inhabited regions in the country, along tree-lined avenues, up mountains, down dales, through ancient forests and by sparkling rivers. I promise you won't be bored.

### THE DRIVE

Head south for 51km on the delightfully green B88, through thick forests and woodlands into Saalfeld.

## 11 SAALFELD

Gables, turrets and gates provide a cheerful welcome to Saalfeld, which has been sitting prim and pretty along the Saale River for 1100 years. Aside from the handsome medieval town centre, you might want to check out the **Feengrotten** (Fairy Grottoes; feengrotten.de) if you're young at heart or travelling with kids. These former alum slate mines (1530–1850) were opened for tours in 1914 and rank among the world's most colourful grottoes, imbued with shades of brown, ochre, sienna, green and blue. Otherwise, take a stroll around the **Markt** then along Brudergasse, uphill to a 13th-century Franciscan monastery, now recycled as the **Stadtmuseum** (City Museum; museumimkloster.de). Its major allure is the celestial building itself, and the collection of local late-Gothic carved altarpieces.

### THE DRIVE

Follow the B281 for 57km until the intersection with the A4 autobahn at exit 56a Hermsdorfer Kreuz. Follow the A7 east for some faster roads for 86km into Chemnitz, at exit 69 Chemnitz Mitte.

## 12 CHEMNITZ

Known from 1953 to 1990 as Karl-Marx-Stadt, Chemnitz, like most former East German cities, had to reinvent itself after reunification. It's done so with some measure of success, at least in its revitalised city centre, which has a pedestrianised

**Feengrotten, Saalfeld**

## Photo Opportunity
Dresden by twilight on the banks of the Elbe.

Dresden

glass-and-steel shopping-and-entertainment district. Although you're here primarily to stretch your legs en route to Dresden, there are some engaging museums that might pique your interest: lovers of modern art should not miss **Museum Gunzenhauser** (kunstsammlungen-chemnitz.de) and its gallery of 20th-century expressionist works, housed in a 1930s former bank building in the austere New Objectivity style. **DAStietz** (dastietz.de) is a beautifully renovated 1913 former department store and now a one-stop shop for art and culture, housing the city library; **Neue Sächsische Galerie** (neue-saechsische-galerie.de), which presents contemporary Saxon art; and the **Museum für Naturkunde** (Natural History Museum; naturkunde-chemnitz.de), whose most interesting exhibit, the **Versteinerter Wald** (petrified forest), can be admired for free in the atrium; some of the stony trunks are 290 million years old.

### THE DRIVE
Take the A4 autobahn from exit 69 Chemnitz Mitte for 70km to exit 78 Dresden Altstadt.

 **DRESDEN**

There are few city silhouettes more striking than that of Dresden, once known fondly as the 'Florence of the North'. The classic view from the Elbe's northern bank takes in spires, towers and domes belonging to palaces, churches and stately buildings, and indeed it's hard to believe that the city was all but wiped off the map by Allied bombings in 1945. Dresden's beloved domed **Frauenkirche** (frauenkirche-dresden.de) collapsed after the WWII bombings, and was rebuilt from a pile of rubble between 1994 and 2005. Other must-sees include **Albertinum** (skd.museum), a Renaissance-era former arsenal transformed into the stunning home of the **Galerie Neue Meister** (New Masters Gallery), and one of Germany's most famous opera houses, the **Semperoper** (semperoper-erleben.de), which opened in 1841 and hosted premieres of works by Strauss, von Weber and Wagner.

### THE DRIVE
Getting back onto the Avenues Route, take the B6 northwest for 60km to the little town of Oschatz, where there has been a settlement since neolithic times. Continue on the B6 through lowlands and fields for another 56km into Leipzig.

### 14 LEIPZIG
When it comes to art, the neo-realistic New Leipzig School has stirred up the international art world for well over a decade with such protagonists as Neo Rauch and Tilo Baumgärtel. Such contemporary art in all media is the speciality of the **Galerie für Zeitgenössische Kunst** (gfzk-leipzig.de), presenting exhibits in a minimalist container-like space and a late 19th-century villa. The city's beloved **Nikolaikirche** (Church of St Nicholas; nikolaikirche.de) has Romanesque and Gothic roots, but since 1797 has sported a striking neoclassical interior with palm-like pillars and cream-coloured pews. The design is certainly gorgeous but the church is most famous for playing a key role in the non-violent movement that led to the downfall of the East German government.

### THE DRIVE
Head north on the B2 for 9km to the junction with the A14 autobahn at exit 23 Leipzig Mitte, then follow the A14 west for 14km to the A9 autobahn at exit 15 Schkeuditzer Kreuz. Head north on the A9 for 48km into Dessau-Rosslau.

TOP TIP:

## Noch Besser Leben

In Leipzig, this locally beloved **bar** (nochbesserleben.com) at the epicentre of the Plagwitz entertainment district is the perfect spot to meet a cool local crowd. With an upstairs band room, funky downstairs bar and bustling patio, it has a communal, friendly vibe for which only the German word *gemütlich* (approximately translated as cosy) will do.

Bacharach (p99)

# Northwestern Germany

**09 North Sea Coast**
Drive this best-followed-in-summer jaunt that hugs the Wattenmeer coast from Emden to Sylt. **p76**

**10 German Fairy Tale Road**
Follow the fantasies and fairy tales in the stories of the Brothers Grimm from the town of their birth (Hanau) to Bremerhaven. **p82**

**11 Cologne & the Ruhr Valley**
Look for the Romans, experience the country's industrial heartland, and join three iconic German cities: Cologne, Dortmund and Paderborn. **p90**

**12 Romantic Rhine**
Fall under the spell of the castle-lined riverscape along the world-famous Rhine on this fabulous drive from Düsseldorf to Mainz. **p94**

**13 Moselle Valley**
Wind through the winery-filled Moselle, from historic Trier to the river's end, where it meets the Rhine at Koblenz. **p102**

**14 German Wine Route**
Bookended by twin gates at Schweigen-Rechtenbach and Bockenheim an der Weinstrasse, this picturesque route links up charming vine-draped villages. **p106**

# Explore

# Northwestern Germany

There's always been a hint of magic about Germany's northwest, nowhere more so than along the Fairy Tale Road, a route that traces the legend of master storytellers, the Brothers Grimm. And you could easily spend weeks following the wine trails along the Rhine and Moselle, and over vine-clad hills everywhere. Throw in a delightful coastal meander, castles, cathedral towns and wonderful smaller cities like Trier and Mainz and it really is a fantastic region for drive touring. And whenever you need a dose of city life, you've signature urban centres like Hamburg, Bremen, Dortmund and Cologne to immerse yourself in.

## Hamburg

Germany's ultimate gateway to the north, Hamburg is one of Germany's coolest, edgiest, most enjoyable cities. Built around neighbourhoods, each with its own offbeat personality, with a waterfront that stretches from a New Age opera house to the old-style fish market, Hamburg has cachet, not to mention a suitably eclectic musical heritage that begins with Brahms and Mendelssohn and ends with the Beatles. It's also brimful of great accommodation and dining options, and its commanding geographic position in the north means that you're well placed for exploring the northwest (and the northeast if that's your thing).

## Kassel

The central German city of Kassel flies a little under the radar when compared to its better-known neighbours. It's an engaging, thoroughly enjoyable city that's one of the best places to eat anywhere in central Germany. It's also a buzzing university town, its cultural highlights include the stunning Bergpark Wilhelmshöhe, and it has an above-average portfolio of places to stay. As a hub for driving around Germany, its location in the heart of the country puts you within reach of just about anywhere from Hamburg to Bavaria; it's especially convenient for exploring the German cultural heartland to west and east.

### WHEN TO GO

The best weather conditions and longest days are from May to September, but avoid July and August if you don't like crowds. The North Sea coast is at its best (and not so crowded) in August and September, the Moselle has wine festivals from late April to early November, and the southern Pfalz region is glorious during the March-to-mid-May spring bloom.

## Cologne

Cologne often ends up being many travellers' favourite German city. And what's not to love? The cathedral here is a miracle wrought in stone, the city's proximity to Germany's best wine regions fuels a culinary experience of the highest quality, and there are enough museums and niche shopping experiences for everyone to fill a few days. The city couldn't be better placed for exploring the Rhine and Moselle, and the infrastructure here in terms of transport connections, hotels and restaurants is world-class. But it does have a downside – most people never want to leave.

## Mainz

They don't call Mainz the City of Churches for no reason – plan on a day just to take it all in. And factor in a visit to the real-life Gutenberg Bible. But Mainz is so much more than the sum total of its attractions. Mainz has a special something, a small city with bucketloads of quiet urban charm. It also has plenty of places to stay, eat and get your trip on the road. Three of northwestern Germany's driving routes begin within less than an hour of the city, and Bavaria is just a short drive away.

**WHERE TO STAY**

Hotels, pensions and guesthouses are everywhere all across northwestern Germany. Clearly the cities will have the biggest array of choices, ranging from contemporary style-temples to converted medieval buildings rich in history and comfort. Watch also for castles and monasteries clinging to the hilltops out in the countryside: some have been converted into high-end and highly atmospheric hotels. Our favourite experiences of sleeping in the region, however, almost always come when staying in the small villages along the way, thanks to the quiet magic that descends on small-town Germany after the tour buses leave.

### TRANSPORT

With so many major cities in the region, getting here is never an issue – Cologne, Hamburg, Düsseldorf and, of course, Frankfurt have excellent regional and international flight connections and lots of car-hire agencies. An excellent network of buses and trains runs mostly north-south through the region if you're looking to join the dots.

**WHAT'S ON**

### Carnival
Some of Europe's most raucous Carnival celebrations take over Cologne and Düsseldorf in February, but the Mainzer Fastnacht runs from 11 November to mid-March.

### Beethovenfest
For three weeks in September (sometimes into October) Bonn celebrates its most famous son with dozens of concerts.

### Christmas markets
Every German city has one, but Trier and Mainz could just be the biggest surprise packets. Trier's is one of Europe's most beautiful.

### Resources

**The Fairy Tale Road** (*deutsche-maerchenstrasse.com*) Plot your path north through the heart of Germany via the stories of the Brothers Grimm.

**Rhineland-Palatinate** (*rlp-tourismus.com*) The official online guide to exploring Germany's best-loved wine country.

**Weinfeste Moselle** (*mosel-weinfeste.de*) Helpful in matching your wine tour to upcoming festivals.

# 09
# North Sea Coast

**BEST FOR OUTDOORS**

Walk the Wadden Sea to an East Frisian Island.

Norderney

| DURATION | DISTANCE | GREAT FOR |
|---|---|---|
| 5–7 days | 613km / 391 miles | History & nature |

| BEST TIME TO GO | August to September: long days and thin crowds. |
|---|---|

From Emden, lightly dusted with the flavours of its Dutch neighbours, travel along the blustery, beautiful Wadden Sea and a take-your-pick selection of enchanting East Frisian Islands, to Bremerhaven, former seat of German emigration, onwards to the high-culture city states of Bremen and Hamburg, before retiring to Sylt, Germany's luxe island resort at the Danish border.

## Link Your Trip

**01 Along the Baltic Coast**

From Hamburg, drive northeast for 65km to Lübeck to join this aquatic excursion, and you'll have Germany's coasts covered.

**02 Design for Life: Bauhaus to VW**

It's 130km of autobahn action from Bremen southeast to Hanover, the final stop of our modern, architecture-themed jaunt.

### 01 EMDEN

You're almost in the Netherlands here: the flat landscape, dykes and windmills outside town and the melodic twang of the local Plattdütsch dialect combine to give this quiet seafaring city a Dutch flavour. Begin your trip with a visit to the **Bunkermuseum** (bunkermuseum. de), to remind yourself that life wasn't always this peaceful here, and check out the **Ostfriesisches Landesmuseum** (Regional History Museum; landesmuseum-emden.de) for an overview of the people whose culture and windblown landscapes

 **03 NORDDEICH**

There's only one real reason to hang about in the busy port of Norddeich: to take the **Reederei Frisia** (reederei-frisia.de) ferry to Norderney or Juist, which you might just want to do. If an East Frisian island visit is on your itinerary, consider spending the night here before or after your trip. Watching the late-night midsummer sun setting from the dykes wall is quite an experience.

### THE DRIVE
Follow Ostermarscher Strasse, which becomes the L5, for 15km to the village of Nessmersiel. This is where you'll alight for walking trips on the Wadden Sea to Baltrum, if you've booked yourself a guide. Otherwise, continue 17km to Benserbiel (for ferries to Langeoog), then onwards for 10km to Neuharlingersiel (ferries to Spiekeroog). It's 29km from here to Jever on the B461: follow the signs.

### Detour
**East Frisian Islands**
Start: 03 Norddeich
Lined up like diamonds in a tiara, from west to east, the seven East Frisian islands are: Borkum, Juist, Norderney, Baltrum, Langeoog, Spiekeroog and Wangerooge. Their long sandy beaches, open spaces and sea air make them a nature lovers' paradise and peaceful retreat. Like their North Frisian cousins Sylt, Amrum and Föhr, the islands are part of the UNESCO World Heritage Wadden Sea (Wattenmeer) National Park.

When the tide recedes on the Wadden Sea, it exposes the mudflats connecting the mainland to the islands, enabling nature lovers to waddle their muddy way to Baltrum and its sister 'isles'. *Wattwandern*,

you're about to explore. Ferries operated by **AG-Ems** (ag-ems.de) depart Emden for Borkum, the largest of the East Frisian Islands, popular with German and Dutch families, who rent houses and come for their summer vacations.

### THE DRIVE
Follow Auricher Strasse north out of town for 3.5km to Landesstrasse and turn left, through the village of Hinte, then turn right onto the K229 for 8km to the village of Jennelt. Turn right onto the L4 for 750m then follow Greetsieler Strasse for about 5km into the delightful village of Greetsiel.

**02 GREETSIEL**

The tiny, photogenic port of Greetsiel was first documented as far back as 1388. There's little to do here but stretch your legs, take a walk around the scenic harbour, check out a windmill or two and admire the handful of handsome buildings along the harbour wall. Why not pick up a souvenir while you're here?

### THE DRIVE
Turning back the way you came, pass the two windmills then turn left at the roundabout towards Norddeich on the L27: the raised bump the road follows on your left-hand side is a dyke. Drive 14km across the moors until you reach the intersection with the K214 and turn left, following the road (and the dyke) for 5km into Norddeich.

### Photo Opportunity
Capture the ethereal light of a late-night North Sea sunset.

**Sylt (p80)**

as it is known, is a no-no without an experienced guide: tidal changes can quickly cut you off from the mainland. Tourist offices in Emden and Jever can hook you up.

If that's not your thing, a day trip or overnight stay on Norderney, Queen of East Frisia, might do the trick. Founded in 1797 by Friedrich Wilhelm II of Prussia, it fast became one of the most famous bathing destinations in Europe. The island's Art Deco **Kurtheater** and the neoclassical **Conversationshaus** (1840), which today houses the tourist office, are worth a visit. But if you need to be pampered, you'll love the sprawling, luxurious **Badehaus** (norderney.de/badehaus) aquatic complex, day spa and sauna housed in the former Art Nouveau seawater baths: reason enough for a day trip.

Tourist season runs from mid-May to September, but opening hours of tourist offices are irregular as are ferry schedules, which are subject to the tides. Same-day return trips are not always possible and advance planning is usually required.

#### 04 JEVER
The capital of the Friesland region is also known for 'Fräulein Maria', who peers out from attractions and shop windows in Jever. She was the last of the so-called *Häuptlinge* (chieftains) to rule the town in the Middle Ages, and although Russia's Catherine the Great got her hands on Jever for a time in the 18th century, locals always preferred their home-grown queen. Having died unmarried and a virgin, Maria is the German equivalent of England's Elizabeth I. Check out her story in Jever's **Schloss** (schlossmuseum.de), then head to the **Friesisches Brauhaus zu Jever** (jever.de) for a brewery tour and a cold pilsner.

#### THE DRIVE
Head south on Mühlenstrasse then east on Silensteder Strasse until you reach the B210. Follow it south for 6km to the A29. Take the A29 south for 18km to Varel, then head east on the B437 for 38km. Pick up the A27 at exit 11 Stotel, heading north for 17km to exit 7, Bremerhaven Mitte.

#### 05 BREMERHAVEN
Bremerhaven's waterfront Havenwelten area, with its old ships and rusty docks juxtaposed against glistening contemporary architecture, is the

# Helgoland

Helgoland's former rulers, the British, really got the better deal in 1891 when they swapped it for then-German-ruled Zanzibar. But Germans today are very fond of this lonesome North Sea outcrop of red-sandstone rock and its fresh air and warm weather, courtesy of the Gulf Stream. The 80m-tall Lange Anna (Long Anna) rock on the island's southwest edge is a compelling sight, standing alone in the ocean. There are also WWII bunkers and ruins to explore, and resurging numbers of Atlantic grey seals. Driving and cycling are not permitted on the tiny 4.2-sq-km island. By an old treaty, Helgoland is not part of the EU's VAT area, so many of the 1130 residents make their living selling duty-free cigarettes, booze and perfume to day-trippers who prowl the main drag, *Lung Wai* ('long way'). To swim, many head to neighbouring Düne, a blip in the ocean that is popular with nudists.

Helgoland makes an easy day trip, but if you want to stay, there are more than 1000 hotel beds. Get more information at helgoland.de. To get here from Hamburg take the **Helgoline** (helgoline.de) ferry or high-speed catamaran from piers 3/4 at the St Pauli Piers.

product of a recent reimagining of its harbour as a place to play and learn. Not only goods have been shipped out for decades from Bremerhaven, one of Europe's busiest ports, but people, too: almost all German emigrants around the world headed off to their new lives from this very place. Hear their stories in the compelling **Deutsches Auswandererhaus** (German Emigration Centre; dah-bremerhaven.de). Continuing on this global theme, the neighbouring **Klimahaus Bremerhaven 8° Ost** (Climate House; klimahaus-bremerhaven.de) takes you on a fascinating journey around the world and its changing climes. If you've an inquisitive mind, both museums are reason enough to come to town.

 **THE DRIVE**
Heading back inland, follow the A7 autobahn for a speedy trip south, 60km into Bremen.

## 06 BREMEN

Bremen, one of Germany's three city states (along with Berlin and Hamburg), has a justified reputation for being among the country's most outward-looking and hospitable places, with a population that strikes a good balance between style, earthiness and good living. Bremen's vibrant districts have a host of fine restaurants, fun bars and a selection of excellent museums. Bremen's must-see **Altstadt** (old town) should be followed by a visit to the **Kunsthalle** (kunsthalle-bremen.de) for its

collection of paintings and artworks: some are over 600 years old. To mix up the new with the old, take a look at the downtown **Übersee Museum** (Overseas Museum; uebersee-museum.de): exhibits on each of the world's continents offer insight into natural evolution with a dazzling collection of exotic artefacts. With over 300 engaging exhibitions housed in a unique, shiny silver building resembling a clamshell, UFO or sperm whale, depending on your interpretation, Bremen's **Universum Science Center** (universum-bremen.de) is one of a kind.

**THE DRIVE**
Pick up the A1 just outside of town for a zippy 105km drive north to Hamburg and its famous port.

## Hamburg: A City Snapshot

Hamburg's commercial character was forged in 1189, when local noble Count Adolf III persuaded Emperor Friedrich I (Barbarossa) to grant the city free trading rights and an exemption from customs duties. This transformed the former missionary settlement and 9th-century moated fortress of Hammaburg into an important port and member of the Hanseatic League.

The city prospered until 1842, when the Great Fire destroyed a third of its buildings. While it managed to recover in time to join the German Reich in 1871, the city was then involved in two devastating world wars. After WWI, most of Hamburg's merchant fleet (almost 1500 ships) was forfeited to the Allies. WWII saw more than half of Hamburg's housing, 80% of its port and 40% of its industry reduced to rubble; tens of thousands of civilians were killed.

In the post-WWII years, Hamburg harnessed its resilience to participate in Germany's economic miracle (*Wirtschaftswunder*). Its harbour and media industries are now the backbone of its wealth. The majority of Germany's largest publications are produced here, including news magazines *Stern* and *Der Spiegel*.

### 07 HAMBURG

Germany's second-largest city, and one of the world's busiest ports, has never been shy. A centre of international trade since the 19th century, it amassed great wealth and remains one of the country's richest cities, infused with a maritime spirit and an openness that has given rise to vibrant multicultural neighbourhoods. Hamburg has more cultural and historical attractions than one can squeeze into a day or three. On **Deichstrasse** you can get a feel for the old canal and merchants' quarter. For bird's-eye views, take the glass lift to a 76.3m-high viewing platform in **Mahnmal St-Nikolai** (Memorial St Nicholas; mahnmal-st-nikolai.de), now a WWII memorial site. Or head to the boisterous **Fischmarkt** in St Pauli, running since 1703, where every Sunday in the wee hours some 70,000 locals and visitors converge. **Hamburger Kunsthalle** (hamburger-kunsthalle.de) is one of Germany's most impressive art galleries, while the incredible scale of **Miniatur Wunderland** (miniatur-wunderland.de) delights young and old.

#### THE DRIVE
Follow the A23 north for 105km until it becomes the B5. Continue for another 70km to Husum.

### 08 HUSUM

Warmly toned buildings huddle around Husum's photogenic Binnenhafen (inner harbour), colourful gabled houses line its narrow, cobbled lanes, and in late March and early April millions of purple crocuses bloom in the Schlosspark. The **Poppenspäler Museum** (pole-poppens paeler.de) has displays of enchanting handmade puppets, and even if you're not familiar with the 19th-century author, the **Theodor-Storm-Haus** (Theodor Storm House; storm-gesellschaft.de) holds appeal for its intimate depiction of a novelist's life in the rooms where he lived and worked.

#### THE DRIVE
Follow the B5 north for 80km to the end of the road and about as far north in Germany as you can go. Congratulations, you made it. You can elect to leave your car on the mainland, or take the car ferry over to the island.

### 09 SYLT

The star of Germany's North Frisian Islands, glamorous Sylt has designer boutiques housed in quintessential reed-thatched cottages, gleaming luxury automobiles jamming the car parks, luxurious accommodation and some of the country's most acclaimed restaurants. Sylt's candy-striped lighthouses rise above wide expanses of shifting dunes, fields of gleaming rapeseed and expanses of heath. On its west coast, fierce surf and strong winds gnaw at the shoreline. In the east, the retreating low-tidal shallows of the Wadden Sea shore expose vast mudflats. Aside from pampering yourself silly and burning a hole in your wallet, you'll want to visit 5000-year-old **Denghoog** (soelring-museen.de), a Stonehenge-esque archaeological site whose outer walls consist of 12 stones weighing around 40 tonnes, as well as the **Erlebnisz-entrum Naturgewalten** (Forces of Nature Centre; naturgewalten-sylt.de), a state-of-the-art ecological museum dedicated to the North Sea.

# 10

# German Fairy Tale Road

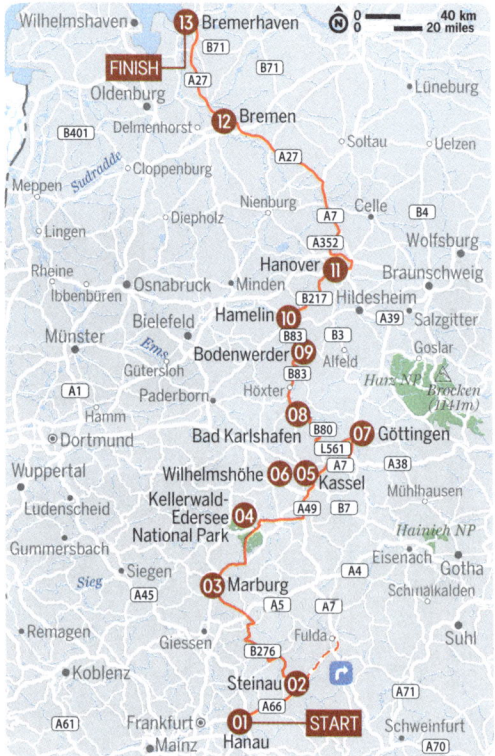

| DURATION | DISTANCE | GREAT FOR |
|---|---|---|
| 5 days | 707km / 439 miles | History, nature & families |
| **BEST TIME TO GO** | Enjoy this trip May to September. | |

Tirelessly roaming the villages and towns of 19th-century Germany, the Brothers Grimm collected 209 folk tales that had been passed down for countless generations. The stories they published often bear little resemblance to the sanitised versions spoon-fed to kids today; rather, they are morality tales with blood, gore, sex, the supernatural, magic and much more. See the locations of the stories and learn about the remarkable brothers on this trip, which includes a few non-Grimm fairy tale sights as well.

### Link Your Trip

**02 Design for Life: Bauhaus to VW**

Join this trip at Hanover to cover iconic German centres of design.

**05 Central Germany's Castles & Palaces**

At Kassel, detour through Germany's heartland to castles and lavish palaces all the way to Leipzig.

### 01 HANAU

A mere 20km east of Frankfurt on the Main River, Hanau is the birthplace of the Brothers Grimm (Jacob in 1785 and Wilhelm in 1786) and the perfect place to begin this trip. Not that their births are especially commemorated here...

Located within Philippsruhe Palace, dating from the early 18th century, the **Historisches Museum Schloss Philippsruhe** (museen-hanau.de) has displays on town history, arts and crafts. The parks and gardens (free) are a beautiful stroll in snow or in summer.

**BEST FOR FAMILIES**

Grimmwelt, Kassel's attraction dedicated to all things Grimm and fairy-tale-worthy.

Grimmwelt, Kassel (p85)

### THE DRIVE
Hop on the A66 for a quick 50km run through the rolling hills to Steinau.

### 02 STEINAU
Steinau is situated on the historic trade road between Frankfurt and Leipzig. (The town's full name is 'Steinau an der Strasse', an important distinction when using your map app as there's another Steinau way up by the North Sea.)

The twin museums, **Brüder Grimm-Haus and Museum Steinau** (brueder-grimm-haus.de), inside the building where the Grimm family lived from 1791 to 1796, have exhibitions on the brothers, their work and the history of Steinau.

### THE DRIVE
Head west on the L3196 for 18km to the B276, where you'll turn north. Weave through the valleys for 64km to the junction with the L3166 and follow the Marburg signs along the L3127, L3089, L3048 and L3125. Picnic spots abound along the route.

### Detour
**Fulda**
Start: 02 Steinau

Although it's not quite on the Fairy Tale Road, photogenic Fulda is well worth a side trip for those interested in sumptuous baroque architecture, historic churches and religious reliquaries. A Benedictine monastery was founded here in 744, and today Fulda has its own bishop.

Inside the baroque **Dom zu Fulda** (bistum-fulda.de), built from 1704 to 1712, you'll find gilded furnishings, plenty of *putti* (infant figures), dramatic statues (eg to the left of the altar) and the tomb of St Boniface, who died a martyr in 754.

Fulda's history started in **Michaelskirche** (St Michael's Church). A still-standing reminder of the abbey that made this town, this remarkable church was the monastic burial chapel. Beneath classic witch's-hat towers, a Carolingian rotunda and crypt recall Fulda's flourishing Middle Ages, when the abbey scriptorium churned out top-flight illuminated manuscripts.

BEST ROAD TRIPS: GERMANY, AUSTRIA & SWITZERLAND

## The Fairy Tale Road

The 600km **Märchenstrasse** (Fairy Tale Road; deutsche-maerchenstrasse.com) is one of Germany's most popular tourist routes, with over 60 stops along the way. It's made up of cities, towns and hamlets in four states (Hesse, Lower Saxony, North Rhine–Westphalia and Bremen), which can often be reached via a choice of roads rather than one single route. The towns are associated in one way or another with the works of Wilhelm and Jacob Grimm. Although most towns can be easily visited using public transport, a car lets you fully explore the route.

Don't miss Fulda's spectacular **Stadtschloss**, built from 1706 to 1721 as the prince-abbots' residence. It now houses the city administration and function rooms. Visitors can enter the ornate **Historiche Räume** (Historic Rooms), including the grandiose banquet hall, and the octagonal **Schlossturm** (castle tower) for great views of the town and magnificent **Schlossgarten** (palace gardens). The palace's fairy tale qualities capture the era's extravagance. Don't miss the amazing **Speigelkabinett** (Chamber of Mirrors) and grandiose **Fürstensaal**, a banquet hall decorated with reliefs of tipsy-looking wine queens. Also, there are pretty views from the **Green Room** over the gardens to the Orangerie.

Fulda is 40km northeast of Steinau on the A66.

Stadtschloss, Fulda

## 03 MARBURG

Hilly, historic and delightful, university town Marburg is 90km north of Frankfurt. It's a delight to wander the narrow lanes of the town's vibrant **Altstadt** (old town), sandwiched between a palace (above) and a spectacular Gothic church (below). On the south side of the focal Marktplatz is the historic **Rathaus** (town hall), dating to 1512. At the base of the Altstadt's Reitgasse is the neo-Gothic **Alte Universität** (1891), still a well-used and well-loved part of Philipps-Universität – the world's oldest Protestant university. Founded in 1527, it once counted the Brothers Grimm among its students.

Perched at the highest point in town, a steep walk up from St-Marien-Kirche or the Marktplatz, is massive **Landgrafenschloss** (uni-marburg.de/uni-museum), built between 1248 and 1300. It offers panoramic views of bucolic hills, jumbled Marburg rooftops and the **Schlosspark**.

 **THE DRIVE**
Head north on the B3; after 18km turn north on the L3073. Continue north for 37km through Gemünden and Frankenau to Edertal, where you'll find the park. Note how the forest gets thicker and darker as you go.

## 04 KELLERWALD-EDERSEE NATIONAL PARK

**Nationalpark Kellerwald-Edersee** (nationalpark-kellerwald-edersee.de) encompasses one of the largest extant red-beech forests in Central Europe, the **Kellerwald**, and the **Edersee**, a serpentine artificial reservoir 55km northeast of Marburg and about the same distance southwest of Kassel. In 2011 this national park, along with Hainich National Park in Thuringia and a cluster of other parks and reserves with large beech forests, became a UNESCO World Cultural Heritage site.

On a fairy tale trip, it's fitting to wander into the deep woods, never forgetting that if your name is Grimm, nothing good is bound to happen. If you're lucky, you may see larger land animals like red deer; overhead, you might spot eagles and honey buzzards and, at night, various species of bat. (The brothers would surely approve.)

For information, head to the striking **visitors centre** (nationalparkzentrum-kellerwald.de) at the western end of the Edersee.

**THE DRIVE**
Drive east on the L3332, B485 and B253 for 28km until you reach the A49 autobahn and zip along northeast until you reach Kassel.

## 05 KASSEL

Visitors to this culture-rich, sprawling hub on the Fulda River discover a pleasant, modern city.

Occupying a prime position atop the Weinberg bunker in the scenic **Weinbergpark** is the truly unmissable attraction on this trip, Kassel's **Grimmwelt** (grimmwelt.de). It could be described as an architect-designed walk-in sculpture housing the most significant collection of Brothers Grimm memorabilia on the planet. Visitors are guided around original exhibits, state-of-the-art

---

**WHY I LOVE THIS TRIP**

Marc Di Duca, writer

Did they give us nightmares or fantasies? Or both? Who can forget hearing the wild stories of the Brothers Grimm as a child? Evil stepmothers, dashing princes, fair maidens, clever animals, mean old wolves and more. With every passing year, these stories become more sanitised. But the real fairy tales are far more compelling, as you'll learn on this trip.

installations and fun, hands-on activities, aided by entries from the Grimms' German dictionary: there was more to these brothers than just fairy tales, didn't you know?

Billed as 'a meditative space for funerary art', the **Museum für Sepulkralkultur** (Museum for Sepulchral Culture; sepulkral museum.de) aims to bury the taboo of discussing death.

### THE DRIVE
The shortest leg of the trip takes you 6km west through Kassel's leafy suburbs. Take Wilhelmshöher Allee.

## 06 WILHELMSHÖHE
Wilhelmshöhe is the classy end of Kassel. You can spend a full day exploring the spectacular baroque parkland, **Bergpark Wilhelmshöhe** (museum-kassel.de), which takes its name from **Schloss Wilhelmshöhe**, the late 18th-century palace inside the expanse. Walk through the forest, enjoy a romantic picnic and explore the castles, fountains, grottoes, statues and water features: the **Herkules** statue and Löwenburg castle are also here.

The palace could star in any fairy tale. Home to Elector Wilhelm and later Kaiser Wilhelm II, the opulent complex today houses one of Germany's best collections of Flemish and Dutch baroque paintings in the **Gemäldegalerie** (painting gallery), featuring works by Rembrandt, Rubens, Jordaens, Lucas Cranach the Elder, Dürer and many others.

### THE DRIVE
Retrace your 6km drive on Wilhelmshöher Allee into Kassel and take the busy A7 right up to Göttingen.

## 07 GÖTTINGEN
With over 30,000 students, this historic town in a corner of Lower Saxony near the Hesse border offers a good taste of university-town life in Germany's north. Since 1734, the Georg-August Universität has sent more than 40 Nobel Prize winners into the world. As well as all those award-winning doctors and scientists, it also produced the fairy-tale-writing Brothers Grimm (as German language teachers).

Stroll around the pleasant **Markt** and nearby Barfüsserstrasse to admire the *Fachwerk* (half-timbered) houses. If you fancy, pop into a pub and make some new friends.

The city's symbol, the **Gänseliesel** (little goose girl) statue on Markt is hailed locally as the most kissed woman in the world – not a flattering moniker, you might think, but enough to make her iconic.

### THE DRIVE
Take the L561 22km west to the B80, then head northwest for another 27km to Bad Karlshafen. Enjoy the curving panoramas as you follow the Weser River, which links several of the Fairy Tale Road towns and cities.

---

## Grimm Fairy Tales

In the early 19th century, the Grimm brothers travelled extensively through central Germany documenting folklore. Their collection of tales, *Kinder- und Hausmärchen* (Children's and Household Tales), was first published in 1812 and quickly gained international recognition. It has 209 tales and includes such fairy tale staples as follows:

• **Hansel and Gretel** – A mother tries to ditch her son and daughter, a witch tries to eat them and Gretel outsmarts her. Kids and father reunited and all are happy (the evil mother had died).

• **Cinderella** – The story that gave stepsisters a bad name. Still, when the prince fits the shoe onto our heroine, all is good with the world, although in the Grimm version, the stepsisters are blinded by vengeful doves.

• **Rapunzel** – An adopted girl with very long hair, a prince who goes blind and some evil older women are combined in this morality play that ends with love when the prince stumbles upon an outcast Rapunzel and his sight is restored. In the first edition of the Grimms' book, Rapunzel had children out of wedlock.

For entertaining synopses of all the Grimm fairy tales, see shmoop.com/grimms-fairy-tales. One thing you'll note is that the Grimm original versions are much bloodier, more violent and earthier than the ultra-sanitised, Disney-fied versions today.

Although best known for their fairy tales, it should be noted that the Brothers Grimm were serious academics who also wrote *German Grammar* and *The History of the German Language*, enduring works that populate reference shelves to this day.

> **Photo Opportunity**
> Bremen's *Bremen Town Musicians* sculpture.

*Bremen Town Musicians* sculpture, Bremen (p89)

 **BAD KARLSHAFEN**

Bad Karlshafen's orderly streets and whitewashed baroque buildings were built in the 18th century for local earl Karl by French Huguenot refugees. The town was planned with an impressive harbour and a canal connecting the Weser and the Rhine to attract trade, but the earl died before his designs were completed. The only reminder of his grand plans is a tiny **Hafenbecken** (harbour basin) transited by white swans.

Take a stroll around the town centre, on the sinuous Weser's south bank, with the Hafenbecken and surrounding square, **Hafenplatz**, at its western end.

The interesting **Deutsches Huguenotten Museum** (German Huguenot Museum; huguenot-museum-germany.com) traces the history of the French Huguenot refugees in Germany, although it fails to mention how many were eaten by big bad wolves on the journey through the forest.

**THE DRIVE**
Stay on the B83 for the 58km to Bodenwerder. You'll enjoy Weser vistas for much of the journey – which might lure you to stop for a picnic.

 **BODENWERDER**

If Bodenwerder's most famous son were to have described his little hometown, he'd probably have painted it as a huge, thriving metropolis on the Weser. But then Baron Hieronymous von Münchhausen (1720–97) was one of history's most shameless liars (his whoppers were no mere fairy tales). He inspired the Terry Gilliam cult film, *The Adventures of Baron Munchausen*.

Bodenwerder's principal attraction, the **Münchhausen Museum** (muenchhausenland.de), tackles the difficult task of conveying the chaos and fun associated with the 'liar baron' – a man who liked to regale dinner guests with his Crimean adventures, claiming he had, for example, tied his horse to a church steeple during a snow drift and ridden around a dining table without breaking one teacup. It holds paintings and displays of Münchhausen books in many languages.

**THE DRIVE**
The B83 again takes you north 23km to Hamelin.

### 10 HAMELIN

According to the Brothers Grimm's *Pied Piper of Hamelin*, in the 13th century *Der Rattenfänger* (Pied Piper) was employed by Hamelin's townsfolk to lure its rodents into the river. When they refused to pay him, he picked up his flute and led their kids away. Today the rats rule once again – fluffy and cute stuffed rats, wooden rats, and tiny brass rats adorning the sights around town.

Rodents aside, Hamelin (Hameln in German) is a pleasant town with half-timbered houses and opportunities for cycling along the Weser, on whose eastern bank lies Hamelin's circular **Altstadt**. The town's heart is its **Markt**.

Many of Hamelin's finest buildings were constructed in the Weser Renaissance style, which has strong Italian influences. Learn more at the town's revamped **Museum Hamelin** (museum-hameln.de).

**THE DRIVE**
Drive 47km northwest on the B217.

### 11 HANOVER

Known for its huge trade shows, Hanover has a past: from 1714, monarchs from the house of Hanover also ruled Great Britain and the British Empire for over a century.

Let your hair down at the spectacularly baroque **Herrenhäuser Gärten** (herrenhaeuser-gaerten.de), the grandiose Royal Gardens of Herrenhausen, which are considered one of the most important historic garden landscapes in Europe. Inspired by Versailles' gardens, they're a great place to slow down and smell the roses for a couple of hours, especially on a blue-sky day. With its fountains, neat flowerbeds, trimmed hedges and shaped lawns, the 300-year-old **Grosser Garten** (Great Garden) is the centrepiece of the experience.

 **THE DRIVE**
Take the A352 16km to the A7, then shoot northwest on that road and the A27 (127km).

### 12 BREMEN

Bremen is well known for its fairy tale character, a unique expressionist quarter and (it must be said, because Bremeners are avid football fans) one of Germany's most exciting, if not overly successful, football teams.

With high, historic buildings rising up from this very compact square, Bremen's **Markt** is one of the most remarkable in northern Germany. The two towers of the 1200-year-old **Dom St Petri** (St Petri Cathedral; stpetridom.de) dominate the northeastern edge, beside the ornate and imposing **Rathaus**, which was erected in 1410. The Weser Renaissance balcony in the middle, crowned by three gables, was added between 1595 and 1618.

In front of the Rathaus is one of the hallmarks of Bremen, the city's 13m-high **Knight Roland statue** (1404). As elsewhere, Roland stands for a city's civic freedoms, especially the freedom to trade independently.

On the western side of the Rathaus you'll find the city's unmissable and famous symbol of the Grimm fairy tale: the *Bremen Town Musicians* (1951) by the sculptor Gerhard Marcks. The story tells of a donkey, a dog, a cat and a rooster who know their time is up with their cruel masters, and so set out for Bremen and the good life. On the way they encounter a forest cottage filled with robbers. They cleverly dispatch the crooks and, yes, live happily ever after. The statue depicts the dog, cat and rooster, one on top of the other, on the shoulders of the donkey. The donkey's nose and front legs are incredibly shiny having been touched by many visitors for good luck.

 **THE DRIVE**
A quick shot up the autobahn (A27) for 65km will bring you to Bremerhaven and the North Sea.

### 13 BREMERHAVEN

Anyone who has had the fairy tale dream of running away to sea will love Bremerhaven's waterfront – part trade machinery, part glistening glass buildings pointing to a more recent understanding of the harbour as a recreation spot.

Bremerhaven has long been a conduit that gathered the 'huddled masses' from the verdant but poor countryside and poured them into the world outside. Of the millions who landed in America, a large proportion sailed from here; an enticing exhibition at the **Deutsches Auswandererhaus** (German Emigration Centre; dah-bremerhaven.de), the city's prime attraction, allows you to share their history. The museum stands exactly in the spot where 7.2 million emigrants set sail between 1830 and 1974. Your visit begins at the wharf where passengers gathered before boarding a steamer. You then visit passenger cabins from different periods (note the improving comfort levels) before going through the immigration process at New York's Ellis Island.

Herrenhäuser Gärten, Hanover

# 11
# Cologne & the Ruhr Valley

**BEST FOR FAMILIES**

Xanten's Römer Museum brings the past alive for all ages.

| DURATION | DISTANCE | GREAT FOR |
|---|---|---|
| 4 days | 404km / 251 miles | History, wine & families |

| BEST TIME TO GO | Enjoy the food, drink and culture any time, but April to October is fun outdoors. |
|---|---|

Dom, Cologne

The Anabaptists were a religious cult that took over the then-pious city of Münster in 1535 – they didn't last but you can learn about their wild ideas at that city's impressive LWL-Museum für Kunst und Kultur. There are also many other fascinating stories here in one of Germany's most historic regions, which boasts dramatic chapters from Roman times till today.

## Link Your Trip

**10 German Fairy Tale Road**
Find out about Cinderella and co. by joining this route at Bad Karlshafen, 66km east of Paderborn on the B64.

**12 Romantic Rhine**
At Cologne, follow the riverscape along the world-famous Rhine.

### 01 COLOGNE

Cologne is like a 3D textbook on history and architecture. Around town you'll stumble upon an ancient Roman wall, medieval churches like the magnificent Dom and more. Many don't realise that Germany's fourth-largest city was founded by the Romans in 38 BC and given the lofty name Colonia Claudia Ara Agrippinensium. Sculptures and ruins displayed outside the entrance of the **Römisch-Germanisches Museum** (Roman Germanic Museum; roemisch-germanisches-museum.de) are the overture to a full symphony of Roman artefacts found along the Rhine. Highlights include the giant

## What's a Ruhrgebiet?

Once known for its belching steelworks and filthy coal mines, the Ruhrgebiet – a sprawling postindustrial region of 53 cities and 5.3 million people – has worked hard in recent years to reinvent itself for the postindustrial future. It includes Duisburg, Essen and Dortmund, all stops on this route.

Poblicius tomb (AD 30–40) and the magnificent 3rd-century **Dionysus mosaic**. Discover more of Cologne's past at the **Archäologische Zone** (miqua.lvr.de), whose deepest level has the Praetorium, with relics of a Roman governor's palace.

### THE DRIVE
Travel at very un-Roman speeds north on the A3 autobahn 73km to Duisburg.

### 02 DUISBURG
Duisburg is home to Europe's largest inland port, whose immensity is best appreciated on a **boat tour** (Harbour Tour; wf-duisburg.de). Embarkation is at the **Schwanentor**, also the gateway to the Innenhafen Duisburg (inner harbour), an urban quarter with a mix of modern and restored buildings. Now a unique performance space and an all-ages adventure playground, **Landschaftspark Duisburg-Nord** (Landscape Park Duisburg-Nord; landschaftspark.de) is a decommissioned iron works where molten iron used to flow 24/7 from its fiery furnaces.

### THE DRIVE
Escape Duisburg on the A40, cross the Rhine and take exit 10 and the L287 north. At Rheinberg, join the B57 (Xantener Strasse). It's a straight shot northwest for 19km to Xanten.

### 03 XANTEN
Xanten has been the hub of the Lower Rhine ever since its founding as a Roman military camp in 12 BC. Within a century it grew into a respectable settlement called Colonia Ulpia Traiana. Revel in all things Roman at the **Archäologischer Park** (Archaeological Park; apx.lvr.de). Its highlight is the **RömerMuseum**, which takes you on a journey through 400 years of Roman presence in the Lower Rhine region.

The crown jewel of Xanten's **Altstadt** (old town) is the **Dom St Viktor** (sankt-viktor-xanten.de), which has Romanesque roots but is now largely Gothic.

### THE DRIVE
Leave Xanten driving south for 14km to the well-signposted A57. Continue south for 18km to the A40 and go east 33km to Essen.

### 04 ESSEN
It's taken a few decades, but Germany's seventh-largest city has transitioned from industrial powerhouse to city of commerce and culture like few others. A grande dame among Germany's art repositories, the free **Museum Folkwang** (museum-folkwang.de) has sparkling premises with galleries radiating out from inner courtyards and

## The Krupp Dynasty

In the Ruhrgebiet, steel and Krupp are virtually synonyms. So are Krupp and Essen, for it's this bustling Ruhrgebiet city that is the ancestral seat of the Krupp family and the headquarters of one of the most powerful corporations in Europe. It all began rather modestly in 1811 when Friedrich Krupp and two partners founded a company to process 'English cast steel', but, despite minor successes, Krupp left a company mired in debt upon his death in 1826. Enter his son Alfred, then a tender 14, who would go on to become a seminal figure of the industrial age.

It was through the production of the world's finest steel that the 'Cannon King' galvanised a company that – by 1887 – employed more than 20,000 workers. It also provided womb-to-tomb benefits to its workers at a time when 'social welfare' had not yet entered the world's vocabulary. In an unbroken pattern of dazzling innovation, coupled with ruthless business practices, Krupp produced steel and machinery that was essential to the world economy.

Krupp will forever be associated, however, with the Third Reich. Not only did the corporation supply the hardware for the German war machine, it also provided much of the financial backing that Hitler needed to build up his political power base. Krupp plants were prime targets for Allied bombers. After the war, the firm slowly lost its way and in 1999 merged with arch-rival Thyssen.

An excellent source for an understanding of what the Krupp family has meant to Germany is William Manchester's brilliant chronicle *The Arms of Krupp* (1964).

---

gardens. Don't miss a visit to the **Zollverein Coal Mine** (zollverein.de), the UNESCO-listed industrial complex whose star is the **Ruhr Museum** (ruhrmuseum.de). Engaging exhibits span the region's history. Just as the coal was transported on conveyor belts, a long escalator whisks you up to the foyer from where you descend into the building's dark bowels.

### THE DRIVE
You are back on the A40 for the 38km to Dortmund. Evidence of the Ruhrgebiet's once-great industrial might are everywhere as you travel.

### 05 DORTMUND
Football is a major Dortmund passion. Borussia Dortmund, the city's team in the Bundesliga (Germany's first league), has been national champion eight times, including for the 2011–12 season (they were runners-up as recently as 2018–19). It's appropriate that the city is home to the **DFB-Museum** (German Football Museum; fussballmuseum.de). Classic scenes of German football triumphs play across the facade of this vast new shrine to the nation's passion. Right outside the Hauptbahnhof, the museum has 6900 sq metres of exhibits dedicated to Germany's footballing prowess.

### THE DRIVE
Leave Dortmund on the B1 heading east for 13km. At the A1 autobahn, turn north to Münster.

### 06 MÜNSTER
One of the most appealing cities between Cologne and Hamburg, Münster has a beautiful centre with many architectural gems. The Altstadt is ringed with beautiful lakes and parks, buzzing with cyclists. The two massive towers of **Dom St Paul** (sankt-viktor-xanten.de) match the proportions of this 110m-long structure and the vast square it overlooks. It's a three-nave construction built in the 13th century. Nearby, the **Historisches Rathaus** (Historic City Hall & Peace Hall) is a Gothic gem. In the **LWL-Museum für Kunst und Kultur** (Museum for Art & Culture; lwl-museum-kunst-kultur.de), explore a collection spanning the Middle Ages to the latest avant-garde creations, and learn about the Anabaptist religious cult.

### THE DRIVE
The next stretch of driving will get you off the autobahn to wander past little villages amid verdant farmland. Take the L585 out of Münster; drive southeast over a series of roads for 42km to Beckum, and switch to the B475 for the final 26km.

### 07 SOEST
One of northwest Germany's most appealing towns, Soest is a tranquil place with half-timbered houses and a clutch of treasure-filled churches that reflect the town's wealth

**Photo Opportunity**
The weirdly green stone of Soest shimmering in the sun.

St Patrokli, Soest

during its Hanseatic League days. It's a maze of idyllic, crooked lanes that has been beautifully rebuilt and preserves much of its medieval character. Soest's one remarkable feature is its stone: a shimmering greenish local sandstone used in the town wall, churches and other public structures. Check out the late-Gothic **St Maria zur Wiese** (Wiesenkirche; wiesenkirche.de) and 10th-century Romanesque **St Patrokli** (sankt-patrokli.de).

### THE DRIVE
Drive 52km from Soest to Paderborn on the B1.

 **PADERBORN**
From the 8th century AD, Charlemagne used Paderborn as a power base to defeat the Saxons and convert them to Christianity, giving him the momentum needed to rise to greater things. Paderborn remains a pious place to this day – churches abound, and religious sculpture and motifs adorn facades, fountains and parks. Start at the massive (104m-long) **Dom** (dom-paderborn.de), a three-nave Gothic hall church.

# 12

# Romantic Rhine

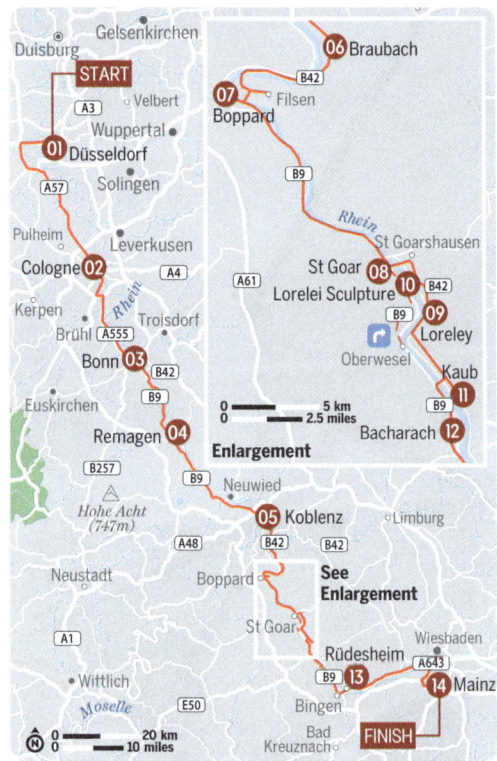

| DURATION | DISTANCE | GREAT FOR |
|---|---|---|
| 5–7 days | 235km / 155 miles | History, wine & nature |

| BEST TIME TO GO | April to October offers the best weather, but July and August can be crowded. |
|---|---|

Boats gliding down the Rhine give passengers mesmerising views of the medieval villages, craggy hillsides, and castle after castle floating past. But on this trip you'll get up close to its mightiest sights, hike through its loftiest vineyards, and discover hidden treasures and romantic hideaways you'd never see from the water. (Though you'll have plenty of opportunities en route to board a cruise, too.)

### Link Your Trip

**11 Cologne & the Ruhr Valley**

At Cologne you can also pick up this absorbing route, visiting vibrant Ruhr cities such as Essen and Münster.

**13 Moselle Valley**

Koblenz sits at the confluence of the Rhine and the Moselle, source of more vineyard-ribboned views and irresistible wines.

### 01 DÜSSELDORF

Survey the mighty Rhine from Düsseldorf's **Medienhafen**. This old harbour area continues to attract red-hot restaurants, bars, hotels and clubs. Crumbling warehouses have transformed into high-tech office buildings, rubbing shoulders with bold new structures designed by celebrated international architects, including Frank Gehry.

Of course, no visit to Düsseldorf is complete without exploring its **Altstadt** (old town), which claims to be the 'longest bar in the world'.

**BEST FOR OUTDOORS**

Hike through the vines above Rüdesheim.

Hiking, Rüdesheim (p100)

**THE DRIVE**
It's a 44km drive south via the B1 and the A57 to Cologne. (Fear not: although this section travels through built-up areas and industrial estates, later stages become much more scenic.)

### 02 COLOGNE

A walking tour is the best way to appreciate this engaging city (Germany's fourth-largest) on the Rhine. Must-sees include Cologne's world-famous **Dom** (Cologne Cathedral; koelner-dom.de), whose twin spires dominate the skyline, as well as superb museums such as the **Römisch-Germanisches Museum** (Roman Germanic Museum; roemisch-germanisches-museum.de); sculptures and ruins displayed outside its entrance are the overture to its symphony of Roman artefacts found along the Rhine.

**THE DRIVE**
Drive south along the B51 on the Rhine's west bank before joining the A555 (29km in total).

### 03 BONN

In a beautiful riverside setting, Ludwig van Beethoven's home town warrants a stop to visit the **Beethoven-Haus Bonn** (Beethoven House; beethoven-haus-bonn.de), where the great composer was born in 1770. Other landmarks include the soaring **Münster Basilica** (bonner-muenster.de), built on the graves of the two martyred Roman soldiers who later became the city's patron saints. It's currently closed for renovations, but the cloister is still partially accessible.

Bonn's old government quarter dates from its time as West Germany's 'temporary' capital, between 1949 and 1991 (when a reunited German government decided to move to Berlin). **Haus der Geschichte** (Museum of History; hdg.de) focuses on history in both Germanies from the end of WWII to the present. Its hugely popular, but the dated, permanent exhibition was retired after

**Burg Neukatzenelnbogen**

30 years in 2024 and replaced with a new one, expected to open December 2025. Alongside it, temporary exhibitions ranging from light-hearted to provocative keep things fresh.

### 🚗 THE DRIVE
Take the B9 southeast for 24km. Once you leave the German state of North Rhine-Westphalia and enter Rhineland–Palatinate, the road returns to the river's west bank; on your right you'll see the hilly wildlife park, Wildpark Rolandseck.

### 04  REMAGEN
Remagen was founded by the Romans in 16 CE as Rigomagus, but the town would hardly figure in the history books were it not for one fateful day in early March 1945. As the Allies raced across France and Belgium to rid Germany of Nazism, the Wehrmacht tried frantically to stave off defeat by destroying all bridges across the Rhine. But the Brücke von Remagen (the steel rail bridge) lasted long enough for Allied troops to cross the river, contributing significantly to the collapse of Hitler's western front. One of the bridge's surviving basalt towers now houses the **Friedensmuseum Brücke von Remagen** (Peace Museum Bridge at Remagen; bruecke-remagen.de), with a well-presented exhibit on Remagen's pivotal role in WWII.

### 🚗 THE DRIVE
Take the B9 southeast for 49km. The Rhine winds back and forth away from the road until you reach Koblenz. Stay on the B9 until you've crossed the Moselle to the town centre, or risk getting lost in a maze of concentric flyovers.

---

### WHY I LOVE THIS TRIP
**Marc Di Duca**, writer

The romance along this stretch of the Rhine is timeless. Poets and painters including Lord Byron and William Turner are among those who have been inspired by this castle-crowned, forest-and-vineyard-cloaked valley. A fabled stop on the original European Grand Tour, the riverscape here is now a designated UNESCO World Heritage site. It doesn't get more classic than that.

**KOBLENZ**
Koblenz sits at the confluence of the Rhine and Moselle rivers – marked by the expansive **Deutsches Eck** ('German Corner'), adjoining flower-filled parks and promenades – and the convergence of three low mountain ranges (the Hunsrück, the Eifel and the Westerwald). Its roots go back to the Romans, who founded a military stronghold (Confluentes) here because of the site's supreme strategic value.

On the Rhine's right bank, the 118m-high fortress **Festung Ehrenbreitstein** (tor-zum-welterbe.de) proved indestructible to all but Napoleonic troops, who levelled it in 1801. To prove a point, the Prussians rebuilt it as one of Europe's mightiest fortifications. It's accessible by car, on foot and by cable car.

Inside Koblenz' striking new glass **Forum Confluentes**, the **Mittelrhein-Museum** (mittelrhein-museum.de) spans 2000 years of the region's history, including 19th-century landscape paintings of the Romantic Rhine by German and British artists.

**THE DRIVE**
Take the B49 to the Rhine's east bank and travel south on the B42; it's 13km to Braubach. At this point of the drive, you leave the cityscapes behind and enter an older world of cobblestones, half-timbered villages, densely forested hillsides and ancient vineyards.

 **BRAUBACH**
Framed by forest, vineyards and rose gardens, the 1300-year-old town of Braubach centres on its small, half-timbered **Marktplatz**. High above are the dramatic towers, turrets and crenellations of the 700-year-old **Marksburg** (marksburg.de), which is unique among the Rhine's fastnesses as it was never destroyed. The compulsory tour takes in the citadel, the Gothic hall and a grisly torture chamber.

**THE DRIVE**
Hug the Rhine's east bank for 11km as it curves around to the car-ferry dock at Filsen. It's a five-minute crossing to charming Boppard.

 **BOPPARD**
Idyllically located on a horseshoe bend in the river, Boppard (pronounced 'bo-*part*') is one of the Romantic Rhine's prettiest towns, not least because its riverfront and historic centre are both on the same side of the railway tracks.

Boppard's riverfront promenade, the **Rheinallee**, has grassy areas for picnicking and a children's playground.

Many of the town's half-timbered buildings house cosy wine taverns, including its oldest, **Weinhaus Heilig Grab** (heiliggrab.de). In summer, sip local Rieslings under the chestnut trees, where live music plays on weekends.

Fantastic hiking trails fan out into the countryside, including the **Hunsrück Trails**, accessed by Germany's steepest scheduled railway route, the **Hunsrückbahn** (hunsrueckbahn.de). Around the **Vierseenblick** (Four-Lakes-View), a panoramic outlook reached by **Sesselbahn** (Chairlift; sesselbahn-boppard.de) creates the illusion that you're looking at four separate lakes rather than a single river.

**THE DRIVE**
Take the B9 south for 15km, passing Burg Maus across the river near the village of Wellmich. Shortly afterwards, you'll spot Burg Rheinfels on the west bank above St Goar.

**08** **ST GOAR**
Lording over the village of St Goar are the sprawling ruins of **Burg Rheinfels** (st-goar.de), once the Rhine's mightiest fortress. Built in 1245 by Count Dieter von Katzenelnbogen as a base for his toll-collecting operations, its size and labyrinthine layout are astonishing. Kids (and adults) will love exploring the subterranean tunnels and galleries (bring a torch). From St Goar's northern edge, follow the Schlossberg road to the castle.

**THE DRIVE**
Take the five-minute car ferry across to the little village of St Goarshausen. From St Goarshausen's Marktplatz, follow the L338 as it twists steeply uphill through thick forest for 1.2km and turn right onto the K89 for 2.5km to reach Loreley.

### Cat & Mouse

Two rival castles stand either side of the village of St Goarshausen. Burg Peterseck was built by the archbishop of Trier to counter the toll practices of the powerful Katzenelnbogen family. The latter responded by building a much bigger castle high on the other side of town, Burg Neukatzenelnbogen, which was dubbed **Burg Katz**, ('Cat Castle'). Highlighting the obvious imbalance of power between the Katzenelnbogens and the archbishop, Burg Peterseck was soon nicknamed **Burg Maus** ('Mouse Castle'). Both are closed to the public.

 **Detour**
**Oberwesel**
Start: 08 St Goar

It's a quick 7.8km south from St Goar along the B9 to the village of Oberwesel.

Every April, Oberwesel crowns not a *Weinkönigin* (wine queen), as in most Rhine towns, but a *Weinhexe* (wine witch) – a good witch, of course – who is said to protect the vineyards. Photos of all the Weinhexen crowned since 1946 are displayed in the cellar of Oberwesel's **Kulturhaus** (kulturhaus-oberwesel.de), along with 19th-century engravings of the Rhine and models of its riverboats.

Hidden sky-high up a vineyard-striped hillside, the flagstone terrace of **Günderode Haus** (guenderodehaus.de) is incredible for a glass of wine, beer or brandy, with sweeping views over the Rhine. The adjacent 200-year-old half-timbered house was used as a film set for Heimat 3 (2004); it now has a cinema room and hosts live music and literary events, as well as wine tastings. From Oberwesel, take the K93 east for 600m, turn right (north) onto the K95; after 1km, the car park's on your right.

## 09 LORELEY

The most storied spot along the Romantic Rhine, Loreley is an enormous, almost vertical slab of slate; it owes its fame to a mythical maiden whose siren songs are said to have lured sailors to their death in the river's treacherous currents. Heinrich Heine told the tale in his 1824 poem 'Die Lorelei'.

On the edge of the plateau 4km southeast of the village of St Goarshausen, visitor centre **Loreley Besucherzentrum** (loreley-touristik.de) covers the Loreley myth and local flora, fauna, shipping and winemaking traditions. A 300m gravel path leads to a **viewpoint** at the tip of the Loreley outcrop, 190m above the river.

 **THE DRIVE**
Return to the B42 at the bottom of the hill; on your left, you'll see Burg Katz. Travel south for 2km to the car park by the breakwater for the next stop, the Loreley Sculpture.

## 10 LORELEY SCULPTURE

At the tip of a narrow breakwater jutting into the Rhine, a bronze sculpture of Loreley's famous maiden perches atop a rocky platform. From the car park, you can walk the 600m out to the sculpture, from where there are fantastic views of both riverbanks. Be aware that the rough path is made from jagged slate (wear sturdy shoes) and the gentler sandy lower path is often underwater.

Pfalzgrafstein, Kaub

 **THE DRIVE**
Take the B42 south for 8km to the little village of Kaub, and park next to the ferry dock.

## 11 KAUB

Kaub is the gateway to one of the river's iconic sights. As if out of a fairy tale, 1326-built, boat-shaped toll castle **Pfalzgrafstein** (burg-pfalzgrafenstein.de),

---

### Driving the Rhine

No bridges span the Rhine between Koblenz and Mainz; the only way to cross the river along this stretch is by **Autofähre** (car ferry).

**Bingen–Rüdesheim** (bingen-ruedesheimer.de)

**Boppard–Filsen** (faehre-boppard.de)

**Niederheimbach–Lorch** (mittelrhein-faehre.de)

**Oberwesel–Kaub** (faere-kaub.de)

**St Goar–St Goarshausen** (faehre-loreley.de)

**Photo Opportunity**
Boat-shaped toll castle Pfalzgrafstein on a Rhine island.

with distinctive white-painted walls, red trim and slate turrets, perches on a narrow Island in the middle of the Rhine. A once dangerous rapid here (since modified) forced boats to use one side of the river, where a chain forced ships to stop and pay a toll. The island makes a scenic picnic spot.

Alongside Kaub's car-ferry dock you can hop on a little **Fährboot** (faehre-kaub.de) passenger ferry (it only runs from this side of the river).

🚗 **THE DRIVE**
Take the car ferry across to the Rhine's west bank and head south on the B9 for 3km.

**12 BACHARACH**
Tiny Bacharach conceals its considerable charms behind a **14th-century wall**. Enter one of the thick arched gateways under the train tracks and you'll find yourself in a medieval old town filled with half-timbered mansions. It's possible to walk almost all the way around the centre on top of the walls. The lookout tower on the upper section of the wall affords panoramic views.

## Cruising the Rhine

If you'd like to let someone else drive for a while and get a different perspective of the Rhine, it's easy to park up and hop on a cruise boat. From around Easter to October (winter services are very limited), passenger ships run by **Köln-Düsseldorfer** (k-d.com) link Rhine villages on a set timetable:

- You can travel to the next village or all the way between Mainz and Koblenz
- Within the segment you've paid for (eg Boppard–Rüdesheim), you can get on and off as often as you like, but make sure to ask for a free stop-over ticket each time you disembark.
- Children up to the age of four travel free, while those up to age 13 are charged a flat fee regardless of distance.
- Return tickets usually cost only slightly more than one-way.
- To bring a bicycle, there's a supplement.

A few smaller companies also send passenger boats up and down the river:

**Bingen-Rüdesheimer** (bingen-ruedesheimer.de)
**Loreley Linie** (loreley-linie.com)
**Rössler Linie** (roesslerlinie.de)

Dating from 1421, **Zum Grünen Baum** (weingut-bastian-bacharach.de) serves some of Bacharach's best whites in rustic surrounds. Its nearby **Vinothèque** (weingut-bastian-bacharach.de), by contrast, is state of the art. Owner Friedrich Bastian is a renowned opera singer, so music (and culinary) events take place year-round, including on Bastian's private river-island with its own vineyard.

### THE DRIVE
Head south on the B9, passing Burg Reichenstein then Burg Rheinstein on your right. Then, on your left, in the river itself, you'll pass the Mäuseturm, a fortified tower used as a signal station until 1974. Drive through Bingen to the car-ferry dock at its eastern edge, and cross the river to Rüdesheim.

 **13 RÜDESHEIM**

Depending on how you look at it, Rüdesheim's town centre – and especially its most famous feature, the tunnel-like medieval alley **Drosselgasse** – is either a touristy nightmare or a lot of kitschy, colourful fun. There's also wonderful walking in the greater area, which is part of the Rheingau wine region, famed for its superior Rieslings.

For a stunning Rhine panorama, head up the wine-producing slopes west of Rüdesheim to the **Niederwald Monument**. Erected between 1877 and 1883, this bombastic monument celebrates the Prussian victory in the Franco-Prussian War and the creation of the German Reich, both in 1871. To save climbing 203 vertical metres, glide above the vineyards aboard the 1400m-long **Seilbahn cable car** (Kabinenbahn; seilbahn-ruedesheim.de). A network of hiking trails extends from the monument.

### THE DRIVE
Head east on the B42 for 23km and turn south on the A643 to cross the bridge over the Rhine. It's then 13km southeast to the centre of Mainz.

 **14 MAINZ**

The Rhine meets the Main at lively Mainz, which has a sizeable university, pretty pedestrian precincts and a *savoir vivre* dating from Napoleon's occupation (1797–1814). Strolling along the Rhine and sampling local wines in an **Altstadt** tavern are classic Mainz experiences. Try the 1791 **Weinstube Hottum** for wines purely from the Rheingau and Rheinhessen regions, or vine-draped **Weingut Michel** (michel-wein.de), which exclusively serves its own wines.

Highlights you won't want to miss include the fabulous **Mainzer Dom** (mainzerdom.bistummainz.de), the ethereal windows of Chagall in **St-Stephan-Kirche** (st-stephan-mainz.bistummainz.de), and the first printed Bible in the **Gutenberg-Museum Mainz** (gutenberg-museum.de). This museum commemorates native son Johannes Gutenberg who ushered in the information age here in the 15th century by perfecting movable type.

Also well worth a visit is the dungeonlike, brilliantly illuminated Roman archaeological site **Heiligtum der Isis und Mater Magna** (roemisches-mainz.de). The easy-to-miss entrance is on the Römer Passage mall's ground floor, just inside the western entrance.

# 13

## Moselle Valley

**BEST FOR WINE**

Bernkastel-Kues offers opportunities to taste the Moselle's famous wines.

Bernkastel-Kues

| DURATION | DISTANCE | GREAT FOR |
|---|---|---|
| 2–4 days | 195km / 121 miles | History, wine & nature |

**BEST TIME TO GO** | Wine festivals abound between late April and early November.

As you wind along the river's edge, and criss-cross over its narrow bridges, you'll pass huddled half-timbered villages, precariously perched hilltop castles (or their crumbling remains), and scores of snug, generations-old wineries serving hearty food and exquisite wines. Pack your hiking boots – from every stop along the route you can head up into the vines for sublime views over the valley.

### Link Your Trip

**12 Romantic Rhine**
Swap one waterway for another: Koblenz sits at the confluence of the Moselle and Rhine rivers, where you can also pick up this route.

**14 German Wine Route**
For more vineyards (and more magnificent wines), drive 129km southeast from Koblenz to the German Wine Route's Bockenheim an der Weinstrasse.

### 01 TRIER

Before hitting the road, history buffs especially will want to explore Germany's oldest city, Trier, at the head of the Moselle Valley. A UNESCO World Heritage site, this is where you'll find the country's finest ensemble of Roman remains, including the 2nd-century 'black gate' **Porta Nigra**; a gladiatorial **Amphitheater**; thermal baths such as the labyrinthine **Kaiserthermen** (Imperial Baths); **Konstantin Basilika** (konstantin-basilika.de), constructed around AD 310 as Constantine's throne room (now a Protestant church); as well as Germany's oldest bishop's church, **Trierer Dom** (trierer-dom. de), which retains Roman sections.

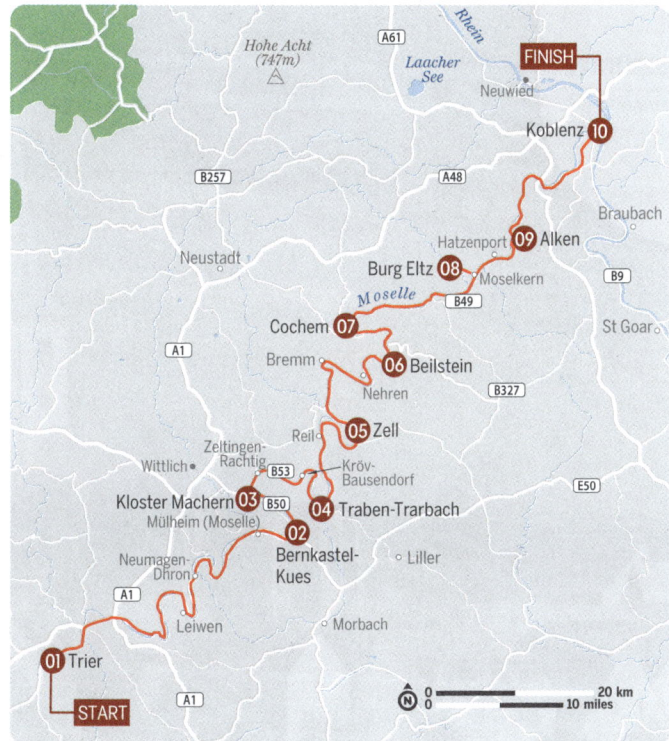

### 🚗 THE DRIVE
From the Bernkastel side of the river, head north, hugging the river as it bends west, for 7km to Zeltingen-Rachtig, then cross to the left (southern) bank: just on your right is one of the trip's biggest surprises.

### 03 KLOSTER MACHERN
The Moselle might be better known for its wine but a former Cistercian monastery, founded in the 13th century, now houses this extraordinary **brewery** (brauhaus-kloster-machern.de), with a bar made from a copper vat and dry hops hanging from the ceiling. There's a wicker-chair-filled terrace, and excellent local cuisine. Brews, including a *Dunkel* (dark), *Hell* (light) and *Hefe-Weizen* (wheat beer), are also sold at its shop. Also here is a museum exhibiting religious iconography, plus puppets, toys and model railways.

### 🚗 THE DRIVE
Follow the B53 downstream as it twists, turns and twists again until you arrive at Traben, one of the twin towns making up Traben-Trarbach.

### 04 TRABEN-TRARBACH
Traben, on the Moselle's left (northern) bank, lost its medieval appearance to three major fires but was compensated with beautiful *Jugendstil* (Art Nouveau) villas, many designed by Berlin architect Bruno Möhring.

Back in Trarbach, Möhring's works include the 1898-built, medieval-style bridge gate, the **Brückentor**, and a 1906 former winery that's now the unlikely home of 2000-plus wood, bronze and paper Buddha statues at the **Buddha Museum** (buddha-museum.de).

Vineyards climbing the hillsides provide a taste of the road trip to come.

### 🚗 THE DRIVE
Cross Germany's oldest bridge, the Römerbrücke (whose 2nd-century stone pilings have held it up since legionnaires crossed on chariots) to the right (western) bank. Turn right onto the B51; after about 1km, the right-hand fork links up to the B53. Following the B53 along the river for 63km brings you to Bernkastel-Kues.

### 02 BERNKASTEL-KUES
On the river's right (eastern) bank, higgledy-piggledy half-timbered houses with beautifully decorated gables cluster around Bernkastel's **Marktplatz**, including the Moselle's oldest half-timbered building, dating from 1416. Shaped like a bird's house, with a narrow base topped by a larger, wonkier upper level to allow carriages to pass through the narrow alley, it's now home to **Weinstube Spitzhäuschen** (spitzhaeuschen.de), where you can taste the Schmitz family's local wines. Looming above Bernkastel is the ruined 13th-century castle **Burg Landshut**.

Kues, on the left bank, is home to the 1458-founded **St-Nikolaus-Hospital** (cusanus.de), where, for more wine tasting, you'll find the **Mosel Vinothek**.

> **Photo Opportunity**
> Europe's steepest vineyard – Calmont.

**Vineyards, Bremm**

Teetering above Trarbach are the ruins of 14th-century **Grevenburg**. Below the castle is **Weingut Louis Klein** (klein-wein.de), which can also arrange vineyard tastings amid the vines.

**THE DRIVE**
From Trarbach follow the B53 north along the river for 20km to the wine-producing town of Zell.

### 05 ZELL

You'll know you've arrived in the charming town of Zell when you come to its roundabout. In the centre is a gigantic black cat, standing on top of a wine barrel raising a full glass and backed by vine-planted hills. So the story goes, in 1863, visiting merchants trying to find the best wine encountered a barrel guarded by a hissing, spitting *Schwarze Katze* (black cat). The merchants snapped up the now-renowned Zeller Schwarze Katz wine; you can taste and buy it at wine shops throughout the town.

**THE DRIVE**
After heading 14km north on the left (western) bank, look up (and up) as you leave the village

of Bremm to spot Europe's, and allegedly the world's, steepest vineyard – Calmont, with a 65-degree gradient. Continuing downriver another 15km and crossing to the right (eastern) bank after Nehren takes you into Beilstein.

### 06 BEILSTEIN

Beilstein's storybook-like half-timbered buildings centre on its 14th-century Marktplatz. Steep slopes lead to the baroque 17th-century Carmelite monastery church, **Karmeliterkirche St Josef** (st-josef-beilstein.de). Its spectacular interior has a vaulted ceiling supported by soaring apricot-coloured columns. Also perched above the village is ruined **Burg Metternich** (burg-metternich.de). Built in 1129, the castle was destroyed by French troops in the Nine Years' War in 1689.

**THE DRIVE**
Continue along the right (eastern) bank for 11km and cross the bridge at busy Cochem.

### 07 COCHEM

Transport hub Cochem is the Moselle at its most touristy. Pastel-coloured, terrace-fronted restaurants line its waterfront. Behind them, Cochem's tangle of narrow, medieval alleyways are crammed with boutiques.

Rising above town is the dazzling **Reichsburg** (reichsburg-cochem.de). This 11th-century castle fell victim to French troops in 1689, then stood ruined for centuries until it was restored to its current – if not always architecturally faithful – glory. Banquets here include a knighting ceremony.

**THE DRIVE**
Stay on the left (west) river bank and follow the B49 as it winds north, then east, for 17km to the village of Moselkern. At Moselkern, leave the river for 8km to reach Burg Eltz.

### 08 BURG ELTZ

At the head of the Eltz, a Moselle side valley, wonderful **Burg Eltz** (burg-eltz.de) is one of the most romantic medieval castles in Germany. Never destroyed, this vision of turrets, towers, oriels, gables and half-timber is still owned by the original family. From the Eltz car park, it's a shuttle bus ride or 1.3km walk to the castle.

**THE DRIVE**
Retrace your route to Moselkern, then follow the B416 along the left (north) bank. After 5.5km you'll pass tiny Hatzenport – vine-shaded riverfront winery Weinhaus Ibald, in the village centre, makes an idyllic stop. From Hatzenport, it's just another 5km (cross the bridge about halfway along) to Alken.

### 09 ALKEN

Alken is one of the Moselle's oldest villages, tracing its roots to Celtic and Roman times. Built on Roman foundations from 1197, its hilltop castle, **Burg Thurant** (thurant.de), has an intriguing history. From 1246 to 1248 it was fought over by the archbishops of Cologne and Trier, and divided in two parts (separated by a wall). Fascinating displays include medieval torture devices; the watchtower is accessible by ladder.

**THE DRIVE**
Along the Moselle's right (east) bank, the B49 squiggles for another 23km to Koblenz.

### 10 KOBLENZ

Koblenz, with intriguing museums, flower-filled parks and a cable-car-accessed fortress, is a fitting last stop: at the broad **Deutsches Eck** ('German Corner'), the Moselle ends, emptying into the Rhine. Specialising in Rhine and Moselle wines by the glass and/or bottle, rustic **Alte Weinstube Zum Hubertus** (weinhaus-hubertus.de) occupies a half-timbered house dating from 1689, with an open fireplace, antique furniture, dark-wood panelling and a summer terrace.

# 14

# German Wine Route

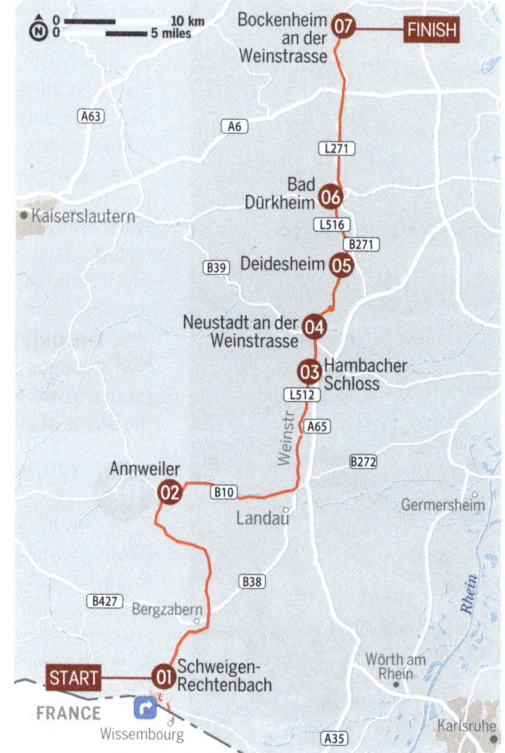

| DURATION | DISTANCE | GREAT FOR |
|---|---|---|
| 2–4 days | 96km / 59 miles | History, wine & nature |

| BEST TIME TO GO | Villages are especially pretty during the spring bloom (March to mid-May). |
|---|---|

From the French border, you'll wind north along this venerable route through Germany's largest contiguous wine-growing area, which is blessed with a temperate climate that allows almonds, figs, lemons and kiwi fruit to thrive, and is scattered with half-timbered villages and castles. The route was inaugurated in 1935, and its western edge weaves through the hilly forest of the Pfälzerwald, a UNESCO Biosphere Reserve with invigorating hiking and cycling trails.

### Link Your Trip

**13 Moselle Valley**
More wines await in the beautiful Moselle Valley, a 129km drive northwest to Koblenz from Bockenheim an der Weinstrasse.

**16 German Castle Road**
From Bad Dürkheim, it's a straight 24km shot east to Mannheim.

## 01 SCHWEIGEN-RECHTENBACH

There's no missing the start of the German Wine Route, which is marked by a towering stone gate, the 1936-built **Deutsches Weintor** (German Wine Gate). Inside is one of Germany's largest wine cooperatives. At this vast **Vinothek** (weintor.de) you can pick up tourist information, stock up on bottles, or sample a variety of wines by the glass

### THE DRIVE

From Schweigen-Rechtenbach, drive north for 16km along the Weinstrasse, which starts as the B38 and becomes the B48 at Bad Bergzabern. Just after pretty Klingenmünster (look out for its castle, Burg Landeck),

**BEST FOR FOODIES**

Epicurean treats abound along the entire route.

Deutsches Weintor, Schweigen-Rechtenbach

the B48 swings west into the forested Pfälzerwald to Annweiler (28km all-up).

### Detour
**Wissembourg, France**
Start: **01** Schweigen-Rechtenbach
From Schweigen-Rechtenbach, it's an easy 5km detour south over the French border to Wissembourg along the B38 (which becomes the D264 when you enter France).

The chic little town's compact centre is awash with centuries-old architectural treasures along with *boulangeries* (bakeries), *fromageries* (cheese shops) and, yes, *caves viticoles* (wine cellars).

Plaques mark 25 key sights around town that you can follow on a walking circuit. Highlights include the 1448-built **Maison du Sel** (Salt House), first a hospital, then a salt warehouse and later a slaughterhouse; the magnificent **Église Sts-Pierre-et-Paul**, incorporating a square tower from an 11th-century abbey church and dazzling stained-glass windows; and the **Couvent des Augustins**, a 1279-founded convent converted into private residences following the French Revolution.

On Wissembourg's main square, Place de la République, the tourist office sells maps outlining the walking route and has details of local hiking and cycling. Alternatively, visit ot-wissembourg.fr for information.

### 02 ANNWEILER

At the westernmost edge of the Palatinate wine-growing region, up in the forested Pfälzerwald, Annweiler has a charming core of half-timbered buildings and cobbled squares bisected by a canal-like stream with giant wooden waterwheels.

It's 8.6km via the K2 to **Burg Trifels** (burgen-rlp.de), looming southeast of the town. Thought to be of Celtic origins, this enormous red-sandstone hilltop castle was first documented in 1081. Between 1125 and 1298 it was the repository of imperial treasures including, allegedly, a nail from Jesus' cross and a tooth from

**Photo Opportunity**
Dürkheimer Riesenfass, the world's largest wine barrel.

**Dürkheimer Riesenfass, Bad Dürkheim**

John the Baptist. Richard the Lionheart (Richard I of England) was imprisoned here from 1193 to 1194 for insulting Leopold V, Duke of Austria (after first having been incarcerated in Austria's Kuenringerburg from 1192 to 1193). Today, Burg Trifels' displays include a replica of the imperial crown jewels. Excavations a decade ago uncovered a probable Saxon-era wooden castle.

**THE DRIVE**
Head east to Albersweiler to rejoin the Weinstrasse (here called the L507) and follow it northeast: Hambacher Schloss is west of the hamlet of Hambach along the one-way K9 to the car park at the top of the hill (27.5km in total).

**03 HAMBACHER SCHLOSS**
Atop a forested Pfälzerwald hill is the monumental **Hambacher Schloss** (hambacher-schloss.de). This 'cradle of German democracy' is where idealistic locals, Polish refugees and French citizens held massive protests for a free, democratic and united Germany on 27 May 1832, hoisting the black, red and gold German flag for the first time. An exhibition commemorates the event, known as the Hambacher Fest. Audioguides and tours are available in English. Inside the castle, opening to a courtyard, **Restaurant 1832** (hambacherschloss.de) is reason enough to make the trip up, with inspired modern German cuisine: liver dumpling soup; tagliatelle with roasted asparagus in fig sauce; fried calf's liver with glazed grapes and potato-and-celery cake; and red mullet, shrimp and clams baked in parchment with cuttlefish risotto.

**THE DRIVE**
Return via the one-way K14 to the Weinstrasse at Hambach and head north for 5.8km into Neustadt an der Weinstrasse. After crossing the railway tracks, turn left for 850m, then right on the B58; after 300m there's a large open-air car park on your left at the edge of the largely pedestrianised Altstadt.

**04 NEUSTADT AN DER WEINSTRASSE**
Vineyards fan out around Neustadt, a busy wine-producing town at the heart of the German Wine Route.

Neustadt's Altstadt teems with half-timbered houses, especially along Mittelgasse, Hintergasse, Metzgergasse and Kunigundenstrasse. It's anchored by the cobbled Marktplatz, which is flanked by the baroque Rathaus (town hall), as well as the Gothic **Stiftskirche** (stiftskirche-neustadt. de). Built from red sandstone, this church, dating from the 14th century, has been shared by Protestant and Catholic congregations since 1708. Recent renovations revealed frescos from 1410 that depict a snapshot of life at the time, with bakers, craftspeople and market traders. Every Saturday at noon guided tours take you into the tower, reached by 184 steps (book ahead).

#### THE DRIVE
Follow the B38 northeast to the roundabout and continue straight ahead onto the L516, which becomes the Weinstrasse; after 8.2km, you'll arrive in Deidesheim.

#### 05 DEIDESHEIM
Draped in pale purple-flowering wisteria in the springtime, diminutive Deidesheim is centred on its charming Marktplatz. This is one of the German Wine Route's most picturesque – and upmarket – villages, with plenty of opportunities for wine tasting, relaxed strolling and sublime dining.

Deidesheim is a 'Cittaslow' town, an extension of the Slow Food movement that aims to rebalance modern life's hectic pace not only through 'ecogastronomy' but also local arts, crafts, nature, cultural traditions and heritage. Galleries and artisans' studios (such as jewellery makers and potters) can be visited along the **Kunst und Kultur** (Art and Culture) Circuit; look for dark-blue-on-yellow 'K' signs.

The town is home to 10 **winemakers** (some closed Sunday) that welcome visitors – look for signs reading *Weingut* (winery), *Verkauf* (sale) and *Weinprobe* (wine tasting) and ring the bell. Many can be found along the small streets west of **Pfarrkirche St Ulrich** (pfarrei-deidesheim.de).

A Marktplatz landmark with a canopied outdoor staircase, the **Altes Rathaus** (old town hall) dates from the 16th century. Inside is the three-storey **Museum für Weinkultur** (Museum of Wine Culture), featuring displays on winemakers' traditional lifestyle and naive-art portrayals of the German Wine Route.

Shutterbugs will love the recently revamped **Deutsches Museum für Foto-, Film- und Fernsehtechnik** (German Photography, Film & TV Museum; 3f-museum.de), tucked down an alleyway across from the Rathaus, with an impressive collection of historic photographic and movie-making equipment.

Signposted walking and cycling routes lead you through vineyards and the Pfälzerwald.

#### THE DRIVE
It's a glorious 6.8km drive north from Deidesheim along the Weinstrasse (L516) through gently rolling hills ribboned with vineyards to Bad Dürkheim.

#### 06 BAD DÜRKHEIM
Adorned with splashing fountains, the spa town of Bad Dürkheim is famous for its thermal springs, lovely parks like the azalea-and-wisteria-filled **Kurgarten**, and what's claimed to be the world's largest wine festival, the **Dürkheimer Wurstmarkt** (duerkheimer-wurstmarkt. de). It also has one of the world's largest wine barrels, the gigantic **Dürkheimer Riesenfass**. It has a diameter of 13.5m and a volume of 1,700,000L, and contains the Restaurant Dürkheimer Fass.

Test the waters at the modern **Kurzentrum** spa. In its lobby, you can taste the salty water (said to be good for your digestion) from a fountain.

*Weinwanderwege* (vineyard trails) from St Michaelskapelle, a chapel atop a little vine-clad hill, lead to Honigsäckel and the Hochmess vineyards (a 6km circuit).

#### THE DRIVE
At Bad Dürkheim, the Weinstrasse becomes the L271; follow it north via the village of Ungstein for 19km to Bockenheim an der Weinstrasse.

#### 07 BOCKENHEIM AN DER WEINSTRASSE
The village of Bockenheim an der Weinstrasse, not to be confused with the Frankfurt district of Bockenheim, marks the end of the German Wine Route.

Spanning the road at the village's northern edge in Roman *castrum* style is the modern, brick-and-tile **Haus der Deutschen Weinstrasse** (House of the German Wine Route, built in 1995 as a counterpart to the Deutsches Weintor at the route's starting point in Schweigen-Rechtenbach. There's a cafe inside, but better dining options are elsewhere.

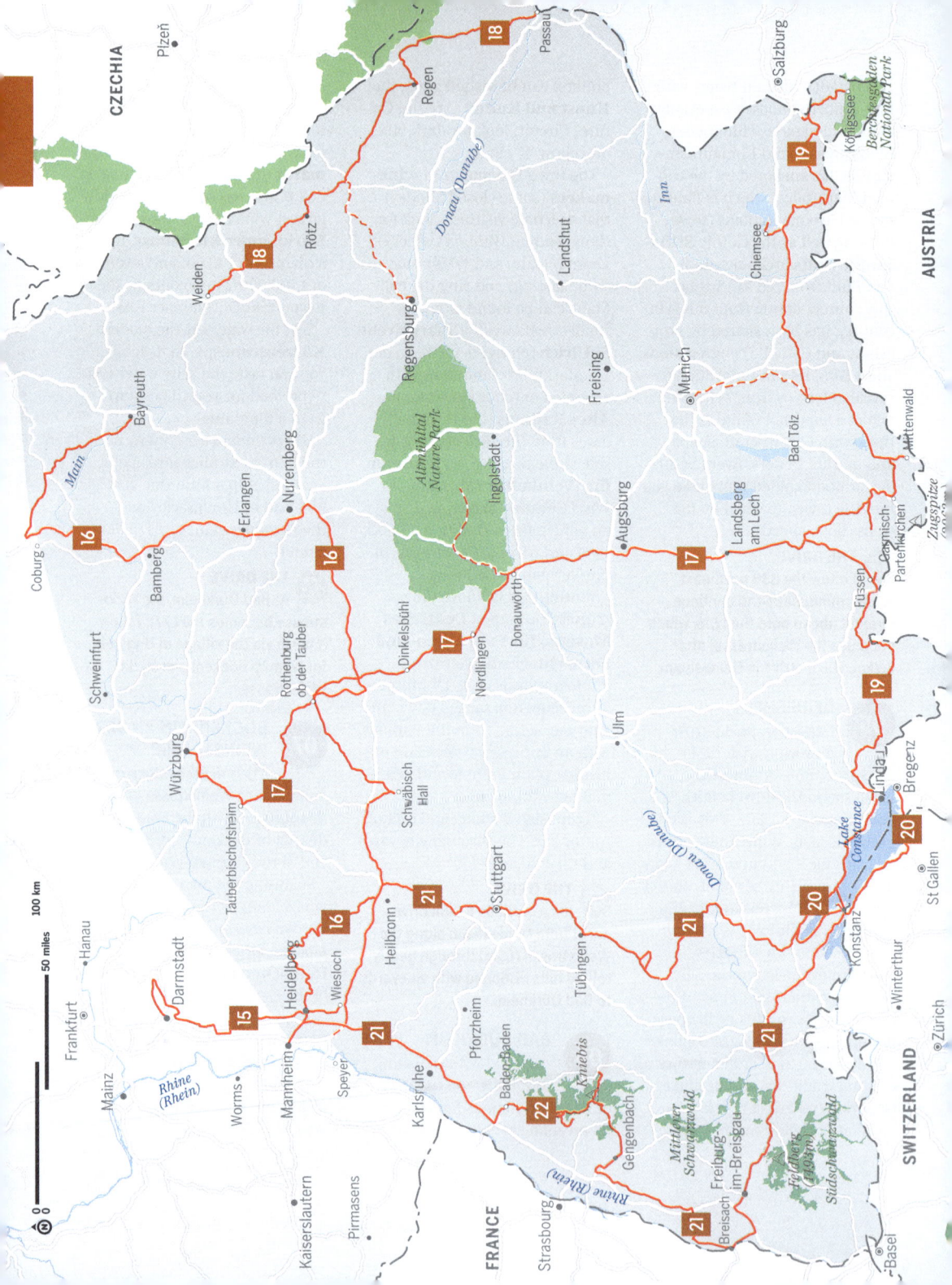

Heidelberg (p116)

# Southern Germany

**15  Bergstrasse**
Drive this diverse route from Darmstadt to Wiesloch (via Heidelberg), tracing an old Roman trade route as you go. **p114**

**16  German Castle Road**
Enjoy castles, palaces and fortresses galore along this storybook route from Mannheim to Bayreuth. **p118**

**17  The Romantic Road**
Spend time driving one of Germany's most famous routes, a ribbon of historical quaintness from Würzburg to Neuschwanstein. **p124**

**18  Glass Route**
Leave the crowds behind and follow this Passau-to-Weiden glass-themed drive through eastern Bavaria's forested border regions. **p132**

**19  German Alpine Road**
Take the high road through Germany's slice of Europe's top peaks, starting out from Lindau all the way to the shores of Königssee. **p136**

**20  Lake Constance**
Stick to the water's edge as you circumnavigate Europes third-largest lake on this beautiful tri-state loop. **p144**

**21  Fantastic Road**
Begin and end in wonderful Heidelberg on this fascinating ring through Baden-Württemberg and the Black Forest. **p148**

**22  Schwarzwaldhochstrasse**
Do some high-altitude motoring through the magnificent landscapes of the Black Forest from Baden-Baden to Freudenstadt. **p152**

BEST ROAD TRIPS: GERMANY, AUSTRIA & SWITZERLAND   111

# Explore

# Southern Germany

When you think of Germany, you're probably thinking of Bavaria and the south. This is the land of Neuschwanstein and the storied hamlets of the Romantische Strasse (Romantic Road), of vast and beautiful Lake Constance and the peerless panoramas of the Alps or the mysteries of the Black Forest. Southern Germany is, quite simply, one of Europe's most beautiful corners, a world of elemental greens and blues and of villages made up entirely of half-timbered homes and stone churches. More than anywhere else in the country, your rewards lie along quiet back roads and far from the clamour of German cities.

### Heidelberg

Could Heidelberg be the world's most beautiful place to attend university? Whether bathed in floodlights or the crisp summer air of the south, Heidelberg has everything you need from a hub town – fabulous restaurants and places to stay, plenty of reasons to stay longer than you planned, and the kind of location where attractions beckon from all corners of the compass.

### Lindau

On the shores of Lake Constance, on the cusp of the Alps, Lindau is the pretty-as-a-postcard hub that you'll never want to leave. At the starting (or end) point of two of the most beautiful road trips anywhere in Germany, Lindau is also convenient for many more. Imagine driving all day with a meal by the lake in Lindau to look forward to at journey's end. Or standing by the lakeshore with Lake Constance and the Alps unfurling to the far horizon on the eve of your trip.

### Nuremberg

Nuremberg is quieter than Munich, it has arguably the world's most memorable Christmas market, and you can be in Munich by train in just over an hour when it's time to leave. It's close to the centre of Bavaria and makes the perfect hub for exploring the south without the clamour and size of Munich to negotiate every time you come and go. And Nuremberg is Munich's match for accommodation, culinary culture and infrastructure for getting you to where you have to go.

### WHEN TO GO

You could drive any of these routes at any time of the year and not be disappointed. But there are nuances. Avoid Lake Constance in winter, when winter fog can obscure your view. Easter to October has the best weather, but July and August can be ridiculously busy. And the Black Forest is simply glorious in spring (flowers) and autumn (leaves).

## Stuttgart

Stuttgart is best-known for its role at the heart of the world of cars – what better way to celebrate a road trip around Germany's south than with a visit to the factories for Porsche and Mercedes-Benz. And don't forget to explore beyond, to the squares and museums that make this such an agreeable place to spend a few days. But Stuttgart is perfectly placed for setting out on just about any route through Germany's picturesque south.

## Würzburg

Where the Romantic Road begins, not to mention all manner of other driving possibilities, Würzburg is an excellent base for driving the south. It has many charms of its own, not least a world-class wine-producing heritage, a respected culinary scene and the exquisite wonder that is the baroque Residenz. But there really is no feeling quite like setting out from Würzburg and knowing that you'll soon be in Rothenburg ob der Tauber and the other magical towns of the Romantic Road.

### TRANSPORT

It couldn't be easier to get to the region – Munich is a major European hub. If you don't feel like driving in the Munich area (although the airport is well outside the city), consider taking a train to Nuremberg or elsewhere and picking up a car there. Main roads generally remain open throughout winter, even in the Alps.

 WHAT'S ON

**Gäubodenfest**
A mid-August rival to Munich's Oktoberfest in Straubing, 30 minutes southeast of Regensburg.

**Fasnacht**
A 500-year-old pre-Lenten folk festival celebrated in southwest Germany to banish winter. Head for Rottweil, Villingen-Schwenningen and Gegenbach.

**Nuremberg Christmas Market**
The undisputed number one, but there's magic everywhere, including Esslingen, Ludwigsburg, Regensburg and anywhere along the Romantic Road.

**Oberammergau Passion Play**
Head to the Alps in 2030 for the once-in-a-decade performance.

### Resources

**Bavaria Travel** (*bavaria.travel*) Everything you need to know for planning road trips through the south.

**Romantische Strasse** (*romantischestrasse.de*) Start dreaming of Europe's most magical road.

**Black Forest** (*blackforestgermany.com*) Your online portal for exploring Germany's most mysterious forest.

**Baden-Württemberg** (*visit-bw.com*) Learn about Germany's stunning southwest.

 WHERE TO STAY

Planning where to sleep isn't just about booking ahead in high season (although you should definitely do this, especially along the Romantic Road). It's also about making sure you get the room that overlooks a cobbled street in Dinkelsbühl. Or securing that lake-facing room in Lindau. Even in the smallest villages in Bavaria, you're likely to have a choice of accommodation. But it's not just the Romantic Road that gets busy – book months in advance around Lake Constance, Füssen (for Neuschwanstein) and the Black Forest (where there are slightly more limited accommodation options) during the summer months.

# 15

# Bergstrasse

| DURATION | DISTANCE | GREAT FOR |
|---|---|---|
| 2–4 days | 125km / 77 miles | History, nature & families |

| BEST TIME TO GO | You'll have the best weather between April and October. |
|---|---|

This Roman trade route along the edge of the Odenwald mountain range might be just 125km, but the diversity you'll encounter is astonishing: *Jugendstil* (Art Nouveau) architecture, archaeological discoveries, the castle that inspired Mary Shelley's *Frankenstein*, a monumental medieval abbey, romantic Heidelberg, Wiesloch (where trailblazer Bertha Benz made motoring history), and Germany's most famous racetrack.

## Link Your Trip

### 16 German Castle Road
For yet more castles, drive 20km northwest from Heidelberg via the A656 to Mannheim to set out on the German Castle Road.

### 21 Fantastic Road
The ancient university city of Heidelberg is the starting point for an unforgettable loop through forest-filled Baden-Württemberg.

### 01 DARMSTADT
Famed for its technical university and the creation of superheavy element Darmstadtium (Ds; atomic number: 110), Darmstadt is a designated *Wissenschaftsstadt* (City of Science). Part of the university is housed in Darmstadt's spectacular **Schloss**, along with a **museum** (schloss museum-darmstadt.de).

The best place to see the city's renowned *Jugendstil* (Art Nouveau) architecture is **Mathildenhöhe** (mathildenhoehe.eu), the former *Künstlerkolonie* (artists colony), established in 1899 by Grand Duke Ernst Ludwig. Surrounded by a fountain-filled hilltop

**BEST FOR DRIVERS**

The Hockenheim-Ring Formula One Grand Prix track.

HockenheimRing (p117)

park, the museum showcases *Jugendstil* furniture, tableware, textiles, ceramics and jewellery.

Or simply splash about at the exquisite 1909 indoor-outdoor *Jugendstil* pool-and-spa complex, **Jugendstilbad** (jugendstilbad.de).

### THE DRIVE
From Darmstadt's Schloss, head east on Alexanderstrasse, which becomes the L3094. Follow it for 10km through beautiful forest; Grube Messel is signposted 300m off on your left.

### 02 GRUBE MESSEL
A UNESCO World Heritage site, this one-time coal-and-shale-oil quarry 10km northeast of Darmstadt, known as **Grube Messel** (Messel Pit; grube-messel.de), is an archaeological wonder, with superbly preserved animal and plant remains from the Eocene era (around 49 million years ago). Fossils of ancient horses found here illustrate the evolutionary path towards the modern beast.

A pretty half-timbered house 3km south of the visitor centre is a fossil-filled **museum** (messelmuseum.de). Better yet, you can visit the pit itself with a German-speaking guide or pre-arrange an English-speaking tour (extra €20 per group).

Other intriguing finds from the site are displayed at the **Hessisches Landesmuseum** (hlmd.de) in Darmstadt and the **Senckenberg Museum** (senckenberg.de) in Frankfurt.

### THE DRIVE
Rejoin the L3094 and travel east towards Dieburg; on its outskirts, turn right (south) on Burgweg. After 1.7km, turn right at the roundabout onto the K128 and follow it for 14km before turning right onto the B426 for 6.7km. Turn left and climb the twisting, precipitous road through shadowed forest to Burg Frankenstein.

### 03 BURG FRANKENSTEIN
Built by Lord Konrad II Reiz von Breuberg around 1250 (who thereafter added *'von und zu Frankenstein'* to

## Photo Opportunity

Wiesloch's statue of Bertha Benz, the world's first road-tripper.

Bertha Benz statue, Weisloch

his name), hulking, partly ruined hilltop castle **Burg Frankenstein** (frankenstein-restaurant.de) was visited by Mary Shelley on her German travels in 1814, inspiring the title of her Gothic novel and its protagonist, Dr Frankenstein. Tours of the castle are in German; you're free to walk around the castle and grounds, or to just stop in for a drink on its restaurant's panoramic terrace.

If you time it right, you can also catch atmospheric events here, including one of Europe's largest – and spookiest – Halloween parties, as well as medieval banquets, costumed adventure castle days, live music including jazz, and theatre nights.

### THE DRIVE

Twist back downhill and take the B426 west for 1.4km before turning left (south) onto the B3. After Zwingenberg you'll see Schloss Auerbach looming on your left above the town of Auerbach. Turn west on the B47 for 2.7km then right onto Bensheimer Strasse in the charming village of Lorsch and follow the signs to Lorsch Abbey (29km all-up).

### LORSCH ABBEY

Founded around AD 760 and UNESCO-listed in 1991, **Lorsch Abbey** (Kloster Lorsch; kloster-lorsch.de) was a significant religious site in its Carolingian heyday (8th to 10th centuries). Preserved medieval buildings include the rare, Carolingian-era Königshalle and the Altenmünster; museum exhibits cover the history of the abbey, life in Hesse, and tobacco, which was cultivated in Lorsch in the late 17th century.

### THE DRIVE

Return to the B3 and take it south for 32km to Heidelberg. En route, look out for castles, including Starkenburg (housing a hostel) on your left above Heppenheim village, and Wachenburg (home to a restaurant) on your left above the town of Weinheim.

## 05 HEIDELBERG

In a spellbinding riverside setting surrounded by forest, Germany's oldest university town is renowned for its baroque, red-roofed **Altstadt** (old town), which emerged from WWII almost unscathed, and for its evocative half-ruined **Schloss Heidelberg** (schloss-heidelberg.de). You can reach the hilltop castle either via a steep, cobbled trail in about 10 minutes or by *Bergbahn* (cogwheel train) from Kornmarkt station. Castle highlights include the world's largest wine cask and fabulous views.

For the best views of the Schloss, cross the **Alte Brücke**, Heidelberg's 200m-long, 1786-built 'old bridge', to the right bank of the Neckar River and the **Schlangenweg** (Snake Path), whose switchbacks lead to the **Philosophenweg** (Philosophers' Walk). Don't drive up here, as the road is narrow and there's nowhere to turn around at the top.

Heidelberg's charms draw 11.8 million visitors a year. They follow in the footsteps of the late 18th- and early 19th-century Romantics, most notably the poet Goethe. Heidelberg also inspired Britain's William Turner to paint some of his greatest landscapes. In 1878, Mark Twain began his European travels in Heidelberg, recounting his observations in *A Tramp Abroad* (1880). Heidelberg's rich literary history, along with its thriving contemporary scene, saw it named a UNESCO City of Literature in 2014.

The longer you spend here, the more heart-stopping panoramas and hidden treasures you'll discover.

## THE DRIVE

It's just 14km south from Heidelberg along the B3 to Wiesloch, at the foot of the Kraichgau hills.

### Detour
### HockenheimRing
**Start:** 05 Heidelberg

One detour no dedicated road-tripper will want to miss is to the hallowed **HockenheimRing** (hockenheimring.de). Signposted 22km southwest of Heidelberg just east of the A6, it has three circuits and stands that accommodate up to 120,000 fans, and hosts some of Germany's most famous car races, including the Formula One German Grand Prix (in even-numbered years).

Start by taking a look behind the scenes on an **Insider Tour**, available in English and German. Tickets are sold at the **Motor Sport Museum** (hockenheimring.de).

While you're here, make time to check out the museum's fantastic collection of historic motorcycles, some a century old, and its ensemble of historic race cars. Upstairs, look out for the reconstruction of the world's first motorcycle, built from wood by Maybach and Daimler in 1885.

If roaring along on a speed-limitless autobahn doesn't get your adrenaline pumping any more, you can take to the Hockenheim track yourself when it isn't being used for a race:

**Renntaxi** Three laps on the Grand Prix course with a professional driver in a superfast racing car, such as a Porsche GT3, a Mercedes SLK 350 or an Audi R8 V10.

**Race'n'Roll** Drive a race car yourself.

**Touristenfahrten** Drive your own car around the track.

## 06 WIESLOCH

Cute little Wiesloch was pivotal in the evolution of road trips: this is where Bertha Benz – business partner and wife of automobile inventor Karl Benz – refuelled on the first-ever long-distance drive in 1888. Bertha stopped at Wiesloch's pharmacy, the **Stadt-Apotheke** (stadtapotheke-wiesloch.de), which provided her with Ligroin (petroleum ether), making it the world's first filling station. Still a pharmacy today, its small **history museum** only opens a handful of days a year. Outside on the cobbled square there's a bronze-and-steel **statue** of Bertha driving her three-wheeled contraption.

Bertha set out with her two teenage sons, without her husband's knowledge, to highlight the possibilities of the machine no one had wanted to buy. Repairs en route included clearing a clogged fuel line with her hat pin, and fixing a broken ignition with her garter. Her circuit – from Mannheim to Pforzheim and back, which she took at an average speed of 16km/h – is now the 194km **Bertha Benz Memorial Route** (bertha-benz.de).

# 16

# German Castle Road

**BEST FOR HISTORY**

Nuremberg is a treasure trove of European history.

| DURATION | DISTANCE | GREAT FOR |
|---|---|---|
| 7 days | 600km / 373 miles | History |

| BEST TIME TO GO | To get the best out of this trip, travel between Easter and October. |
|---|---|

Nuremberg (p121)

This romantic trip will take you castle-hopping across 600km of southern Germany and through 1000 years of the country's history. From Germany's biggest baroque pile in Mannheim to Bayreuth's Altes Schloss, it's a castle a day on this route. When palace fatigue sets in, there's nothing easier than escaping to a contemporary art gallery, fascinating museum, or traditional tavern to sample the local sausages and unsurpassed beer.

## Link Your Trip

### 17 The Romantic Road
The Castle Road and the Romantic Road meet in Rothenburg ob der Tauber.

### 18 Glass Route
Bayreuth is 60km northwest of Weiden, the northern end of the Glass Route.

### MANNHEIM

The Castle Road kicks off in style at the gates of **Barockschloss Mannheim** (schloss-mannheim.de). The city's most famous sight is Germany's largest baroque palace. Now occupied by the city's university, the 450m-long structure was built over the course of 40 years in the mid-1700s but was almost completely destroyed during WWII. Off the main courtyard are the **Schloss Museum**, where you can see the impressively rococo Kabinettsbibliothek, saved from wartime destruction (having been stored off-site), and several baroque halls – each a feast of stucco, marble, porcelain and chandeliers – rebuilt after the war.

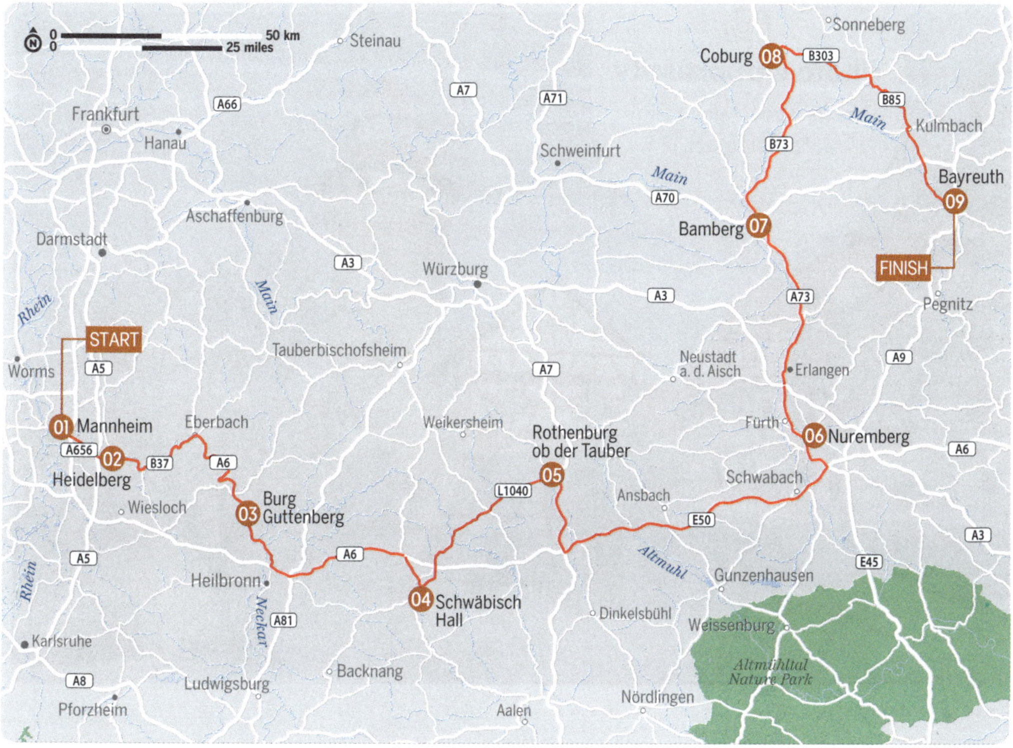

The **Schlosskirche** was constructed between 1720 and 1731, and rebuilt post-WWII. Mozart performed here in 1777. It belongs to the Alt-Katholiken (Old Catholics), a movement that split with Rome over papal infallibility in the 1870s and is now part of the Anglican Communion.

### THE DRIVE
To reach Heidelberg from Mannheim, take the B36 then the A656 heading southeast. Traffic can be heavy on these roads. Heidelberg is just 19km from Mannheim, meaning it can also be tackled as a day trip by public transport; Mannheim's S-Bahn and regional trains make the run every few minutes.

### 02 HEIDELBERG
Towering over the **Altstadt** (old town), the ruins of Renaissance **Schloss Heidelberg** (schloss-heidelberg.de) cut a romantic figure, especially across the Neckar River when illuminated at night. It's a steep climb, but once you arrive up top, you'll be struck by the far-reaching views over the Neckar and the Altstadt rooftops. The only way to see the interior is by tour, which can be safely skipped. After 6pm you can stroll the grounds for free.

Another sight that tourists gravitate to is the **Marktplatz**, the focal point of Altstadt street life. The trickling **Hercules fountain** in the middle – that's him up on top of the pillar – is where petty criminals were chained and left to face the mob in the Middle Ages.

### THE DRIVE
To reach the next stop at Burg Guttenberg, the quickest route is to take the A6 autobahn, a journey of 62km which you should cover in a snappy 45 minutes. However, a much more picturesque but considerably slower way to go is to follow country roads along the Neckar Valley where several dramatic castle ruins wait to be discovered.

### 03 BURG GUTTENBERG
Rising high above the Neckar Valley, lonely **Burg Guttenberg** (burg-guttenberg.de) is one of the most dramatic castles on this part of the route and a fine example of an intact 14th-century castle. In addition to the gobsmacking views of the surrounding vineyards and

### Photo Opportunity
The view from Nuremberg's Sinwell Tower.

**Sinwell Tower, Nuremberg**

forests, the award-winning exhibition inside acquaints visitors with the life of medieval knights. The castle has a tavern with great views.

🚗 **THE DRIVE**
From Burg Guttenberg continue south along the attractive Neckar Valley until you reach the town of Neckarsulm. From there, take the A6 autobahn as far as exit 43 for Schwäbisch Hall. The whole journey is 72km and should take little more than an hour.

**04 SCHWÄBISCH HALL**
Out on its rural lonesome near the Bavarian border, Schwäbisch Hall is an unsung gem. It's a medieval time capsule of higgledy-piggledy lanes, soaring half-timbered houses built high on the riches of salt, and covered bridges that criss-cross the Kocher River – story book stuff.

Buzzy cafes and first-rate museums add to the appeal of this town, known for its rare black-spotted pigs, which can be seen at the **Hohenloher Freilandmuseum** (wackershofen.de), an open-air farming museum that will be a sure-fire hit with the kids. It's 6km northwest of Schwäbisch Hall and served by bus 7. However, Schwäbisch Hall's top attraction is the **Kunsthalle Würth** (kunst.wuerth.com), a contemporary gallery housed in a striking limestone building that preserves part of a century-old brewery. Stellar temporary exhibitions have recently spotlighted Viennese art and Henri Matisse. Guided tours are in German only but audioguides in English are available

🚗 **THE DRIVE**
The best way to reach the next halt – at Rothenburg ob der Tauber, 55km away to the northeast – is to take the L2218 country road back to the A6 motorway. After a short stretch of superfast autobahn driving, take exit 45 and the L1040, which will take you all the way to your destination. You are now in Bavaria.

**05 ROTHENBURG OB DER TAUBER**
A medieval gem, Rothenburg ob der Tauber is also a top stop along the Romantic Road (Trip 17). With its web of cobbled lanes, crooked medieval houses and towered walls, the town is a fairy tale in bricks and plaster.

A striking feature here is the **Stadtmauer** (Town Walls), which form a 2.5km uninterrupted ring around the historical core.

At the **Käthe Wohlfahrt Weihnachtsdorf** (wohlfahrt.com) you can buy a mind-boggling assortment of high-quality Yuletide decorations, so you can celebrate Christmas every day of the year if you want. Next door is the **Deutsches Weihnachtsmuseum** (Christmas Museum; weihnachtsmuseum.de) – also an odd experience in July.

Rothenburg's most popular museum is the **Mittelalterliches Kriminalmuseum** (Medieval Crime & Punishment Museum; kriminalmuseum.eu), where you can view medieval implements of torture and punishment.

### THE DRIVE
There are several ways of getting to your next stop, the city of Nuremberg. The simplest is to head south to the autobahn, which will see you get through the 111km in around 1½ hours. Slower routes go via Ansbach, which also has a magnificent Residenz (palace).

### 06 NUREMBERG
Bavaria's second city is a lively, energetic and moodily historic place. For centuries, it was the undeclared capital of the Holy Roman Empire and the preferred residence of most German kings, who kept their crown jewels at the **Kaiserburg** (Imperial Castle; kaiserburg-nuernberg.de). This enormous castle complex above the Altstadt poignantly reflects Nuremberg's medieval might. The main attraction is a tour of the newly renovated residential wing to see the lavish Knights' and Imperial Hall, a Romanesque double chapel, and an exhibition on the Holy Roman Empire. This segues to the Kaiserburg Museum, which focuses on the castle's military and building history. Elsewhere, enjoy panoramic views from the Sinwell Tower or peer 48m down into the Deep Well.

Nuremberg's other stellar sight is the **Germanisches Nationalmuseum** (German National Museum; gnm.de), the German-speaking world's biggest and most important museum of Teutonic culture.

**TOP TIP:**

### Nürnberg Card

The Nürnberg Card allows admission to all 40 of the city's museums and access to the excellent public transport system. It's available from tourist offices in Nuremberg or viatourismus.nuernberg.de.

### Nuremberg for Kids

No city in Germany's south has more for kids to see and do than Nuremberg. In fact keeping the little 'uns entertained in the Franconian capital is child's play.

**Museums**

**Children & Young People's Museum** (kindermuseum-nuernberg.de) Educational exhibitions and lots of hands-on fun – just a pity it's not open more often.

**School Museum** Re-created classroom plus school-related exhibits from the 17th century to the Third Reich.

**Deutsche Bahn Museum** (dbmuseum.de) Feeds the kids' obsession for trains.

**Play**

**Playground of the Senses** (erfahrungsfeld.nuernberg.de) Some 80 hands-on 'stations' designed to educate children in the laws of nature, physics and the human body. Take the U2 or U3 to Wöhrder Wiese.

**Toys**

**Playmobil** (playmobil-funpark.de) This theme park has life-size versions of the popular toys. It's located 9km west of the city centre in Zirndorf; take the S4 to Anwanden, then change to bus 151. Free admission if it's your birthday.

**Käthe Wohlfahrt Christmas shop** (wohlfahrt.com) The Nuremberg branch of this year-round Christmas shop.

**Spielzeugmuseum** (Toy Museum) Some 1400 sq metres of Matchbox, Barbie, Playmobil and Lego, plus a great play area.

## Continuing into Czechia

In 1994 the Castle Road was extended into Czechia, a country as rich in castle architecture as southern Germany. The route crosses the border between Bavaria and Czechia at Cheb. Be aware that cars hired in Germany cannot normally be taken into Czechia without additional insurance.

Castle highlights of the Czech section of the route include idyllic **Loket**, with its perfectly preserved medieval town; **Bečov nad Teplou**, with its famous reliquary; **Křivoklát Castle**, set dramatically against the forests of Central Bohemia; 14th-century **Karlštejn Castle**, built to house the imperial crown jewels of the Holy Roman Empire; and of course **Prague Castle**, the daddy of all Central European royal residences, where a millennium of history is presented in fascinating exhibitions.

### THE DRIVE
From busy Nuremberg head north along the A73 via Forchheim, a trip of about 61km. To the east of the road extends the so-called Fränkische Schweiz (Franconian Switzerland), a soothing area of wooded hills, lazy rivers and village breweries producing Franconia's countless types of tasty *Landbier* (regional beer).

### 07 BAMBERG
A disarmingly beautiful architectural masterpiece with an almost complete absence of modern eyesores, Bamberg's entire **Altstadt** is a UNESCO World Heritage site and one of Bavaria's unmissables. Generally regarded as one of Germany's most attractive settlements, the town is bisected by rivers and canals and was built on seven hills, earning it the inevitable nickname of 'Franconian Rome'. Make your way across its bridges and along the narrow medieval streets to the gaggle of hilltop sights, beginning with the **Neue Residenz** (New Residence). This splendid episcopal palace gives you an eyeful of the lavish lifestyle of Bamberg's prince-bishops who, between 1703 and 1802, occupied its 40-odd rooms. Nearby rises the **Bamberger Dom** (erzbistum-bamberg.de), a cathedral packed with artistic treasures, most famously the life-size equestrian statue of the **Bamberger Reiter** (Bamberg Horseman), whose true identity remains a mystery.

### THE DRIVE
The B73 is your road today as you head 53km north to Coburg. Along the way you pass through Lichtenfels, a small town renowned for its basket-weaving traditions and its commanding baroque basilica visible for miles around.

### 08 COBURG
Coburg is most famous for its associations with the British royal family – Prince Albert of Saxe-Coburg-Gotha famously married his cousin Queen Victoria in 1840. Albert spent his childhood at **Schloss Ehrenburg** (schloesser-coburg.de), a lavish palace and erstwhile residence of the Coburg dukes. Queen Victoria stayed here in a room with Germany's first flushing toilet (1860). The splendid **Riesensaal** (Hall of Giants) has a baroque ceiling supported by 28 statues of Atlas. Prince Albert's statue can be found on Coburg's **Marktplatz**.

However, Coburg's blockbuster attraction is **Veste Coburg** (kunstsammlungen-coburg.de), a storybook medieval fortress towering over the old centre. With its triple ring of fortified walls, it's one of the most impressive fortresses in Germany. It houses the vast collection of the **Kunstsammlungen**, with works by star painters such as Rembrandt, Dürer and Cranach the Elder. The elaborate **Jagdintarsienzimmer** (Hunting Marquetry Room) is a superlative example of carved woodwork.

Also famous in Coburg are its sausages. Around 30cm long, they are grilled over the embers of pine cones, giving them a sappy, smoky flavour. The tasty result is

**Bamberg**

then served in a tiny bread bun with a dollop of mustard. The best places to try them are the unpresuming kiosks on Marktplatz.

### 🚗 THE DRIVE
The most attractive way to cover the 74km between Coburg and Bayreuth is to take the B303 and then the B85 via Kulmbach, where the hilltop Plassenburg is worth stopping to explore.

### 09 BAYREUTH
Bayreuth is best known for its Wagner connections, but its glory days began in 1735 when Wilhelmine, sister of King Frederick the Great of Prussia, was forced to marry stuffy Margrave Friedrich. Bored with the local scene, the cultured Anglo-oriented Wilhelmine invited the finest artists, poets, composers and architects in Europe to court. The period bequeathed some eye-catching buildings, still on display for all to see. The **Altes Schloss** was Wilhelmine's summer residence. Visits to the palace are by guided tour only and take in the **Chinese Mirror Room** where Countess Wilhelmine penned her memoirs. The **Neues Schloss** lies a short distance south of the main shopping street, **Maxmilianstrasse**. A riot of rococo style, the Margrave's residence post-1753 features a vast collection of 18th-century Bayreuth porcelain. The **Spiegelscherbenkabinett** (Broken Mirror Cabinet), which is lined with irregular shards of broken mirror, is supposedly Margravine Wilhelmine's response to the vanity of her era.

---

### WHY I LOVE THIS TRIP
**Marc Di Duca**, writer

Think of Central Europe and castles – medieval, Renaissance and in all manner of 'neo' styles – probably come to mind. This route satisfies the longing many history fans have to take a peek at the way dukes, royals, prince-bishops and assorted other gentry once lived, a world away from the crooked medieval streets of the towns that surround them.

SOUTHERN GERMANY  16  GERMAN CASTLE ROAD

# 17

# The Romantic Road

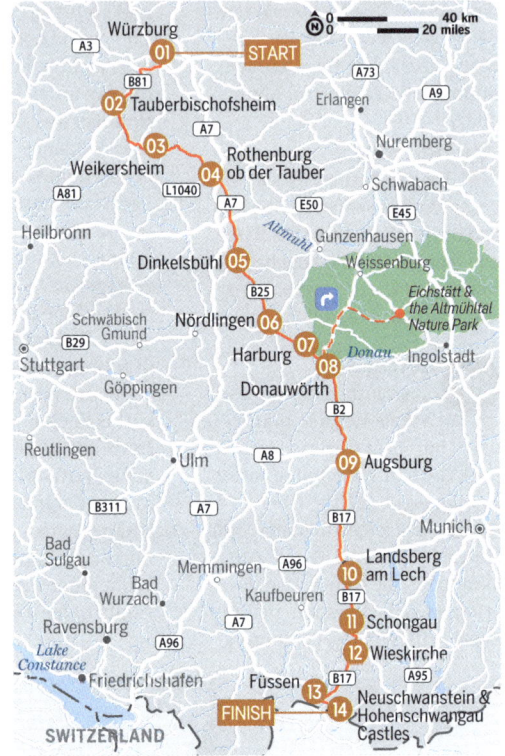

| DURATION | DISTANCE | GREAT FOR |
|---|---|---|
| 10 days | 350km / 217 miles | History & families |

| BEST TIME TO GO | Any time of year. |
|---|---|

From the vineyards of Würzburg to the foot of the Alps, the Romantic Road (Romantische Strasse) is by far the most popular of Germany's touring routes. This well-trodden trail cuts through a cultural and historical cross-section of southern Germany, coming to a climax at the gates of King Ludwig II's crazy castles. The route links some of Germany's most picturesque towns, many appearing untouched since medieval times.

### Link Your Trip

**16 German Castle Road**

The Romantic and the German Castle Roads intersect in Rothenburg ob der Tauber.

**19 German Alpine Road**

The German Alpine and the Romantic Roads meet in Füssen.

### 01 WÜRZBURG

This scenic town in Bavaria's northeast corner straddles the Main River and is renowned for its art, architecture and delicate wines. A large student population keeps things lively and hip nightlife pulsates through its cobbled streets.

Top billing goes to the **Würzburg Residenz** (residenz-wuerzburg.de), a vast UNESCO-listed palace built by 18th-century architect Balthasar Neumann as the home of the local prince-bishops. It's one of Germany's most important and beautiful baroque palaces. The wonderful zigzagging Treppenhaus (Staircase) is capped by the world's

## BEST TWO DAYS

The stretch between stops 4 and 6 takes in the most romantic towns of the Romantic Road.

Dinkelsbühl (p127)

largest fresco, a masterpiece by Giovanni Battista Tiepolo depicting allegories of the four then-known continents (Europe, Africa, America and Asia). The **Dom St Kilian** (dom-wuerzburg.de) is a highly unusual cathedral with a Romanesque core and baroque Schönbornkapelle, also by Neumann.

### THE DRIVE
Take the B19 south to join the A3 motorway; follow this to meet the B81, which goes all the way to Tauberbischofsheim (37km).

### 02 TAUBERBISCHOFSHEIM
The main town of the pretty Tauber Valley, this small settlement has a picturesque marketplace dominated by a neo-Gothic town hall and lined with typical half-timbered houses. Follow the remains of medieval town walls to the Kurmainzisches Schloss, housing the **Tauberfränkisches Landschaftsmuseum** (tauberfraenkisches-landschaftsmuseum.de), where you can learn about Tauberbischofsheim's past.

### THE DRIVE
The 34km dash to Weikersheim passes through Lauda-Königshofen, a pretty stop in the Tauber Valley.

### 03 WEIKERSHEIM
Top billing in under-visited Weikersheim is **Schloss Weikersheim** (schloss-weikersheim.de), the Romantic Road's finest palace.

### WHY I LOVE THIS TRIP
**Marc Di Duca**, writer

This 350km-long ribbon of historical quaintness is the Germany you came to see, but things can get crowded in the summer months, taking away a bit of the romance. Do the trip in winter when Bavaria's chocolate-box towns look even prettier under a layer of snow.

Renaissance to the core, it's surrounded by beautiful formal gardens inspired by Versailles. Highlights include the enormous

**Photo Opportunity**

The half-timbered buildings of Rothenburg ob der Tauber's Plönlein.

Knights Hall dating from around 1600 and over 40m long. The rich decor includes a huge painted ceiling, each panel depicting a hunting scene, and the amazingly ornate fireplace. The unforgettable rococo mirror cabinet, with its gilt-and-red decor, is also part of the guided tour, after which you can wander the elegantly laid-out gardens.

### THE DRIVE
The short 28km journey between Weikersheim and Rothenburg ob der Tauber follows minor country roads all the way. You could also detour via Creglingen, a minor stop on the Romantic Road.

### 04 ROTHENBURG OB DER TAUBER
A well-preserved historical town, Rothenburg ob der Tauber is the Romantic Road's most popular stop. Once you're finished with the main sights, there are some less obvious attractions here.

You'll often see the **Plönlein** in brochures and tourist bumf, a gathering of forks in the cobbled road (Obere Schmiedgasse) occupied by possibly the quaintest, most crooked half-timbered house you'll ever see.

Hidden down an alley is the **Alt-Rothenburger Handwerkerhaus**, where numerous artisans – coopers, weavers, cobblers and potters – have their workshops, and mostly have had for their house's 700 years or more of existence. It's half museum, half active workplace; you can easily spend an hour or so watching the artisans at work.

### THE DRIVE
The quickest way to Dinkelsbühl is the A7 motorway (50km). For a slower and longer experience,

## Rothenburg's Snowballs

Where can you get your hands on a snowball in July? Why, in Rothenburg ob der Tauber, of course. The town's speciality are *Schneeballen* (snowballs), ribbons of dough shaped into balls, deep-fried then coated in icing sugar, chocolate and other dentist's foes. Some 24 types are made at **Diller's Schneeballen** (schneeballen. eu); a smaller range can be enjoyed all over town.

follow the official Romantic Road route along country roads via Schillingsfürst, another quaint halt.

### 05 DINKELSBÜHL
Immaculately preserved Dinkelsbühl is arguably the Romantic Road's most authentically medieval stop. Like Rothenburg, it is ringed by medieval walls, boasting 18 towers and four gates. The joy of Dinkelsbühl is aimless wandering through the crooked lanes, but for a history lowdown visit the **Haus der Geschichte** (House of History; hausdergeschichte-dinkelsbuehl. de), in the same building as the tourist office.

### THE DRIVE
Just 32km separate Dinkelsbühl from Nördlingen along the B25, accompanied by the Wörnitz River for the first part of the journey. A few kilometres short of Nördlingen is Wallerstein, a small market town with the beautiful Church of St Alban, also a Romantic Road stop.

Rothenburg ob der Tauber

## Willy Wonka's Nördlingen

If you've seen the 1971 movie *Willy Wonka & the Chocolate Factory*, you've already looked down upon Nördlingen from a glass lift – aerial shots of the town were used in the film's final sequences.

### 06 NÖRDLINGEN

Charmingly medieval, Nördlingen lies within the Ries Basin, a massive impact crater gouged out by a meteorite more than 15 million years ago. The crater – some 25km in diameter – is one of Earth's best preserved, and has been declared a special 'geopark'. Nördlingen's 14th-century walls, all original, mimic the crater's rim and are almost perfectly circular: **Rieskrater Museum** tells the story. Next door is the **Stadtmuseum**, giving an interesting rundown of Nördlingen's story so far.

On a completely different note, the **Bayerisches Eisenbahnmuseum** (bayerisches-eisenbahn museum.de) near the train station is a retirement home for locos that have puffed their last. The museum runs steam trains up to Dinkelsbühl, Feuchtwangen and Gunzenhausen several times a year; the website has details.

**THE DRIVE**
The 19km drive to Harburg is along the arrow-straight B25.

### 07 HARBURG

Looming over the Wörnitz River, the medieval covered parapets, towers, turrets, keep and red-tiled roofs of 12th-century **Schloss Harburg** (burg-harburg.de) are so perfectly preserved they almost seem like a film set. Tours tell the Schloss's long tale and evoke the ghosts said to use the castle as a hang-out.

From the castle, the walk to Harburg's cute, half-timbered **Altstadt** (old town) takes 10 minutes, slightly more the other way (uphill). A fabulous village-and-castle panorama can be admired from the 1702 stone bridge spanning the Wörnitz.

**THE DRIVE**
Follow the B25 12km to Donauwörth.

### 08 DONAUWÖRTH

Sitting pretty at the confluence of the Danube and Wörnitz rivers, the small town of Donauwörth had its heyday as a Free Imperial City in the 14th century. WWII destroyed 75% of the medieval old town but three gates and five town-wall towers still guard it today. The main street is Reichstrasse, which is where you'll discover the **Liebfraukirche**, a 15th-century Gothic church with original frescos and a sloping floor that drops 120cm. Swabia's largest church bell (6550kg) swings in the belfry. The town's other major attraction is the **Käthe-Kruse-Puppen-Museum** (kaethe-kruse.de). In a former monastery, it's a nostalgia-inducing place of old dolls and dollhouses from world-renowned designer Käthe Kruse (1883–1968).

**THE DRIVE**
Augsburg is 47km away via the B2 and the A8 motorway. The scenic route via back roads east of the A8 passes close to the pretty town of Rain, another minor stop on the Romantic Road.

**Detour**
### Eichstätt & the Altmühltal Nature Park
Start: 08 Donauwörth

A short 55km off the Romantic Road from Donauwörth lies the town of Eichstätt, the main jumping-off point for the serenely picturesque 2900-sq-km Altmühltal Nature Park, which follows the wooded valley of the Altmühl River. Canoeing is a top activity here, as is cycling and camping. The park is an ideal break from the road and a relaxing place to spend a few days in unspoilt natural surroundings. Eichstätt itself has a wealth of architecture, including the richly adorned medieval **Dom** (bistum-eichstaett.de/dom), with its museum, the baroque **Fürstbischöfliche Residenz**, where local prince-bishops once lived it up, and the **Willibaldsburg**, a 14th-century castle that houses a couple of museums.

### 09 AUGSBURG

Augsburg is the Romantic Road's largest city and one of Germany's oldest, founded by the stepchildren of Roman emperor Augustus over 2000 years ago. This attractive city of spires and cobbles is an engaging stop, though less quaint than others along the route.

Augsburg's top sight is the **Fuggerei** (fugger.de), Europe's oldest Catholic welfare settlement, founded by banker and merchant Jakob Fugger in 1521. Around 200 people inhabit the complex today; see how the residents of yesterday lived by visiting the **Fuggereimuseum**.

Two famous Germans have close associations with Augsburg. Protestant Reformation leader Martin Luther stayed here in 1518 – his story is told at **St Anna Kirche**. The birthplace of poet and playwright Bertolt Brecht is now a museum, the **Brechthaus** (brechthaus-augsburg.de).

**Nördlingen**

 **THE DRIVE**
Drive 41km to Landsberg am Lech along the B17. The route mostly follows the valley of the Lech River. Look out for signs to the saucily named town of Kissing.

**10 LANDSBERG AM LECH**
A walled town on the Lech, lovely Landsberg has a less commercial ambience than others on the route. Just like the Wieskirche further south, the small baroque **Johanniskirche** was created by architect Dominikus Zimmermann, who lived in Landsberg and served as its mayor. **Neues Stadtmuseum** (museum-landsberg.de) tells Landsberg's tale from prehistory to the 20th century.

 **THE DRIVE**
The 28km drive along the B17 to Schongau should take 30 minutes. En route you pass through Hohenfurch, a pretty little town regarded as the gateway to the Pfaffenwinkel, a foothill region of the Alps.

**11 SCHONGAU**
One of the lesser-visited stops on the Romantic Road, attractive Schongau is known for its largely intact medieval defences. The Gothic **Ballenhaus** served as the town hall until 1902 and has a distinctive stepped gable; it now houses a cafe. Other attractions include the **Church of Maria Himmelfahrt**, with a choir by baroque architect, Dominikus Zimmermann.

### Landsberg's Dark Literary Connections

Landsberg am Lech can claim to be the town where one of the German language's best-selling books was written. Was it by Goethe, Remarque, Brecht? No, unfortunately, it was by Adolf Hitler. It was during his 264 days of incarceration in a Landsberg jail, following the 1923 beer-hall putsch, that Hitler penned his hate-filled *Mein Kampf*, a book that sold an estimated seven million copies when published. The jail later held Nazi war criminals and is still in use.

**THE DRIVE**
Take the B17 south until you reach Steingaden. From there country roads lead east and then south to Wies. This is where Bavaria starts to take on the look of the Alps, with flower-filled meadows in summer and views of the high peaks when the weather is clear.

**12 WIESKIRCHE**
Located in the village of Wies, the **Wieskirche** is one of Bavaria's best-known baroque churches and a UNESCO-listed site, the monumental work of legendary artist-brothers, Dominikus and Johann Baptist Zimmermann. In 1730, a Steingaden farmer claimed he'd witnessed his Christ statue shedding tears. Pilgrims poured into the town in such numbers over the next decade that the local abbot commissioned a new church to house the weepy work. Inside the almost-circular structure, eight snow-white pillars are topped by gold capitals and swirling decorations. The unsupported dome must have seemed like God's work in the mid-17th century, its surface adorned with a pastel ceiling fresco celebrating Christ's resurrection.

 **THE DRIVE**
Backtrack to Steingaden and rejoin the B17 to reach Füssen (27km). The entire journey is through the Alps' increasingly undulating foothills, with gorgeous views of the ever-nearing peaks along the way.

**13 FÜSSEN**
Sitting at the foot of the Alps, tourist-busy Füssen is all about the nearby castles of Neuschwanstein and Hohenschwangau, but there are other reasons to linger. The town's **historical centre** is worth half a day's exploration and, from here, you can easily escape the crowds into a landscape of gentle **hiking trails** and Alpine vistas. Or, take an hour or two in Füssen's very own castle, the **Hohes Schloss**, today home to an art gallery.

 **THE DRIVE**
To drive to King Ludwig II's castles, take the B17 across the river until you see signs for Hohenschwangau. Parking is at a premium in summer. However, as the castles are a mere 4km from Füssen's centre, it's probably not worth driving at all. RVO buses 78 and 73 (rvo-bus.de) run there from Füssen Bahnhof (at least hourly, tickets from the driver).

**14 NEUSCHWANSTEIN & HOHENSCHWANGAU CASTLES**
The undisputed highlights of any trip to Bavaria, these two castles make a fitting climax to the Romantic Road.
**Schloss Neuschwanstein** (neuschwanstein.de) was the model for Disney's *Sleeping Beauty* castle. King Ludwig II planned

---

**TOP TIP:**

## Visiting Neuschwanstein & Hohenschwangau Castles

The castles can only be visited on guided tours (35 minutes). Buy timed tickets from the **Ticket Centre** (hohenschwangau.de) at the foot of the castles. In summer, arrive as early as 8am to ensure you get in that day.

---

**Schloss Neuschwanstein**

this fairy tale pile himself, with the help of a stage designer rather than an architect. He envisioned it as a giant stage on which to re-create the world of Germanic mythology, inspired by the operatic works of his friend Richard Wagner.

It was at nearby **Schloss Hohenschwangau** (hohenschwangau.de) that King Ludwig II grew up and later enjoyed summers until his death in 1886. His father, Maximilian II, built this palace in a neo-Gothic style atop 12th-century ruins. Less showy than Neuschwanstein, it has a distinctly lived-in feel, where every piece of furniture is a used original. It was at Hohenschwangau where Ludwig first met Wagner.

### Museum of the Bavarian Kings

Palace-fatigued visitors often overlook the worthwhile **Museum der Bayerischen Könige** (Museum of the Bavarian Kings; museumderbayerischenkoenige.de), installed in a former lakeside hotel 400m from the castle ticket office (towards Alpsee Lake) in Hohenschwangau. The big-window views across the beautiful lake (a great picnic spot) to the Alps are almost as amazing as the Wittelsbach bling on show, including Ludwig II's famous blue-and-gold robe. The architecturally stunning museum is packed with historical background on Bavaria's first family and is well worth the extra legwork. A detailed audioguide is included in the ticket.

# 18

# Glass Route

**BEST FOR SHOPPING**

**JOSKA Bodenmais** for authentic local glassware.

| DURATION | DISTANCE | GREAT FOR |
|---|---|---|
| 7 days | 270km / 167 miles | History & nature |

| BEST TIME TO GO | Easter to October when all sights are open. |
|---|---|

JOSKA Bodenmais, Bodenmais (p134)

Think Bavaria, think Alpine meadows, tankards of beer and fast cars – but few may know that the eastern part of the region along the Czech border has a long tradition of making glass. However, viewing the region's glazed and glittering creations is just one of the delights of this low-key route – you'll also be passing through the semiwilderness of the mysterious and undervisited Bavarian Forest National Park.

## Link Your Trip

### 16 German Castle Road
Weiden, the northern terminus of this route, is just 60km southeast from Bayreuth to link up with the castle route.

### 19 German Alpine Road
Passau, at this route's southern end, is a 145km drive north from Berchtesgaden on the Alpine Road. (The route passes through Austria so you'll need an Austrian motorway vignette.)

**01 PASSAU**

Passau is a delightful town, its **Altstadt** (old town) is stacked atop a narrow peninsula that jabs its sharp end into the confluence of three rivers: the Danube, the Inn and the Ilz. The glass highlight here is the **Passauer Glasmuseum** (glasmuseum.de) within the Hotel Wilder Mann. This warren-like museum is filled with some 30,000 priceless pieces of glass and crystal from the baroque, classical, Art Nouveau and Art Deco periods. Much of what you see hails from Bohemia's glassworks, but there are also works by Tiffany and famous Viennese producers.

Passau's other unmissable sight is the **Dom St Stephan**, a late 17th-century confection by a team of Italians, notably architect Carlo Lurago and stucco master Giovanni Battista Carlone. The interior is a top-heavy baroque affair with a mob of saints and cherubs gazing down at the congregation from countless cornices and capitals.

### THE DRIE
A mere 22km on the B85 separates Passau from Tittling, an easy drive across rolling farmland.

### 02 TITTLING
Tiny Tittling on the southern edge of the Bavarian Forest is home to a big attraction – the **Museumsdorf Bayerischer Wald** (museumsdorf.com), the largest open-air museum in Europe. This 20-hectare site hosts 150 typical Bavarian Forest timber cottages and farmsteads, as well as mills, schools and stables, all from the 17th to 19th centuries. Exhibitions range from clothing and furniture to pottery and farming implements. You certainly get a lot for the admission price – you could spend hours ducking in and out of the various buildings. If you are feeling peckish at the end of your tour, drop into the on-site **Gasthaus Mühlhiasl** for some belly-filling east Bavarian fare.

### THE DRIVE
This section of the route takes you deep into the dark hills of the Bavarian Forest as you head north for 38km on minor road 2132 then the B85. Along the way you'll pass by Grafenau, which has one of the best places to stay in the Bavarian Forest.

### 03 FRAUENAU
For as long as the region has been producing glass, Frauenau has been a key location and still boasts three glass factories. So when it came to deciding where to put the region's dazzlingly modern **Glasmuseum** (glasmuseum-frauenau.de), Frauenau won the day. The superb exhibition covers four millennia of glass-making history, starting with the ancient Egyptians and ending with modern glass art from around the world. Demonstrations and workshops for kids are regular features, as are superb temporary exhibitions. It goes without saying that the museum is an essential stop on any trip along the Glasstrasse.

### THE DRIVE
From Frauenau it's a short 8km jaunt to your next stop in Zwiesel. Most base themselves in Zwiesel and make day trips out to Frauenau. The two towns, and several others, are linked by the Waldbahn, a private railway line serving the communities of the Bavarian Forest.

### 04 ZWIESEL
Zwiesel is the main settlement in the Bavarian Forest National Park and the traditional centre of glass production in the region. The **Zwieseler Glasfachschule** (Zwiesel Glassmaker's School) is where many of the artisans of eastern Bavaria learn their trade. The town's main place of interest is the **Waldmuseum** (waldmuseum.zwiesel.de), housed in a former brewery. This 'Forest Museum' has exhibitions on local customs, flora and fauna, life in the forest and, of course, glass-making.

## Bavarian Forest National Park

A paradise for outdoor fiends, the Bavarian Forest National Park extends around 243 sq km along the Czech border, from Bayerisch Eisenstein in the north to Finsterau in the south. Its thick forest, most of it mountain spruce, is criss-crossed by hundreds of kilometres of marked hiking, cycling and cross-country skiing trails; some now link up with a similar network across the border. The region is home to deer, wild boar, fox, otter and countless bird species.

Around 1km northeast of the village of Neuschönau (a short detour north of your route from the village of Grafenau) stands the **Hans-Eisenmann-Haus** (nationalpark-bayerischer-wald. de), the national park's main visitor centre. The free exhibition has hands-on displays to shed light on topics such as pollution and tree growth, plus a children's discovery room, a shop and a library.

### THE DRIVE
This 16km drive takes you through more wooded hills on country roads to the next stop at the castle of Weissenstein (for the Gläserne Wald), 5km south of the town of Regen.

### 05 GLÄSERNE WALD

One of the more unusual sights along the Glass Route is the **Gläserne Wald** (Glass Forest; glaeserner-wald.de) near the town of Regen. Here glass artist Rudolf Schmid has created a forest of glass trees, some as much as 8m tall. The trees, in a number of transparent shades, are set in a flowery meadow next to Weissenstein Castle and are an intriguing sight; many more are set to be added in coming years.

### THE DRIVE
Some 16km divide the Glass Forest from the next halt in Bodenmais, following roads 2135 and 2132 through the thickly forested landscape.

### 06 BODENMAIS

The glass highlight of the small town of Bodenmais is **JOSKA Bodenmais** (joska.com), a crystal theme park complete with crystal shops, public artworks, a beer garden, a year-round Christmas market, a crystal gallery and a workshop where visitors can try their hand at glass-blowing.

### THE DRIVE
The biggest distance of the route; it's around 117km to Weiden, sticking to the 2132 and B22. You quickly leave the Bohemian forest and enter a hilly landscape of huge agricultural fields, passing through the towns of Cham and Rotz.

 **Detour**
### Regensburg
**Start: 06 Bodenmais**

It would be a pity to pass through eastern Bavaria without calling in at one of the state's most engaging cities, Regensburg. A Roman settlement completed under Emperor Marcus Aurelius, the city was the first capital of Bavaria, the residence of dukes, kings and bishops, and for 600 years a Free Imperial City. Two millennia of history bequeathed the city some of the region's finest architectural vestiges, a fact recognised by UNESCO in 2006.

One of Regensburg's top attractions is the **Schloss Thurn und Taxis** (thurnundtaxis.de). In the 15th century, Franz von Taxis (1459–1517) set up the first European postal system, which remained a monopoly until the 19th century. In recognition of his services, the family was given the former Benedictine monastery St Emmeram, henceforth known as Schloss Thurn und Taxis. It soon became one of the most modern palaces in Europe, and featured such luxuries as flushing toilets, central heating and electricity. Tours include the **Basilika St Emmeram**.

A chunk of Regensburg's Roman heritage has survived in the shape of the Roman Wall in a street called Unter den Schwibbögen. Dating from AD 179, the rough-hewn Porta Praetoria arch is the tallest Roman structure in Bavaria and formed part of the city's defences for centuries. A short walk away is the **Steinerne Brücke** (Stone Bridge), a 900-year-old bridge that was at one time the only fortified crossing of the Danube. Neglected and damaged for centuries (especially by the buses that once used it), the bridge has recently been restored. At the old-town end of the bridge, the **World Heritage Visitors Centre** (regensburg-welterbe.de) focuses on the city's UNESCO sites using interesting interactive multimedia exhibits.

### 07 WEIDEN

With several sheet-glass factories, the large town of Weiden often hosts glass-art exhibitions (ask the tourist office for details), many of them in cooperation with partners across the border in Czechia, which itself has a huge glass- and crystal-producing tradition. Otherwise the town is a pleasantly low-key place to end your exploration of Bavaria's glassy traditions.

**Photo Opportunity**

The confluence of three rivers in Passau.

# 19
# German Alpine Road

**BEST FOR OUTDOORS**

Vista-rich hiking trails ring the Königssee.

Königssee (p143)

| DURATION | DISTANCE | GREAT FOR |
|---|---|---|
| 7 days | 450km / 280 miles | Nature |

| BEST TIME TO GO | From Easter to October for warmer weather and better road conditions. |
|---|---|

The Alpenstrasse, as it's known in German, was the country's first touring road, dating from 1858. Since then generations of horse riders, motorbikers, cyclists and campervanners have been discovering the magnificence of the Bavarian Alps. A bonus of this route is its variety – one day you can be exploring one of King Ludwig II's castles, the next picnicking on an Alpine meadow, and the day after that taking a boat trip across a glassy Alpine lake.

## Link Your Trip

**17 The Romantic Road**
The Romantic and German Alpine Roads come together in Füssen.

**20 Lake Constance**
Lindau starts both the Lake Constance and German Alpine Road routes.

### 01 LINDAU
Brochures rhapsodise about Lindau being Germany's 'Garden of Eden' and the 'Bavarian Riviera'. Paradise and southern France it ain't but it is, well, pretty special. Cradled in the southern crook of Lake Constance and almost dipping its toes into Austria, this is a good-looking, outgoing little town, with a candy-coloured postcard of an Altstadt (old town), Alpine views (on clear days) and lakefront cafes that use every sunray to the max. It's the lake that really is the main draw here, and the harbourside **Seepromenade**, with its palms, bobbing boats and folk sunning themselves in pavement

cafes, is an unmissable part of the experience. Out at the harbour gates, looking across the Alps, is Lindau's signature 33m-high **Neuer Leuchtturm** (New Lighthouse), which can be climbed for cracking views out over Lindau and the lake.

Lindau's biggest architectural stunner is the 15th-century step-gabled **Altes Rathaus** (Old Town Hall), a frescoed frenzy of cherubs, merry minstrels and galleons.

### THE DRIVE
The most scenic way to go from Lindau to Füssen is to follow the B308 then the B310 via Immenstadt. This 104km route takes in many minor stops along the Deutsche Alpenstrasse.

### 02 FÜSSEN
Bustling with tourist traffic year-round, Füssen is one of the liveliest towns in the Alps. Most stay here to access King Ludwig II's castles at nearby Hohenschwangau. But there are other attractions. For fabulous views of the Alps and the Forggensee, take the **Tegelbergbahn** (tegelbergbahn.de) to the top of the Tegelberg (1730m), a prime launch point for hang-gliders and parasailors. From here it's a wonderful hike down to the castles (two to three hours; follow the signs to Königsschlösser).

The river that flows through Füssen is the Lech – walk a kilometre south from the bridge across the river to the Lechfall where the chilly water squeezes through a tight gorge. There are forest trails to the castles from here, too.

**TOP TIP:**

### Guest Card

Wherever you stay in the Alps, make sure your hotel reception supplies you with a guest card. This grants free or discounted admission to local attractions plus free use of public transport within a given area.

**Photo Opportunity**
Pretty Schloss Linderhof makes for a beautiful shot.

**Schloss Linderhof**

### THE DRIVE
A hefty chunk of the Alps stands between Füssen and Oberammergau, making for a photogenic if roundabout route. Take the B17 as far as Steingaden, then the minor St2058 to the Ammer River, where you head south along the B23.

### 03 OBERAMMERGAU
Quietly quaint Oberammergau occupies a wide valley surrounded by the dark forests and snow-dusted peaks of the Ammergauer Alps. The centre is packed with traditional painted houses, woodcarving shops and awestruck tourists who come here to learn about the town's world-famous Passion Play.

The top attraction here is the **Passionstheater** (passionsspiele-oberammergau.de), where the Passion Play is performed every decade (the next one is in 2030). The building can be visited as part of a guided tour, which provides ample background on the play's history and lets you peek at the costumes and sets. Also unmissable is the **Oberammergau Museum** (oberammergaumuseum.de), one of the best places to view exquisite examples of Oberammergau's famously intricate woodcarving art. Local crafts-people can produce anything from an entire nativity scene in a single walnut shell to a life-size Virgin Mary.

### THE DRIVE
The next stop at Schloss Linderhof is a short, snappy transfer along a picturesque valley.

The monastery at Ettal is just a few kilometres off this route and worth a stop to sample the monks' Ettaler Klosterlikör, a sugary herbal digestif.

### Detour
**Fünfseenland**
Start: 03 Oberammergau
Once a royal retreat and still a popular place of residence with the rich and famous, the Fünfseenland (Five Lakes District) is set in a glacial plain to the southwest of Munich.

The most popular of the five lakes is the **Starnberger See**, also the largest at 21km long. Those on the King Ludwig II trail should make a beeline for the tiny village of Berg on the eastern shore. It was here that the 'mad king' famously (and mysteriously) drowned along with his doctor in just a few feet of water.

The spot where his body was found is marked with a large solemn cross backed by a Votivkapelle (Memorial Chapel). Berg is 5km from the town of Starnberg and can be reached on foot in around an hour.

The other lakes – **Ammersee, Pilsensee, Wörthsee** and **Wesslinger See** – are smaller and offer more secluded charm. Swimming, boating and windsurfing are popular activities on all lakes, and the district is also criss-crossed by a whopping 493km network of bike paths and 185km of hiking trails.

One unmissable sight by the Ammersee is the gorgeous hilltop monastery of **Kloster Andechs**, founded in the 10th century. Long a place of pilgrimage, today visitors come here primarily to slurp the Benedictines' fabled ales. After inspecting the church, which contains the remains of Carl Orff, the composer of *Carmina Burana*, plunge into the nearby **Bräustüberl**, the monks' beer hall and garden. There are seven varieties of beer on offer, from the rich and velvety *Doppelbock* dark to the fruity unfiltered *Weissbier* (wheat beer).

Andechs and Starnberg are around an hour by car from Oberammergau.

**04** **SCHLOSS LINDERHOF**

A trove of weird treasures, **Schloss Linderhof** (schlosslinderhof.de) was Ludwig II's smallest but most sumptuous palace, and the only one he lived to see fully completed. Finished in 1878, the palace hugs a steep hillside in a fantasy landscape of French gardens, fountains and follies. Linderhof was inspired by Versailles and dedicated to Louis XIV, the French 'Sun King'.

Linderhof's myth-laden, jewel-encrusted rooms are a monument to the king's excesses. The **private bedroom** is the largest, heavily ornamented and anchored by an enormous 108-candle crystal chandelier weighing 500kg. An **artificial waterfall**, built to cool the room in summer, cascades just outside the window.

Created by the famous court gardener Carl von Effner, the gardens and outbuildings (open April to October) are as fascinating as the palace itself. The highlight is the **Moorish Kiosk**, where Ludwig would preside over nightly entertainment from a peacock throne.

 **THE DRIVE**
Backtrack along the valley to the B23, which joins the B2 at Oberau. The journey to Garmisch-Partenkirchen is 26km and should take no more than 30 minutes.

**05** **GARMISCH-PARTENKIRCHEN**

An incredibly popular hang-out for outdoorsy types, skiing fans and day-trippers from Munich, the double-barrelled resort of Garmisch-Partenkirchen (G-P) is blessed with a fabled setting a snowball's throw from the Alps. The area offers some of the best skiing in the land, including runs on Germany's highest peak, the 2964km **Zugspitze** (zugspitze.de).

No visit to G-P would be complete without a Zugspitze **train trip**. The round trip starts in Garmisch aboard a *Zahnradbahn* (cogwheel train) that chugs along the mountain base to the Eibsee, an idyllic forest lake. From here, the Eibsee-Seilbahn, a supersteep cable car, swings to the top. When you're done admiring the views, the Gletscherbahn cable car brings you to the Zugspitze glacier at 2600m, from where the cogwheel train heads back to Garmisch.

Easily accessible from town, the narrow and dramatically beautiful 700m-long **Partnachklamm** (partnachklamm.eu) is a hikeable gorge with walls rising up to 80m.

 **THE DRIVE**
Just 18km separate Garmisch-Partenkirchen from Mittenwald, along the B2. Most tackle it as a day trip and trains run hourly between the two.

**06** **MITTENWALD**

Nestled in a cul-de-sac under snow-capped peaks, sleepily alluring Mittenwald is the most natural spot imaginable for a resort. This drowsy village is known far and wide for its master violin makers, and its citizens seem almost bemused by its popularity. The air is ridiculously clean, and on the main street the loudest noise is a babbling brook.

Skiing on the **Karwendel** ski field is the main attraction, but there is one fascinating off-piste sight – the **Geigenbaumuseum** (geigenbaumuseum-mittenwald. de), a collection of over 200 locally crafted violins and the tools used to fashion them. It's also the venue for occasional concerts.

#### THE DRIVE
The 57km scenic route between Mittenwald and Bad Tölz follows the B11 north to the stunningly beautiful Walchensee. Take the 2072 along the lakeshore, then through some marvellous Alpine terrain to the B13, Lengries and on to Bad Tölz.

### 07 BAD TÖLZ
A pretty spa town straddling the Isar River, Bad Tölz is a delightful spot known for its attractive, frescoed houses. It's also the gateway to the Tölzer Land region and its emerald-green lakes, the **Walchensee** and the **Kochelsee**. The town is worth a couple of hours' wander, perhaps followed by a climb up the **Kalvarienberg** (Cavalry Church), the destination for the town's famous **Leonhardifahrt** (Leonhardi pilgrimage; toelzer-leonhardi fahrt.bayern).

#### THE DRIVE
Some 72km divide Bad Tölz from the shores of the Chiemsee. The quickest route is along the B72 and the A8, but there are other more picturesque options.

####  Detour
#### Munich
**Start:** 07 **Bad Tölz**

Just over 50km north of Bad Tölz, Munich is one of Germany's top cities and a magnet for tourists from all over the globe. You could explore this affluent, stylish city for weeks and not see everything, but a few days can give you a taste of what Bavaria's capital is all about.

Most people start their exploration at the **Marienplatz**, a popular gathering spot that packs a lot of personality into a compact frame. It's anchored by the Mariensäule (Mary's Column). From here it's a short walk to the city's top attraction, the **Residenz**. All the trappings of the lifestyles of Bavaria's Wittelsbach rulers are on display at the Residenzmuseum, which takes up around half of the palace.

Not far from the Residenz is the **Hofbräuhaus** (hofbraeuhaus.de), Munich's most famous beer hall, although there are many others that are just as characterful. Of the city centre's churches, two stand out: the landmark **Frauenkirche** and the late-baroque **Asamkirche**.

Munich has often been dubbed the 'city of art and beer' and when you've tried the beer, next comes the **Kunstareal** (kunstareal.de), a whole district of world-class art museums including the Alte Pinakothek, the Museum Brandhorst, the Neue Pinakothek and the Pinakothek der Moderne.

### 08 CHIEMSEE
Most foreign visitors arrive at the shores of the **Bavarian Sea** – as Chiemsee is affectionately known – in search of King Ludwig II's Schloss Herrenchiemsee. This is Bavaria's

Mittenwald (p139)

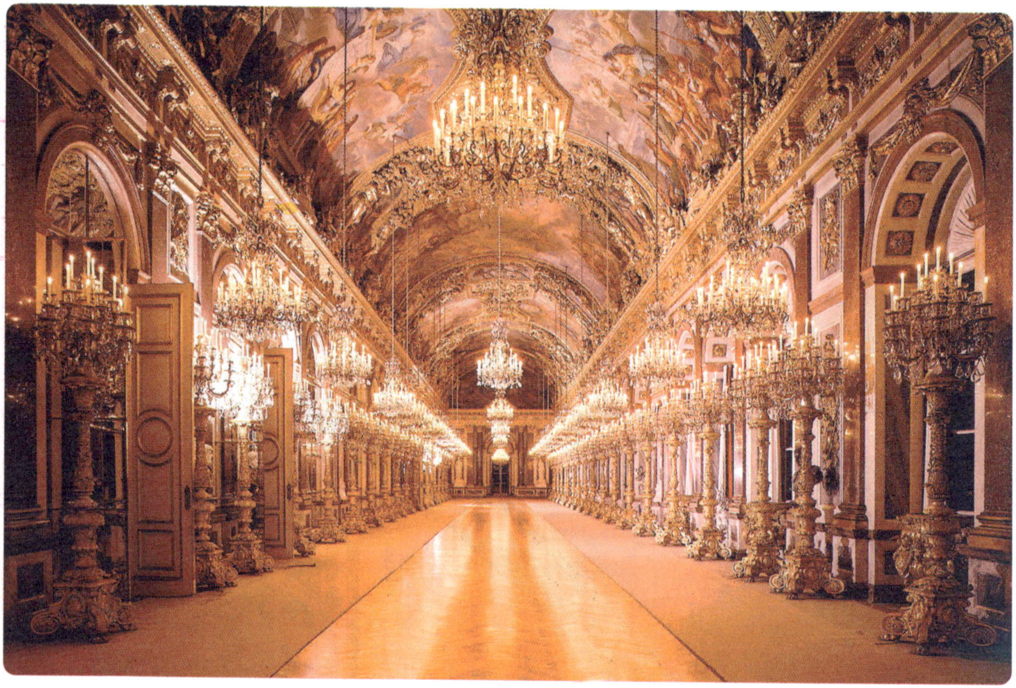

SMITH ARCHIVE/ALAMY, BUILDING SHOWN COURTESY OF THE BAVARIAN PALACE ADMINISTRATION, WWW.SCHLOESSER.BAYERN.DE

Grosse Spiegelgalerie, Schloss Herrenchiemsee

### WHY I LOVE THIS TRIP

**Marc Di Duca**, writer

It's no wonder this was chosen by Bavaria's nobility as the original touring route – a more varied and picturesque string of places you couldn't hope to find anywhere else in Germany. Towering 2000m-high peaks, quaint Bavarian taverns, rivers flowing jade-green with snowmelt and some of Germany's most intriguing castles – the magic of the German Alps meets you at every corner.

biggest lake (if you don't count Lake Constance, which is only partially in the state), and its natural beauty and water sports make the area popular with Munich folk – many of the city's affluent residents own weekend retreats by the shimmering waters.

The towns of **Prien am Chiemsee** and, about 5km south, **Bernau am Chiemsee** are good bases for exploring the lake. Of the two towns, Prien is by far the larger and livelier.

**THE DRIVE** There's no car ferry to the Herreninsel. Take the hourly or half-hourly passenger ferry from Prien-Stock or from Bernau-Felden. From the boat landing on Herreninsel, it's a 20-minute walk through pretty gardens to the palace.

## 09 SCHLOSS HERRENCHIEMSEE

An island just 1.5km across the Chiemsee from Prien, **Herreninsel** is home to Ludwig II's Versailles-inspired castle, **Schloss Herrenchiemsee** (herrenchiemsee.de). Begun in 1878, it was never intended as a residence, but as a homage to absolutist monarchy, as epitomised by Ludwig's hero, Louis XIV. Ludwig splurged more money on this palace than on Neuschwanstein and Linderhof combined, but when cash ran out in 1885, one year before his death, 50 rooms remained unfinished. Ludwig spent only 10 days here.

The vast **Gesandtentreppe** (Ambassador Staircase), a double staircase leading to a frescoed gallery and topped by a glass roof, is the first visual knock-out on the guided tour, but that fades in comparison to the stunning **Grosse Spiegelgalerie** (Great Hall of Mirrors). This tunnel of light runs the length of the garden (98m, or 10m longer than that in Versailles).

Other highlights include the **Paradeschlafzimmer** (State Bedroom), featuring a canopied bed perching altar-like on a pedestal behind a golden balustrade, and the king's bedroom, the **Kleines Blaues Schlafzimmer** (Little Blue Bedroom), encrusted with gilded stucco and wildly extravagant carvings.

### THE DRIVE
The easy-going way to cover the 90km from Prien to Berchtesgaden is to head south to Reit im Winkl, then east almost to Bad Reichenhall on the B305 nearly all the way. Stay on the B305 to Berchtesgaden. The journey takes a little under 1¾ hours and passes through the dramatic Chiemgauer Alpen range.

### 10 BERCHTESGADEN
Wedged into Austria and framed by six formidable mountain ranges, the **Berchtesgadener Land** is a drop-dead gorgeous corner of Bavaria. The area includes the **Watzmann** (2713m), Germany's second-highest mountain, and the pristine **Königssee**, perhaps the country's most photogenic body of water.

Away from the stunning Alpine views, Berchtesgaden has some dark tourism sights bequeathed by the Nazis who chose nearby Obersalzberg as their headquarters. **Dokumentation Obersalzberg** (obersalzberg.de) tells the story.

The **Eagle's Nest** (Kehlsteinhaus; kehlsteinhaus.de) was built as a mountaintop retreat for Hitler, and gifted to him on his 50th birthday. It took some 3000 workers only two years to carve the precipitous 6km-long mountain road, cut a 124m-long tunnel, install a brass-panelled lift through the rock, and build the lodge itself (now a restaurant). It can only be reached by special shuttle bus from the Kehlsteinhaus bus station.

### THE DRIVE
It's a short 6km drive to Schönau on the northern shore of the Königssee. Electric boats depart for lake tours.

### 11 KÖNIGSSEE
Crossing the serenely picturesque, emerald-green **Königssee** makes for some once-in-a-lifetime photo opportunities. Cradled by steep mountain walls some 5km south of Berchtesgaden, Königssee is Germany's highest lake (603m), with pure, drinkable waters shimmering into fjordlike depths.

Escape the hubbub of the bustling lakeside tourist village of **Schönau** by taking an electric-boat tour to **St Bartholomä**, a quaint onion-domed chapel on the western shore. At some point, the boat will stop while the captain plays a horn towards the **Echo Wall** – the sound will bounce seven times. From St Bartholomä, an easy trail leads to the wondrous **Eiskapelle** (ice chapel) in about one hour.

You can also skip the crowds by meandering along the lake shore. It's a nice and easy 3.5km return walk to the secluded **Malerwinkel** (Painter's Corner), a lookout famed for its picturesque vantage point.

## Hitler's Mountain Retreat

Of all the German towns tainted by the Third Reich, Berchtesgaden has a burden heavier than most. Hitler fell in love with nearby Obersalzberg in the 1920s and bought a small country home, later enlarged into the imposing Berghof.

After seizing power in 1933, Hitler established a part-time headquarters here and brought much of the party brass with him. They bought, or often confiscated, large tracts of land and tore down farmhouses to erect a 7ft-high barbed-wire fence. Obersalzberg was sealed off as the fortified southern headquarters of the NSDAP (National Socialist German Workers' Party). In 1938, British prime minister Neville Chamberlain visited for negotiations (later continued in Munich), which led to the infamous promise of 'peace in our time' at the expense of Czechoslovakia's Sudetenland.

Little is left of Hitler's Alpine fortress today. In the final days of WWII, the Royal Air Force levelled much of Obersalzberg, though the Eagle's Nest, Hitler's mountaintop eyrie, was left strangely unscathed. The historical twist and turns are dissected at the impressive Dokumentation Obersalzberg.

# 20
# Lake Constance

**BEST FOR HISTORY**

Meersburg's castle double act is unmissable for history fans.

| DURATION | DISTANCE | GREAT FOR |
|---|---|---|
| 7 days | 180km / 112 miles | History & nature |

**BEST TIME TO GO** | Easter to October: winter fog doesn't obscure views and all sights are open.

*Altes Schloss, Meersburg*

Shared by three countries (Germany, Austria and Switzerland), Lake Constance is Central Europe's third-largest body of water. Taking in meadows and vineyards, orchards and wetlands, beaches and Alpine foothills, the lake's landscapes make a 'greatest hits' of European scenery. Add to that heaps of culture, medieval architecture and relaxed lakeside promenades and you have yourself a highly enjoyable drive with many reasons to stop along the way.

## Link Your Trip

**19 German Alpine Road**
Both this Lake Constance route and the German Alpine Road kick off in Lindau.

**29 Northern Switzerland**
This route in Switzerland starts in St Gallen, only about 13km southwest of Rorschach.

### 01 LINDAU

Some of the town's lesser-known attractions are also worth an hour or two of exploration. The **Peterskirche** is a 1000-year-old church now transformed into a war memorial, but still hiding exquisite time-faded frescos of the Passion of Christ by Hans Holbein the Elder. The cool, dimly lit interior is a quiet spot for contemplation. Lions and voluptuous dames dance across the trompe l'oeil facade of the flamboyantly baroque Haus zum Cavazzen, the town's museum.

### THE DRIVE
The 19km drive from Friedrichshafen to Meersburg hugs the lakeshore most of the way as it follows the B31. En route, the town of Immenstaad is a pretty stop, its old town gathered around a small promontory and pier.

### 03  MEERSBURG
Tumbling down vine-streaked slopes to Lake Constance and crowned by a perkily turreted medieval castle, Meersburg lives up to all those clichéd knight-in-armour, damsel-in-distress fantasies. And if its tangle of cobbled lanes and half-timbered houses filled with jovial banter doesn't sweep you off your feet, the local Pinot noir served in its cosy *Weinstuben* (wine taverns) certainly will.

Meersburg's two castles are the town's premier attractions. Looking across Lake Constance from its high perch, the **Altes Schloss** is an archetypal medieval stronghold, complete with keep, drawbridge, knights' hall and dungeons. The **Neues Schloss** (neues-schloss-meersburg.de) was built in 1710 by Prince-Bishop Johann Franz Schenk von Stauffenberg, and is a dusky pink, lavishly baroque affair. A visit to the now state-owned palace takes in the extravagant bishops' apartments, replete with stucco work and frescos, Balthasar Neumann's elegant staircase, and gardens with inspirational lake views.

### THE DRIVE
The quickest way to go between Meersburg and the next stop, the Wallfahrtskirche Birnau, is to stick to the B31 all the way (9km). The lakefront road is not a suitable route.

### THE DRIVE
This anticlockwise route follows a simple rule: if the lake is on your right, you're going the wrong way. From Lindau take the L116 as far as Kressbronn. From there take the L334 to Eriskirch, where you join the B31 as far as Friedrichshafen. The journey is around 30km.

### 02  FRIEDRICHSHAFEN
Zeppelins, the cigar-shaped airships that first took flight in 1900 under the stewardship of high-flying Count Ferdinand von Zeppelin, will forever be associated with Friedrichshafen. Near the eastern end of its lakefront promenade, Seestrasse, is the **Zeppelin Museum** (zeppelin-museum.de), housed in the Bauhaus-style former Hafenbahnhof, built in 1932. The centrepiece is a full-scale mock-up of a 33m section of the *Hindenburg* (LZ 129), the largest airship ever built, measuring an incredible 245m long and outfitted as luxuriously as an ocean liner. The hydrogen-filled craft tragically burst into flames, killing 36, while landing in New Jersey in 1937. Other exhibits provide technical and historical insights, including an original motor gondola from the famous *Graf Zeppelin*, which made 590 trips and travelled around the world in 21 days in 1929.

A promenade runs through the sculpture-dotted lakefront Stadtgarten park along Uferstrasse, a great spot for a picnic or stroll.

BEST ROAD TRIPS: GERMANY, AUSTRIA & SWITZERLAND   145

**Photo Opportunity**
Aerial shots from a Zeppelin over Lake Constance.

### 04 WALLFAHRTSKIRCHE BIRNAU

The exuberant, powder-pink **Wallfahrtskirche Basilika Birnau** is one of Lake Constance's architectural highlights. It was built by the rococo master Peter Thumb of Vorarlberg in 1746. When you walk in, the decor is so intricate and profuse that you don't know where to look first. At some point your gaze will be drawn to the ceiling, where Gottfried Bernhard Göz worked his usual fresco magic.

#### THE DRIVE
There are two ways of reaching Konstanz. The short way is to backtrack to Meersburg and take the ferry. The long way is to head to the north of the lake then southeast along the western shore, a journey of around 46km.

### 05 KONSTANZ

Sidling up to the Swiss border, bisected by the Rhine and outlined by the Alps, Konstanz sits prettily on the northwestern shore of Lake Constance. Roman emperors, medieval traders and the bishops of the 15th-century Council of Constance have all left their mark on this alley-woven town, which was mercifully spared the bombs of WWII.

Crowned by a filigreed spire and looking proudly back on 1000 years of history, the sandstone **Münster** was the church of the diocese of Konstanz until 1821. The cathedral's interior is an architectural potpourri of Romanesque, Gothic, Renaissance and baroque styles. It's worth ascending the tower for broad views over the city and lake. On the lake itself, the sculpture-dotted promenade lures inline skaters, cyclists, walkers and ice-cream lickers. Just 4km northeast of the centre, the **Strandbad Horn** has sunbathing lawns, a kiddie pool and sports facilities.

#### THE DRIVE
The border with Switzerland doesn't come straight after the bridge over the Rhine in Konstanz, but a couple of kilometres further on. Have your passport ready just in case. After that, road 13 hugs the lake's shore all the way to Rorschach, a journey of around 40km.

### 06 RORSCHACH

The quiet waterfront resort of Rorschach on the Swiss side of the lake is backed by a wooded hill. Although something of a faded beauty, the town has some fine 16th- to 18th-century houses with oriel windows. Out on the lake is the 1920s Badhütte (Bathing Hut), attached to land by a small, covered bridge; it is a pleasant place for a drink.

#### THE DRIVE
From Rorschach take road 7 east to the A1 highway. Stay on this until the signs for the exit to the border crossing with Austria. From there the B202 heads into Bregenz, crossing the Rhine Canal on the way. The journey is 27km long.

### 07 BREGENZ

Bregenz enjoys the most stupendous of views, with the lake spreading out like a liquid mirror; behind you the Pfänder (1064m) climbs to the Alps; to the right you see Germany, to the left the faint outline of Switzerland.

## Come Fly With Me

Real airship fans will justify the splurge on a trip in a high-tech, 12-passenger **Zeppelin NT** (zeppelin-nt.de). Flights last between 30 and 45 minutes for trips covering lake destinations such as Schloss Salem and Lindau, while longer ones drift across to Austria or Switzerland. Takeoff and landing are in Friedrichshafen. The flights aren't cheap but little beats floating over Lake Constance with the Alps on the horizon, and their slow pace means that you can make the most of the legendary photo ops.

Three attractions stand out in Vorarlberg's capital. Designed by Swiss architect Peter Zumthor, the giant glass-and-steel cube of the **Kunsthaus** (kunsthaus-bregenz.at) is said to resemble a lamp, reflecting the changing light of the sky and lake. The stark, open-plan interior is perfect for rotating exhibitions of contemporary art. The striking home of the **Vorarlberg Museum** (vorarlbergmuseum.at) is a white cuboid that homes in on Vorarlberg's history, art and architecture. For an outdoor experience, the **Pfänder Cable Car** (pfaenderbahn.at) whizzes to the peak of the Pfänder, a wooded mountain rearing above Bregenz with a breathtaking panorama.

Zeppelin flight, Lake Constance

# 21

# Fantastic Road

| DURATION | DISTANCE | GREAT FOR |
|---|---|---|
| 4–6 days | 753km / 468 miles | History & nature |

| BEST TIME TO GO | June to August offers the loveliest summer weather. |
|---|---|

On this ring encircling the German state of Baden-Württemberg, you'll be dazzled by its jewels: the ancient university city of Heidelberg, a string of storybook castles, sparkling Alp-framed lakes, a lush island-set garden, and a swathe of thick Black Forest. Treasures include half-timbered villages huddled around cobbled squares, and the yesteryear grandeur of Baden-Baden, with its temple-like spa and opulent casino.

## Link Your Trip

### 15 Bergstrasse
Pick up the castle-lined, mountain-backed Bergstrasse in Heidelberg.

### 22 Schwarzwaldhochstrasse
Baden-Baden is the starting point for a glorious drive through the Black Forest along the Schwarzwaldhochstrasse.

### 01 HEIDELBERG
Spirited Heidelberg is famed for its centuries-old university. The three-room **Universitätsmuseum** (uni-heidelberg.de), inside the Alte Universität building, has paintings, portraits, photos and documents about the university's mostly illustrious history.

From 1823 to 1914, students convicted of misdeeds such as public inebriation, duelling, loud nocturnal singing or freeing the local pigs were sent to its student jail, the **Studentenkarzer** (Student Jail; uni-heidelberg.de), for at least 24 hours. Judging by the inventive wall graffiti, some found their stay

**BEST FOR FOODIES**

Black Forest gateau on its home turf.

Black Forest gateau

highly amusing. Delinquents were let out to attend lectures or take exams. In certain circles, a stint in the Karzer was considered a rite of passage.

Heidelberg's student atmosphere peaks in its pubs, including its most historic, **Zum Roten Ochsen** (Red Ox Inn; roterochsen.de), with black-and-white frat photos on its dark wooden walls and names carved into the tables.

**THE DRIVE**
Zooming along 120km of autobahn is the easiest way to reach Stuttgart. Southwest of Heidelberg take the A5 south for 9km. Join the eastbound A6 for 52km, and turn off onto the southbound A81 for another 52km.

**02 STUTTGART**
The city where Bosch invented the spark plug and Daimler pioneered the gas engine has plenty to interest road-trippers, not least its two high-powered motoring museums. The **Mercedes-Benz Museum** (mercedes-benz.com) takes a chronological spin through the Mercedes empire. Look out for legends like the 1885 Daimler Riding Car, the world's first gasoline-powered vehicle, and the record-breaking Lightning Benz that hit 228km/h at Daytona Beach in 1909. At the **Porsche Museum** (porsche.com/museum), groovy audioguides race you through the history of Porsche

from its 1948 beginnings. Stop to glimpse the 911 GT1 that won Le Mans in 1998.

**THE DRIVE**
From Stuttgart, it's 43km south via the B27 to Tübingen.

**03 TÜBINGEN**
In this bewitchingly pretty city, cobbled lanes lined with half-timbered townhouses twist up to a turreted 16th-century castle, **Schloss Hohentübingen** (unimuseum. uni-tuebingen.de). An ornate Renaissance gate leads to the courtyard and the laboratory where Friedrich Miescher discovered DNA in 1869. Inside the castle, view the world's oldest

BEST ROAD TRIPS: GERMANY, AUSTRIA & SWITZERLAND

**Photo Opportunity**

Schloss Hohentübingen's terrace overlooks the river, old town and vine-streaked hills beyond.

Schloss Hohentübingen, Tübingen (p149)

figurative artworks, the locally unearthed 35,000-year-old Vogelherd figurines, at the **Museum Alte Kulturen**.

### THE DRIVE

Back on the B27, drive south for 25km. At the Hechingen-Süd exit, take the K7111 (which becomes the K7110) for 2.3km to reach the lower and upper car parks for Burg Hohenzollern, from where it's an 800m or a 600m walk, respectively, to the castle.

### 04 BURG HOHENZOLLERN

Rising dramatically from an exposed crag, its medieval battlements and silver turrets often veiled in mist, neo-Gothic **Burg Hohenzollern** (burg-hohenzollern.com) dates from 1867. It's the ancestral seat of the Hohenzollern family, the first and last monarchical rulers of the short-lived second German Empire (1871–1918).

### THE DRIVE

From Burg Hohenzollern, it's 110km southeast to Meersburg. When you cross the Danube at Sigmaringen, look out for the stunning Schloss Sigmaringen (rarely open to the public). The B31 bringing you into Meersburg skirts Lake Constance's eastern shore.

### 05 MEERSBURG

Tumbling down vine-laced slopes to Lake Constance, Meersburg's tangle of cobbled lanes and half-timbered houses are the stuff of medieval fantasies. Looking across the lake from its lofty perch, the **Altes Schloss** is an archetypal medieval stronghold, complete with keep, drawbridge, knights' hall and dungeons. Founded by Merovingian king Dagobert I in the 7th century, the fortress is among Germany's oldest. The bishops of Konstanz used it as a summer residence between 1268 and 1803.

In 1710 Prince-Bishop Johann Franz Schenk von Stauffenberg, perhaps tired of the dinginess and rising damp, swapped the Altes Schloss for the dusky pink, lavishly baroque **Neues Schloss** (neues-schloss-meersburg.de). A visit to the now state-owned palace takes in the extravagant bishops' apartments, replete with stucco work and frescos, Balthasar Neumann's elegant staircase, and gardens with inspirational lake views.

**THE DRIVE**
From Meersburg's harbour, take the car ferry across Lake Constance to the B33 and follow it into Konstanz (10km including the ferry ride).

## 06 KONSTANZ

Konstanz is a highlight on a road filled with highlights, with its stunning location on the northwestern shore of Lake Constance, magnificent architecture and a fascinating history spanning Roman emperors, medieval traders and the bishops of the 15th-century Council of Constance. It also has a spirited student scene.

**THE DRIVE**
Take the B33 northwest for 50km and turn left (southwest) onto the B31. Pass beautiful Freiburg (well worth a stop if you have time); 6km later turn left onto the A5 towards Basel for 12km, before taking the B31 for 11km to reach Breisach.

### Detour
**Mainau Island**
Start:  Konstanz

From Konstanz, it's a quick 6km drive north via the B33 and L219 to the car park for Mainau Island, which is reached by a pedestrian-only causeway. (If you want to leave the car behind for a while, you can also take a ferry here from Konstanz.)

Jutting out over the lake, the lusciously green islet of Mainau is a 45-hectare Mediterranean **garden** (mainau.de) dreamed up by the Bernadotte family, relatives of the royal house of Sweden.

Crowds especially flock on weekends to admire sparkly lake and mountain views from the baroque castle, and to wander sequoia-shaded avenues and hothouses bristling with palms and orchids. Crowd-pullers include a butterfly house, an Italian Cascade integrating patterned flowers with waterfalls, and a petting zoo. Tulips and rhododendrons bloom in spring, hibiscus and roses in summer.

## 07 BREISACH

Breisach is where the Black Forest meets the French border. Lording over the town, the Romanesque and Gothic **St Stephansmünster** shelters a faded fresco cycle, Martin Schongauer's *The Last Judgment* (1491), and a magnificent altar triptych (1526) carved from linden wood.

Breisach's cobbled streets are lined with pastel-painted houses, and you'd never guess that 85% of the town was flattened in WWII, so successful has been the reconstruction. Vauban's star-shaped French fortress-town of Neuf-Brisach (New Breisach), which made the UNESCO World Heritage list in 2008, sits 4km west of Breisach.

**THE DRIVE**
Vineyards fan out around you on this stretch of the trip. Head north via the L104 to reach the A5. Take it north towards Offenburg for 39km and link up with the B33. Following the B33 east brings you to Gengenbach (a 77km drive in total), within the Black Forest.

## 08 GENGENBACH

Chocolate-box Gengenbach's chief sight is its scrumptious **Altstadt** (old town) of half-timbered houses framed by vineyards and orchards. It's especially atmospheric during its Christmas festivities.

**THE DRIVE**
It's a 96km journey to Baden-Baden. Take the B33 south; at Biberach, wind northeast for 35km to reach the high-altitude B500 (aka the Schwarzwaldhochstrasse or Black Forest High Road, which you can explore on Trip 22). For the next 46km, views stretch over the mist-wreathed Vosges Mountains, heather-flecked forests and glacial lakes.

## 09 BADEN-BADEN

Baden-Baden recalls the grandeur of yesteryear with its colonnaded buildings and turreted Art Nouveau villas beneath a backdrop of forest-covered mountains.

Gleaming with marble and glistening with mosaics, the palatial 19th-century Friedrichsbad thermal baths put the *baden* (bathe) in Baden.

Marlene Dietrich called Baden-Baden's sublime **casino** (casino-baden-baden.de) 'the most beautiful casino in the world'. Gents must wear a jacket and tie. To marvel at the opulence, take a guided tour.

**THE DRIVE**
From Baden-Baden, it's a quick 90km back to Heidelberg. Take the B500 (Schwarzwaldhochstrasse) northwest for 6.3km and turn northeast onto the A5. Along the way, you'll pass the town of Karlsruhe, which was the model for Washington, DC.

# 22 Schwarzwaldhochstrasse

**BEST FOR FAMILIES**

Mehliskopf for its zippy bob run and high-rope course.

| DURATION | DISTANCE | GREAT FOR |
|---|---|---|
| 2–4 days | 60km / 37 miles | Wine, nature & families |

| BEST TIME TO GO | Spring to autumn for seasonal colour (flowers and foliage). |
|---|---|

Grobbach stream near Geroldsauer Wasserfälle

Road trips in the deep, dark Black Forest don't get any lovelier than the Schwarzwaldhochstrasse. Why? This is a road with altitude, where the views over hill and dale are constant. Wind down the window for pine-fresh air as you wiggle south from the spa town of Baden-Baden to Freudenstadt, passing heather-flecked woodlands, luscious meadows, waterfalls, lakes and stout farmhouses. Autumn brings a dash of gold to the picture.

## Link Your Trip

### 15 Bergstrasse
From Baden-Baden, drive 86km north to Wiesloch and the Bergstrasse, a road trip taking in castles and vineyards aplenty.

### 16 German Castle Road
Like nothing better than a good castle? You'll be in your element on this history-packed road trip. Hook onto it in Heidelberg, 90km north of Baden-Baden.

### 01 BADEN-BADEN
Baden-Baden's air of old-world luxury and curative waters have attracted royals, the rich and celebrities over the years – Obama and Bismarck, Queen Victoria and Victoria Beckham included. This chic Black Forest town boasts grand colonnaded buildings and whimsically turreted Art Nouveau villas spread across the forested hillsides. Top billing goes to the grand neoclassical **Trinkhalle** (Pump Room), a pump room embellished with 19th-century frescos of local legends, the sublime gilded casino and the architecturally innovative **Museum Frieder Burda** (museum-frieder-burda.de),

## Spa Time

The bath-loving Romans were the first to discover the healing properties of Baden-Baden's springs in the city they called Aquae Aureliae. Rheumatism, arthritis, respiratory complaints, skin problems – all this and a host of other ailments can be healed, apparently, by this mineral-rich spring water. To take the waters yourself, you could abandon modesty (and clothing) to wallow in thermal waters at **Friedrichsbad** (carasana.de), a palatial 19th-century marble- and mosaic-festooned spa, with a strict regime of hot-and-cold bathing, dunking and scrubbing. If you'd rather keep your bathing togs on, slip over to **Caracalla Spa** (carasana.de), a modern glass-fronted spa with a cluster of indoor and outdoor pools, grottos and surge channels.

whose stellar collection features Picasso, Gerhard Richter and Jackson Pollock. If the sun's out, join the locals for a lazy mooch along the **Lichtentaler Allee**, a 2.3km ribbon of greenery shadowing the sprightly Oosbach river, studded with fountains and carpeted with flowers.

### THE DRIVE
The B500 south of Baden-Baden soon begins its steady climb through high meadows and spruce, pine and larch forest. After 7.5km, just after Gasthaus Auerhahn, bear left onto Geroldsauerstrasse, which soon becomes Wasserfallstrasse. It's a further 2km drive to Geroldsauer Wasserfälle.

### 02 GEROLDSAUER WASSERFÄLLE
Word has it that German composer Brahms and French painter Courbet had a soft spot for the wispy **Geroldsauer Wasserfälle**, which plunge over mossy boulders into a green pool. The 1.5km walk through forest and along the Grobbach stream is deliciously cool on a hot day and looks freshly minted for a kids' picture book about water sprites. The falls are at their loveliest when the rhododendrons are in bloom (early May to June).

### THE DRIVE
Backtrack to the B500 and follow it as it meanders south, affording bucolic views over forested hills, to Mehliskopf, 14km away.

### 03 MEHLISKOPF
The slopes of 1007m **Mehliskopf** (mehliskopf.de) are a magnet for families seeking low-key outdoor adventure. You can whizz downhill year-round on the bob run, picking up speeds of up to 40km/h on its hairpin bends and 360-degree loop, or on the downhill carts (over 14-year-olds only). There's also a high-rope course in the forest and a lookout tower, with far-reaching views across the Northern Black Forest and the Rhine Plain. In winter, the focus switches to the snow park's rails and obstacles, and downhill skiing.

## Gourmet Pit Stop

Swinging along country lanes 6km north of Freudenstadt brings you to Baiersbronn. It looks like any other Black Forest town, snuggled among meadows and wooded hills, but on its fringes sit two of Germany's finest restaurants, both holders of the coveted three Michelin stars.

**Schwarzwaldstube** (traube-tonbach.de) commands big forest views from its rustically elegant dining room. Here Harald Wohlfahrt performs culinary magic, while carefully sourcing and staying true to French cooking traditions.

Claus-Peter Lumpp has consistently won plaudits for his brilliantly composed, French-inflected menus at **Restaurant Bareiss** (bareiss.com). Dishes that appear deceptively simple on paper become things of beauty.

**THE DRIVE**
Sidling up to Mehliskopf is the peak of Hundseck – your next stop.

### 04 WALDERLEBNIS-STATION HUNDSECK

A sure-fire hit with the kids, this **forest discovery area** has child-geared trails including a circular 500m hunting path and a 2km quiz path, as well as a shorter barefoot path for feeling different textures underfoot.

**THE DRIVE**
Press on south along the panoramic B500, veering right onto the L86 after around 5km. After a couple of kilometres you'll reach the Wildgehege Breitenbrunnen.

### 05 WILDGEHEGE BREITENBRUNNEN

If wildlife encounters rank highly on your wish list, factor in a stop at this **game reserve** to come eye to eye with stags, roe deer and wild boar.

**THE DRIVE**
Head back to the B500 for the dreamy drive overlooking a ripple of wooded hills to Mummelsee, around 3.5km south.

### 06 MUMMELSEE

This glacial **cirque lake** makes a beautiful splash on a vast tract of forest. Lore has it that an underwater king and nymphs dwell in its inky depths – and indeed the lake is pure Grimm fairy tale stuff. You can pedal across it by boat or stroll its shores. Should you want to ramble further, hike 1.5km up to 1164m Hornisgrinde, the highest peak in these parts, commanding far-reaching views over the Black Forest from its lookout tower.

**THE DRIVE**
From Mummelsee, bear south past slopes that fill with skiers in winter, then turn right onto the L87 (Ruhesteinstrasse) for the drive to Ottenhöfen, 14km away.

### 07 OTTENHÖFEN

As storybook Black Forest villages go, **Ottenhöfen** (ottenhoefen-tourismus.de) fits the bill nicely with its plethora of lovingly restored watermills (best explored on the 12km Mühlenweg), slender-spired church and farmhouses snuggled among low-rise, wooded hills. Climbers and hikers can head up to the knobbly peak of Karlsruher Grat. The surrounding area is criss-crossed with family-friendly walking trails and mountain-bike routes.

**THE DRIVE**
The K5371 is a minor country road leading southeast of Ottenhöfen to Allerheiligen, 7.5km away.

### 08 ALLERHEILIGEN WASSERFÄLLE

Allerheiligen's 90m-high **waterfalls** spill in silky threads over several cascades. From here, a short, round trail leads over bridges and up steps through the wooded gorge to a ruined Gothic abbey – an evocative sight with its nave open to the sky.

**THE DRIVE**
From Allerheiligen, take the winding K5370 north back to the B500, then turn right heading south, where you'll pass Schliffkopf Wellness & Nature Hotel en route to the Lotharpfad. It's a 16km drive in total.

### 09 LOTHARPFAD

Hurricane Lothar swept across Europe in 1999, flattening some parts of the Northern Black Forest: trees fell like dominoes in wind speeds of up to 200km/h. The Lotharpfad is an 800m adventure trail that gives an insight into how the area is now being reforested.

**THE DRIVE**
Back behind the wheel, drive gently south to reach the little village of Kniebis, 7km distant.

### 10 KNIEBIS

Serene and family-friendly, **Kniebis** (kniebis.de) backs onto a terrific landscape for all manner of outdoor activities – from hiking and biking to cross-country skiing and sledding. To cool off in summer, head over to the forest-rimmed **Waldschwimmbad** (waldschwimmbad-kniebis.de), with its outdoor pool, kids' splash area and volleyball court.

### Photo Opportunity

Snap the Black Forest peaks wreathed in morning mist.

**Black Forest**

### THE DRIVE
It's an easy 11km drive east on the B28, past forested hills, pastures and farmhouses, to Freudenstadt, marking the southern terminus of the Schwarzwaldhochstrasse.

### 11 FREUDENSTADT

Duke Friedrich I of Württemberg built a new capital in Freudenstadt in 1599, which was bombed to bits in WWII. Though its centre is underwhelming, statistics lovers will delight in ticking off Germany's biggest square (216m by 219m, for the record), **Marktplatz**, whose arcades harbour rows of shops and cafes with alfresco seating, and the 17th-century red-sandstone **Stadtkirche**, with an ornate 12th-century Cluniac-style baptismal font, Gothic windows, Renaissance portals and baroque towers. The glass-fronted **Panorama-Bad** (panorama-bad.de) is a relaxation centre with pools, steam baths and saunas.

### Nationalpark Schwarzwald

An outdoor wonderland of heather-speckled moors, glacial cirque lakes, deep valleys, mountains and near-untouched coniferous forest, the **Nationalpark Schwarzwald** (Black Forest National Park; nationalpark-schwarzwald.de), which finally achieved national park status on 1 January 2014, is the Black Forest at its wildest and untamed best. Nature is left to its own devices in this 100-sq-km pocket in the Northern Black Forest, tucked between Baden-Baden and Freudenstadt and centred on the Schwarzwaldhochstrasse, the Murgtal valley and the Mummelsee.

Hiking and cycling trails abound, as do discovery paths geared towards children. Stop by the information centre in Seebach for the lowdown and to pick up maps. Details of guided tours and online maps are also available on the website.

Burg Hochosterwitz (p189)

# Austria

**23** **Along the Danube**
Follow the Danube's scenic spread of abbey-set towns, artistic cities, idyllic villages and castle ruins as it ribbons through Austria. p160

**24** **The High Alpine Trio – Grossglockner to Silvretta**
Ascend to peak heights on three iconic mountain passes during this wonderous, winding journey from stately Salzburg to lakeside Bregenz. p164

**25** **Mountain Valleys of Tyrol & Vorarlberg**
Valley-hop between hike-worthy villages and picture-book ski towns of western Austria, home to Alpine landscapes primed for outdoor adventures. p170

**26** **Castles of Burgenland & Styria**
Take the ancient path through Roman towns and past medieval hilltop castles between the culture-crammed cities of Vienna and Graz. p176

**27** **Salzkammergut**
Tour the shimmering teal-hued waterways and Alpine-framed hamlets of Austria's famed lake district on a breathtaking loop drive from Salzburg. p182

**28** **Carinthian Lakes**
Boat and bathe the turquoise Carinthian Lakes and weave through the shoreline towns and Roman foundations of Austria's sunny south. p188

# Explore

# Austria

Austria's dreamscape spread of nature and heritage unfolds on the open road. Cross-country autobahns and high mountain passes link the eastern prairies to the western peaks, passing history-stacked towns, culture-steeped cities, lakeside hamlets and deep-set valleys. When the engine stops, new adventures await: skiing, hiking, biking and tobogganing mountain ranges and parkland swathes; diving, boating and bathing in glistening lakes; descending into ice caves, cellars and salt mines; and musing on Roman strongholds, medieval castles and imperial palaces. All are fuelled by a culinary scene as diverse as the terrain, from mountain huts to Michelin-star eats, and coffee houses to vineyards.

### Vienna

Austria's capital and cultural heavyweight will keep you on your toes. Move from Roman ruins to medieval backstreets in the cathedral-stamped, UNESCO-listed historical centre, romp through Habsburg palaces and grand parks and gardens, and sip in time-capsule coffee houses. Switch gears from classic to contemporary in avant-garde galleries and bohemian districts and sample a cutting-edge culinary scene beyond the imperial staples.

### Salzburg

Famous for *The Sound of Music* and as the birthplace of Mozart, Salzburg is a sublime baroque city jewel crowned by a hilltop fortress and framed by Alpine peaks. Walk the clifftop paths hugging the city, bike the Salzach River, stroll from quaint old-town lanes to the Schloss Mirabell gardens, and soak up beer-hall culture at Augustiner Bräustübl.

### Graz

Austria's under-the-radar second city, cultural epicentre and 'Culinary Capital' packs a lot into its compact core. Unwind in the UNESCO–listed historical centre among frescoed facades and Italian Renaissance architecture, wind up the hill for sweeping views from the clocktower, step inside the bulbous, blue, 'Friendly Alien' Kunsthaus modern art museum, and dine out on a farm-to-fork cuisine.

### WHEN TO GO

Temperatures peak in July and August and drop in December and January. April and November are the wettest. The shoulder seasons of May to June (up to 25°C) and September to October (up to 15°C) are prime for city breaks and outdoor pursuits, though mountain weather is unpredictable. High mountain passes close during winter, typically between December and March.

### Innsbruck

The serrated ridges of the Nordkette mountain range rise above and around the pastel abodes and cobblestone Aldstadt of the

Tyrolean capital, Innsbruck. It's an urban basin where you can snack on strudel; take a romp around an imperial palace; glide to Alpine viewpoints, powdery ski slopes and forested hiking tracks on futuristic funiculars; and sleep in centuries-old hotels.

## Bregenz

Alpine Vorarlberg's capital is a culture and art hub that spreads along the shoreline of Europe's third-largest lake, Lake Constance (Bodensee). Walk the harbourside promenade, peruse lakeside art galleries, take a leisurely cruise to Germany and Switzerland, rent bikes for the 273km Bodensee Radweg loop trail, or unwind at a shoreside camp site.

## St Wolfgang

Cafes, bars and restaurants fill the historic streets of this lakeshore town. Bathe in Wolfgangsee's glistening waters or hire watersport equipment in town, criss-cross the lake's other towns by ferry, and head up the 1783m Schafberg mountain by cable car or steam railway for spectacular views of the lake-set mountain ranges.

## Klagenfurt

Stamping the eastern fringe of Carinthia's largest lake, Wörthersee, the regional capital, Klagenfurt, is a worthy pitstop on a tour through Austria's southernmost state. It's around 4km from the Renaissance centre to the shoreline, dotted with bathing beaches, waterside hiking and biking trails and boat trips that zip you around other lakeside towns.

### TRANSPORT

Vienna's international airport is the primary hub for entry, while the smaller airports at Innsbruck, Salzburg and Graz serve European routes. Bregenz, in Austria's westernmost state, stands between the borders of Germany and Switzerland, allowing for a multicountry drive. An extensive rail network of intercity and suburban trains connects all corners of the country, making transfers between key regions for car hire easy.

 **WHAT'S ON**

**Spring and summer festivals**
Festival season takes hold from May to July and includes the week-long classical-music Styriarte in Graz; Vienna's island music festival, Vienna Donauinselfest; Bregenz's performing arts stage Bregenzer Festspiele; and the mega music showcase Salzburg Festival.

**Alpine classic car rallies**
In June and July, watch vintage vehicles circle dreamy Alpine circuits at the Silvretta Classic Rally Montafon, Kitzbühel's Alpenrallye, and the Arlberg Classic Car Rally.

### Resources

**Austria Tourism** (austria.info/en-gb) Austria's tourism website has seasonal highlights and destination tips across all nine federal states.

**Bergfex** (bergfex.at) A compendium of ski, hiking and biking trails, weather tips and tours. Also available via app.

**Austrian Automobile Club (ÖAMTC)** (oeamtc.at/laenderinfo/austria) Lists traffic forecasts, route planners, petrol stations, digital vignettes and traffic regulations.

 **WHERE TO STAY**

Road-trippers have a pick of accommodation across Austria, mixing in-the-thick-of-it urban and off-grid rural stays, reflective of regional character and with the country's sustainability ethos at the fore. In cities, options include historic palaces and villas repurposed into boutique or art hotels alongside trendy midrange options and international chains. Small towns offer a more personal experience, with family-run hotels, traditional inns and Pensionen (B&Bs). In Alpine regions, eco-conscious stays abound, with wellness-focused spa hotels, rustic Gasthäuser (inns), and cosy farmhouse lodgings (Bauernhof). Campsites are found mainly in the lake regions, and those with shoreline access fill up fast.

BEST ROAD TRIPS: GERMANY, AUSTRIA & SWITZERLAND

# 23 Along the Danube

**BEST FOR ART**

Linz' contemporary Lentos gallery.

Stift Melk, Melk (p163)

| DURATION | DISTANCE | GREAT FOR |
|---|---|---|
| 2–4 days | 293km / 198 miles | History, wine & nature |

| BEST TIME TO GO | Aim for spring or summer: many places close between November and March. |
|---|---|

Follow the course of the river made world-famous by Johann Strauss II's *Blue Danube* waltz through hedged green forests, hilltop castles, horseshoe bends and hamlet-fringed vineyards. Though most spectacular in its Wachau stretch between Melk and Krems an der Donau, this route also packs a cultural punch with the pioneering arts city of Linz and two centuries-old monasteries still crafting beer and wine.

### Link Your Trip

**26 Castles of Burgenland & Styria**

Vienna is the starting point of this castle-strewn route.

**27 Salzkammergut**

From Passau, it's 115km southwest to Salzburg, from where you can explore the Salzkammergut's mountain-ringed lakes.

### 01 PASSAU

Just inside the German border, Passau's pastel-shaded Altstadt (old town) sits atop a narrow peninsula jutting into the confluence of three rivers: the Danube, the Inn and the Ilz. Christianity generated prestige as Passau evolved into the largest bishopric in the Holy Roman Empire, as testified by the mighty cathedral **Dom St Stephan**.

Stroll the old town, which remains much as it was when the powerful prince-bishops built its tight lanes, tunnels and archways with an Italianate flourish.

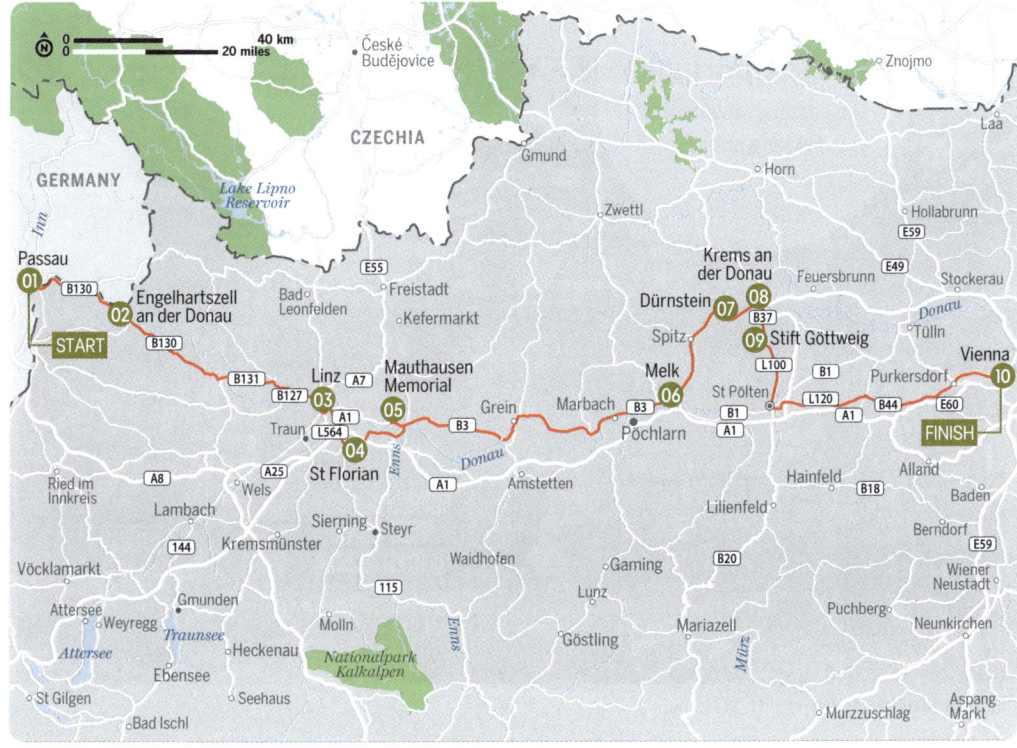

### THE DRIVE
Cross the Inn River where it joins the Danube via the Marienbrücke and head east on the ST2125 which, 3.3km later, becomes the B130 on entering Austria, and follows the Danube's southern bank. On your right, you'll pass Burg Krempelstein, built on the site of a Roman watch-house. It's 26km in total to Engelhartszell an der Donau.

### 02 ENGELHARTSZELL AN DER DONAU
The little riverside village of Engelhartszell an der Donau is home to one of only eight licensed Trappist breweries outside Belgium, and the only one in Austria. At the 1293-founded abbey **Engelszell** (stift-engelszell.at), you can purchase monk-made brews (dark Gregorius, amber Benno, blond Nivard and the lager, 1293er); the shop also sells liqueurs and cheeses produced here. Adjoining the shop is the abbey's gorgeous rococo church, completed in 1764.

### THE DRIVE
Take the B130; at Aschach an der Donau, cross the river on the B131, and continue east to Ottensheim to join the B127 to Linz (52km in total). For a nature detour around 17km in, turn off the B130 into Schlögenleiten, where you can park up and take a leisurely forest climb to the Schlögener Schlinge viewpoint overlooking the head-turning Danube River horseshoe bend.

### 03 LINZ
The Austrian saying *In Linz beginnt's* (It begins in Linz) sums up this technology trailblazer. Its leading-edge **Ars Electronica Center** (aec.at) has labs for interacting with robots, animating digital objects, converting your name to DNA and (virtually) travelling to outer space. After dark, the LED glass skin kaleidoscopically changes colour. Directly across the Danube is the world-class contemporary-art gallery, the glass-and-steel **Lentos** (lentos.at), with works by Warhol, Schiele and Klimt, among others.

The creative arts thread continues at the **Mariendom** (dioezese-linz.at) – the neo-Gothic giant of a cathedral with its riot of pinnacles and flying buttresses conceals a gallery of chromatic modern-art stained glass windows.

**Photo Opportunity**
The dazzling interior of St Florian's abbey.

Library, Augustiner Chorherrenstift, St Florian

**THE DRIVE**
Take the B1 southeast to Ebelsberg, then continue on the L564 to St Florian (21km in total).

**04 ST FLORIAN**
Rising like a vision above St Florian is its magnificent abbey, **Augustiner Chorherrenstift** (stift-st-florian.at). Dating to at least 819, it has been occupied by the Augustinian Canons, living under Augustinian rule, since 1071. Today its imposing yellow-and-white facade is overwhelmingly baroque.

Compulsory guided tours of the abbey's interior take in the resplendent apartments adorned with rich stuccowork and frescos, including 16 emperors' rooms (once occupied by visiting popes and royalty) and a galleried library housing 160,000 volumes.

Tours include entrance to the **Stiftsbasilika** (stift-st-florian.at) – an exuberant affair with an altar carved from 700 tonnes of pink Salzburg marble, and the gilded 18th-century 'Bruckner Organ'.

**THE DRIVE**
Head northeast on the L566 to join the B1. Follow it for 7.5km then turn east on the B123 to cross the Danube, before turning west on the B3. After 2.4km take the L1411 for 2.5 signposted kilometres to the Mauthausen Memorial (22km in total).

**05 MAUTHAUSEN MEMORIAL**
Nowadays Mauthausen is a peaceful small town on the north bank of the Danube, but in WWII, the Nazis turned the quarrying centre into the **KZ Mauthausen** concentration camp. Prisoners were forced into slave labour in the granite quarry and many died on the so-called *Todesstiege* (stairway of death) leading from the quarry to the camp. Some 100,000 prisoners perished or were executed in the camp between 1938 and 1945. The complex is now a **memorial** (mauthausen-memorial.org); English-language audioguides and guided tours relate its sobering history. It's not recommended for under 14s.

**THE DRIVE**
Travelling east on the B3 for for 76km brings you to Melk. Along the river at Grein, look out for the dramatic castle Greinburg rising to your left.

## 06 MELK

Historically, Melk was of great importance to the Romans and later to the Babenbergs, who built a castle here. In 1089 the Babenberg margrave Leopold II donated the castle to Benedictine monks, who converted it into the fortified **Stift Melk** (Benedictine Abbey of Melk; stiftmelk.at). Fire destroyed the original edifice; today its monastery church dominates the complex with its twin spires and high octagonal dome. The exuberantly Baroque interior has regiments of cherubs, gilt twirls and polished faux marble. The theatrical high-altar scene depicts St Peter and St Paul (the church's two patron saints).

### THE DRIVE
The Wachau is the loveliest stretch along the mighty river's length: both banks here are dotted with ruined castles and terraced with vineyards. From Melk, follow the river northeast along the nothern bank for 28km, passing medieval villages Spitz, Wösendorf in der Wachau and Weissenkirchen, to reach Dürnstein.

## 07 DÜRNSTEIN

Picturesque Dürnstein is best known for the **Kuenringerburg** – the now-ruined castle above the town where Richard the Lionheart (Richard I of England) was imprisoned from 1192 to 1193, before being moved to **Burg Trifels** in Germany.

Of the 16th-century buildings lining Dürnstein's hilly, cobbled streets, the blue and white spired Dürnstein **Chorherrenstift Abbey** (stiftduernstein.at) is the most impressive. It's all that remains of the former Augustinian monastery originally founded in 1410, and received its baroque facelift in the 18th century.

### THE DRIVE
Head east along the river on the B3 for 7.5km to reach Krems an der Donau.

## 08 KREMS AN DER DONAU

Against a backdrop of terraced vineyards, Krems has an attractive cobbled centre and gallery-dotted **Kunstmeile** (Art Mile; kunstmeile-krems.at). Its flagship is **Landesgalerie NÖ** (landesgalerie-noe.at), a futuristic stretched cube structure containing ever-changing exhibitions of edgy modern art and contemporary installations.

### THE DRIVE
Leave Krems an der Donau on the B37 and cross the southbound L100. Stift Göttweig is well-signposted (9km altogether from Krems).

## 09 STIFT GÖTTWEIG

Rising upon a Wachau hill and surrounded by grape-laden vines is the UNESCO–listed **Stift Göttweig** (Göttweig Abbey; stiftgoettweig.at). Though founded in 1083, the abbey you see today is mostly baroque. Highlights include the Imperial Staircase, with a heavenly ceiling fresco painted by Paul Troger in 1739, and the luminous baroque interior of the Stiftskirche (which has a Kremser Schmidt work in the crypt). Best of all is the opportunity to sip wine made here by the monks – including an exquisite Messwein rosé – on the panoramic garden terrace above the valley (you can also buy it at the abbey's shop).

### THE DRIVE
From Stift Göttweig, it's 79km to Vienna. The most scenic route, through farmland and forest, is south on the L100 to St Pölten, then east on the L120 to join the eastbound B44 at Ebersberg. Continue through the Wienerwald to the Austrian capital.

## 10 VIENNA

Vienna's grand mix of Roman ruins, medieval remnants and imperial Habsburg heritage in palaces and world-class art museums melds with a modern metropolis hit of avant-garde galleries and bohemian *Bezirke* (districts). The best way to explore the city – starting with the UNESCO-listed historic centre Innere Stadt (1st district) – is on foot, criss-crossing cobblestoned lanes and opulent shopping streets within the *Palais*-fringed Ringstrasse road. An atmospheric (if touristy) alternative is clip-clopping the city highlights aboard a **Fiaker**, a traditional two-horse-drawn carriage (bowler-hatted drivers can be found at Stephansplatz, and Michaelerplatz at the Hofburg). Trams, buses and a metro system conveniently link the inner city to the outer district Schönbrunn and Belvedere big-hitter palaces and surrounding green spaces. This includes the **Prater Park** between the Danube and Danube Canal – best known for its **Wurstelprater** amusement park thrills (praterwien.com/en/home), where you can take a city-view turn on the 64.75m, 1897-built Wiener Riesenrad Ferris wheel of *The Third Man* movie fame.

# 24

# The High Alpine Trio – Grossglockner to Silvretta

**BEST FOR DRIVERS**

The Grossglockner's 36 heart-in-your-mouth hairpin bends.

| DURATION | DISTANCE | GREAT FOR |
|---|---|---|
| 5–7 days | 711km / 442 miles | Nature |

| BEST TIME TO GO | Tackle this trip in summer. Some high mountain passes close in winter. |
|---|---|

Silvretta High Alpine Road (p169)

This Alpine-set adrenaline route tackles three of Austria's most iconic mountain passes, famed for their dramatic switchbacks and dizzying ascents, along with a year-round hit of spectacular high-altitude scenery and activity, from skiing to white-water rafting. It's a track best suited to confident drivers; those who'll find this roading rollercoaster challenging can opt for the gentler route: Mountain Valleys of Tyrol & Vorarlberg.

### Link Your Trip

**25 Mountain Valleys of Tyrol & Vorarlberg**

To make a mega-circuit of the Austrian Alps, pick up the Tyrol & Vorarlberg route in Bregenz.

**28 Carinthian Lakes**

Wind around the Carinthian Lakes from lively Lienz.

## 01 SALZBURG

Salzburg's **trophy sights** huddle in the pedestrianised, UNESCO World Heritage–listed Altstadt (old town). The tangled lanes are made for a serendipitous wander, leading to hidden courtyards and medieval squares framed by burgher houses and baroque fountains. You'll also see plenty of iconic spots from the musical *The Sound of Music*.

Beyond city strolling, there are plenty of opportunities to get active, from swimming at **Freibad Leopoldskron**, Salzburg's biggest lido, with diving boards, waterslides and volleyball, to hiking up Salzburg's rival mountains, the 540m **Mönchsberg** and 640m **Kapuzinerberg**. Both mountains are thickly wooded and criss-crossed by walking trails, with photogenic views of the historic centre, spread across the right and left banks of the Salzach river.

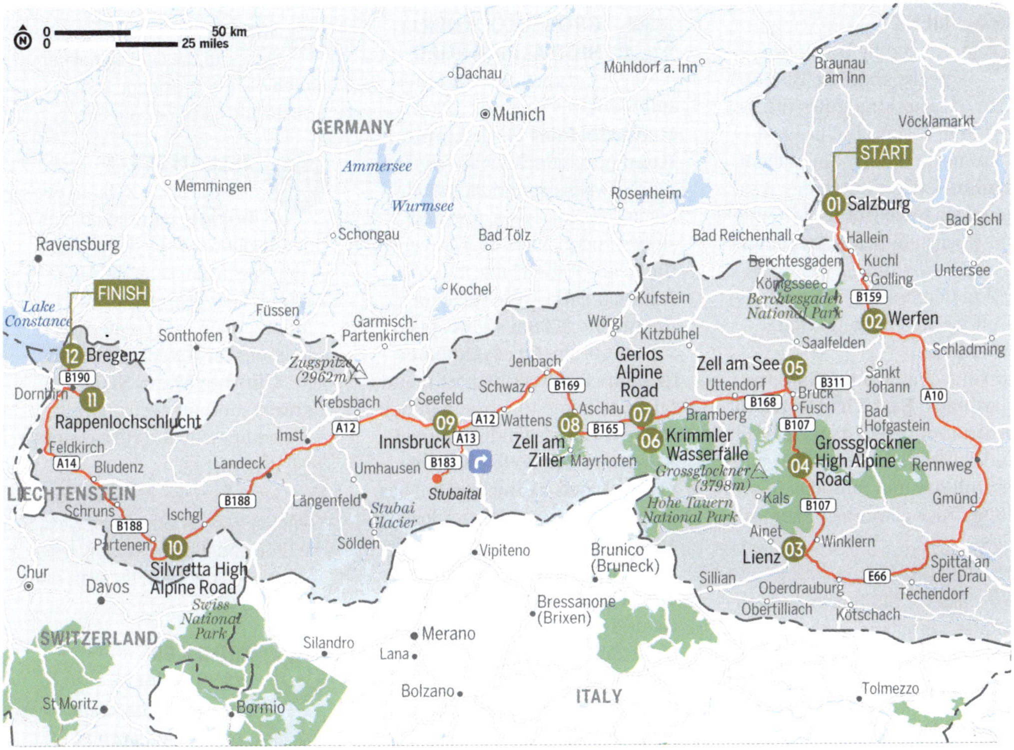

### THE DRIVE
It's 45km south from Salzburg on the B159 to Werfen, mostly along the Salzach River. After passing through a wide valley, you'll enter a tight, steep gorge; follow it until Werfen.

### 02 WERFEN
More than 1000m above Werfen in the Tennengebirge mountains is **Eisriesenwelt** (eisriesenwelt.at). Billed as the world's largest accessible ice caves, this spectacle spans 30,000 sq metres and 42km of narrow passages. A highlight is the cavernous **Eispalast** (ice palace), where the frost crystals twinkle when a magnesium flare is held up to them. Wear sturdy shoes for the 134m climb via steep tracks, and wrap up for subzero temperatures. Photography is not permitted.

On a wooded clifftop beneath the majestic peaks of the Tennengebirge range formidable **Burg Hohenwerfen** (Hohenwerfen Fortress; burg-hohenwerfen.at/en) dates from 1077. Time your visit to be at the castle by 11am or 3pm for the falconry shows.

### THE DRIVE
Take the A10 south to the Millstätter See (which you can visit on Trip 28 through the Carinthian Lakes) and turn west onto the B100/E66 through the Drau Valley to Lienz (166km in total).

---

### TOP TIP:
### Alpine Road Tolls

Be aware that this trip's three top-draw drives – Grossglockner High Alpine Road, Gerlos Alpine Road and Silvretta High Alpine Road – incur hefty tolls. There's also a smaller toll on the detour to the Stubaital. Toll booths accept cash and credit cards; you can also book ahead online.

### 03 LIENZ

Ringed by Dolomite peaks, the East Tyrolean town of Lienz stradddles the Isel and Drau Rivers, and lies just 40km north of Italy. An ancient **Roman settlement**, today it's a famed ski town (for its Zettersfeld and Hochstein peaks, 21 kilometres of slopes and especially its 100km of cross-country trails), but it has an energetic vibe year-round.

If you want to get up into the mountains, **East Tirol tourism** (osttirol.com/en) lists registered guides who can lead you on half-day, full-day and multiday hiking, biking, rock climbing or summit trips.

#### THE DRIVE
Take the B107 north, passing picturesque villages including Winklern (with a wonderful Alpine hotel) and Heiligenblut (look for the needle-thin spire of its pilgrimage church) to the Grossglockner High Alpine Road toll gates (43km in total) on the Carinthia side.

#### WHY I LOVE THIS TRIP
**Marc Di Duca**, writer

Awe-inspiring mountainscapes and adrenaline-pumping activities abound on this Alpine itinerary, but the ultimate draw is the drive itself, peaking with its trio of dizzying high-altitude switchback passes – the Grossglockner High Alpine Road, Gerlos Alpine Road and Silvretta High Alpine Road. This is a route that reminds you that the highlight of road-tripping isn't the destination but the journey.

### 04 GROSSGLOCKNER HIGH ALPINE ROAD

A stupendous feat of 1930s engineering, the 48km **Grossglockner High Alpine Road** (grossglockner.at) spectacularly twists around 36 switchbacks, passing lakes, forested slopes and glaciers as it traverses the heart of the Hohe Tauern National Park, – the stage for the mighty 3798m snowcapped summit of the **Grossglockner** (3798m), Austria's highest mountain and home to more than half of the country's wildlife species.

En route, flag-dotted **Kaiser-Franz-Josefs-Höhe** (2369m) has memorable views of Grossglockner and the 8km-long (though rapidly retreating) Pasterze Glacier (best appreciated on the short and easy Gamsgrubenweg and Gletscherweg trails). Allow time to see the glacier-themed exhibition at the visitor centre and the Wilhelm-Swarovski observatory.

Get your camera handy for **Fuscher Törl** (2428m), with super views on both sides of the ridge, and Fuscher Lacke (2262m), a gemstone of a lake nearby. A exhibition in the original roadmaker's house documents the construction of the road, built by 3000 men over five years during the Great Depression.

A 2km side road corkscrews up to **Edelweiss Spitze** (2571m), the road's highest viewpoint. Climb the tower for 360-degree views of more than 30 peaks topping 3000m.

Between toll gates, all attractions are free. Check the forecast before you hit the road, as the drive is not much fun in heavy fog, snow or a storm. It's often bumper-to-bumper by noon, especially in July and August; beat the crowds by setting out early.

#### THE DRIVE
Descend the Grossglockner on the B107 to Bruck and take the B311 northeast to Zell am See.

### 05 ZELL AM SEE

Resort town Zell am See's brightly painted chalets line the shore of the deep-blue Zeller See, framed by the Hohe Tauern's snow-capped peaks.

Mountain breezes create ideal conditions for watersports on the lake; **Günther Maier SUP-Center** (supcenter-zellamsee.at) rents equipment and runs courses.

#### THE DRIVE
From the lake, it's 54km to the Krimmler Wasserfälle. Head west on the B168 and B165 to Krimml; when you arrive in the town the waterfalls come into view.

### 06 KRIMMLER WASSERFÄLLE

Europe's highest falls, at 380m, are the thunderous, three-tier **Krimmler Wasserfälle** (Krimml Falls; wasserfaelle-krimml.at). The **Wasserfallweg** (Waterfall Trail), which starts at the ticket office and weaves uphill through mixed forest, has up-close viewpoints. It's 4km one way (about a 2½-hour round-trip walk).

#### THE DRIVE
From the falls, it's 7.7km (and eight hairpin bends) to the Gerlos Alpine Road toll gates.

### 07 GERLOS ALPINE ROAD

Open year-round, the **Gerlos Alpine Road** (gerlosstrasse.at) winds 12km through high moor and spruce forest, reaching an elevation of 1630m. The lookout above the turquoise *Stausee* (reservoir) is a great picnic stop, with a tremendous view of the Alps.

**Photo Opportunity**

Europe's highest waterfalls, the three-tiered Krimmler Wasserfälle.

Grossglockner High Alpine Road (p166)

If you have the urge to burst into song as you skip through wildflower-strewn meadows, take the 4.8km-long **Jodel Wanderweg** (Yodel Hiking Trail; jodelweg.at) in Königsleiten. You can go it alone and practise your high notes at eight stops with giant cowbells, Alpine horns and listen-repeat audio clippings. The melodic trail begins at the top station of the village cable car. Alternatively, join a free guided sing 'n' stroll hike with trail founder Christian Eder. The three-hour ambles begin at 11am on selected Wednesdays from July to mid-September at the **Dorfbahn** cable-car station; reserve by 5pm the previous day by phone.

 **THE DRIVE**
Continue west on the B165, passing the reservoir Durlassboden, before descending to Zell am Ziller along six hairpin bends (63km in total).

**08 ZELL AM ZILLER**
At the foot of knife-edge Reichenspitze (3303m), Zell am Ziller is a former gold-mining centre and popular ski base.

Between May and October, you can take a wild toboggan ride on the 1.45km-long **Arena Coaster** (zillertalarena.com), which incorporates both a 360-degree loop and a 540-degree loop. It starts at the valley station of the Rosenalmbahn cable car.

**Aktivzentrum Zillertal** (aktivzentrum-zillertal.at) offers summertime paragliding, white-water rafting on the Ziller, canyoning, *via ferrata* climbing and monster scooter tours.

 **THE DRIVE**
Zell am Ziller sits 60km from Innsbruck. Take the B169 north then the A12 west to the city.

**09 INNSBRUCK**
Walk through Innsbruck's historic centre with its cobblestone streets and baroque facades. Then, head up to the **Bergisel Olympic ski jump** (bergisel.info) for a spectacular city and mountain panorama and to watch high-flyers jump from the glass-and-steel structure designed by Iraqi architect Zaha Hadid. Hadid also designed the space-age funicular **Nordkettenbahnen** (nordkette.com) which whizzes from the old town to the

Alpine Zoo, mountainside viewing areas, the slopes and the top of Innsbruck – the 2,300m-high Hafelekar – every 15 minutes. Walking trails head off in all directions from Hungerburg and Seegrube.

### THE DRIVE
Leave Innsbruck on the westbound A12 and veer southwest on the B188, passing a string of ski towns, to the Silvretta High Alpine Road toll gates in Galtür (118km in total).

### Detour
**Stubaital**
Start: **09 Innsbruck**
In less than an hour, you can find yourself on the year-round ice ridge, Stubai Glacier. The ski season here runs slightly longer than other Alpine resorts, from October to May, with 26 lifts accessing 62km of slopes between 2900m and 3165m and a daredevil 20m-high ice climbing tower. July to mid-September is prime hiking, rock climbing and via ferrata season. The views across the Dolomites from the 'Top of Tyrol' platform at 3210m can be seen during winter and summer.

Lower down in the Stubai Valley, the Wildewasserweg waterfall trail wends for 9.7km (one way) to Sulzenau Glacier. En route, it passes the spectacular Grawa falls, best viewed from the Grawa Observatory platform.

The Stubai Glacier is just 38km south of Innsbruck. Take the A13 south to the toll gates; keep right to take the B183 southwest along the valley.

## 10 SILVRETTA HIGH ALPINE ROAD
Silhouetted by the glaciated Silvretta range and crowned by the 3312m arrow of Piz Buin, the Montafon Valley remains one of the most unspoilt in the Austrian Alps.

The 23km-long **Silvretta High Alpine Road** (silvretta-bielerhoehe.at) twists and turns beneath peaks rising to well over 2500m before climbing over the 2032m Bielerhöhe Pass via 34 knuckle-whiteningly tight switchbacks. At the top of the pass, the **Silvretta Stausee** (2030m), an aquamarine reservoir, mirrors the surrounding peaks on bright mornings.

### THE DRIVE
It's 100km to Rappenlochschlucht. From the official road end at Partenen, continue on the B188 join the A14 at Bludenz (home to the Milka chocolate factory; there's an outlet shop but alas, no tours). Continue northwest to Dornbirn, from where Rappenlochschlucht is 4km southeast on Gütlestrasse.

## 11 RAPPENLOCHSCHLUCHT
The **Rappenlochschlucht** (Rappenloch Gorge; rappenloch.at) was gouged out by the Dornbirner Ache stream. From the car park you can pick up the one hour Circular Trail – a rock-carved track that leads to the turquoise **Staufensee** lake.

### THE DRIVE

Return to Dornbirn and head north on the B190 for 16km to Bregenz.

## 12 BREGENZ
Bregenz sits on the shores of Lake Constance, Europe's third-largest lake. The views here are extraordinary: before you the mirror-like lake; behind you, 1064m-high mountain the Pfänder; to the right, Germany; to the left, Switzerland.

A **cable car** (pfaenderbahn.at) glides up the Pfänder. At the top, a 30-minute circular trail brings you close to the ibex, deer and marmot residents at the year-round **Alpine Wildlife Park** (pfaender.at).

Some 5km south of central Bregenz, where the Rhine flows into Lake Constance, is the nature reserve **Rheindelta** (rheindelta.org). Its mossy marshes, reeds and woodlands attract more than 300 bird species.

BEST ROAD TRIPS: GERMANY, AUSTRIA & SWITZERLAND

# 25
# Mountain Valleys of Tyrol & Vorarlberg

**BEST FOR FOODIES**

The Bregenzerwald Käsestrasse (Bregenz Forest Cheese Road).

| DURATION | DISTANCE | GREAT FOR |
|---|---|---|
| 5–7 days | 383km / 295 miles | History & wine |

| BEST TIME TO GO | Year round is possible; you'll need snow tyres and chains in winter. |
|---|---|

Cable car, Bregenz

The leisurely drive between lake-side Bregenz and storybook Salzburg shows a different side to the Alps from its dizzying high Alpine roads. One filled with cable car-connected valleys, castle-crowned hills and ski-piste towns turned summer hiking pastures. A region shaped as much by its food as by its dramatic mountainscapes, this is also a delicious trail through Alpine dairies, schnapps distilleries and farm-to-fork seasonal fare.

## Link Your Trip

**24 The High Alpine Trio – Grossglockner to Silvretta**
Salzburg is the starting point for an action-packed trip through the Alps.

**27 Salzkammergut**
Set off from Salzburg to the Salzkammergut's sparkling mountain-ringed lakes.

### 01 BREGENZ

In a postcard-perfect setting on the shores of Lake Constance, framed by towering Alps, Bregenz offers plenty of swimming, boating and walking opportunities.

The white cuboid **Vorarlberg Museum** (vorarberg museum.at) is emblazoned with 16,656 flowers made from the imprints of PET bottles in concrete. Permanent exhibitions home in on Vorarlberg state's history, art and architecture, and archaeological finds from Roman Brigantium, and paintings by Angelika Kauffmann.

Bregenz is most famous for the **Bregenzer Festspiele** (Bregenz Festival; bregenzerfestspiele.com),

when open-air opera and musical productions are performed on a floating stage on the lake.

Palm-shaded **Beach Bar Bregenz** (wirtshausamsee.at) is perfect for enjoying cool cocktails and chilled DJ beats in a deckchair.

### THE DRIVE
It's a quick 33km zip from Bregenz via the southbound A14 to Feldkirch.

## 02 FELDKIRCH
On the banks of the turquoise Ill River, Feldkirch sits at the foot of wooded mountains, vineyards and a castle-crowned hill. Its cobbled, arcaded lanes and pastel-coloured townhouses wing you back to late-medieval times. Towers surviving from the old fortifications include the 40m-high **Katzen-**

**turm** (Hirschgraben), where a bell weighing 7500kg still tolls.

Red-turreted **Schloss Schattenburg** (schattenburg.at) was once the seat of the counts of Montfort. The castle now houses a small museum displaying religious art, costumes and weaponry.

Distinguished by its slender spire, Feldkirch's cathedral, **Domkirche St Nikolauas**, has a large, forbidding interior complemented by late-Gothic features and dazzling stained glass.

### THE DRIVE
You'll know you're in the Alps on this 50km drive. From Feldkirch, take the B190 southeast, then the precipitous B193 northwest up to Schoppernau. Wind down your car windows to hear the melodic clanging of cowbells.

## 03 SCHOPPERNAU
Discover the Bregenzerwald's mountain cheese-making secrets (including why Emmentaler is holey) at show dairy **Bergkäserei Schoppernau** (bergkaeserei.at). It's famed for its award-winning tangy Bergkäse, matured for up to 12 months. For a full palate workout, book wine, beer and cheese tastings, *Käsknöpfle* cooking classes and dairy tours (register by 5pm the day before at the tourist office on Argenau 376).

If the dairy whets your appetite for more melt-in-your-mouth cheese produced from the pristine Alpine pastures, set off from Schoppernau on a detour of the Bregenzerwald Käsestrasse (Bregenz Forest Cheese Road).

### THE DRIVE

From Schoppernau, it's an ultra-scenic 47km through deep valleys, steep ascents and switchback descents along the B200 and B198 to St Anton am Arlberg. Stop in Lech Zürs am Alberg along the way to see Vorarlberg's majestic ski slopes glimmer emerald green with the changing of the seasons.

### Detour
### Bregenzerwald Käsestrasse
**Start: 03 Schoppernau**

Explore the Bregenzerwald's rolling dairy country and local *Sennereien* (dairy farms) on the **Bregenzerwald Käsestrasse** (Bregenz Forest Cheese Road; kaesestrasse.at), which refers to the cheese-producing region rather than a specific route.

From Schoppernau, it's a 49km round trip. Country lanes lead to the pretty village of Egg en route to Lingenau. Peek inside the huge cellars of the ultramodern **Käsekeller Lingenau** (kaesekeller-bregenzer wald.at) to see robots brushing wagon-wheel-sized cheeses with salt water, watch a free 12-minute film (in English) and savour a tasting with local wine.

Book ahead to take a factory tour of **Käse-Molke Metzler** (molke produkte.com). Tours include a lavish buffet of cheeses like creamy *Wälderkäsle*, made from cow's and goat's milk. Or you can try your hand at the Alpine craft in a cheese-making workshop at the dairy school.

Old farmhouses tiled with wood shingles and studded with scarlet geraniums crowd the narrow streets of Schwarzenberg. Contemplate neoclassical art in the **Angelika Kauffmann Museum** (angelika-kauff mann.com). Admission covers entry to the neighbouring **Heimat Museum** (Heritage Museum), a pristine Alpine chalet. Displays focus on rural 19th-century life with traditional painted furniture, extraordinary headwear, hunting paraphernalia and filigree iron crosses. Dine on cheesy *Kässpätzle* (hand-rolled noodles with cheese, topped with crispy fried onion) in the wood-panelled parlour or garden at **Gasthof Hirschen** (hotel-hirschen-bregenzerwald.at).

From Schwarzenberg, head southeast via peaceful Au back to Schoppernau.

**Käsekeller Lingenau**

## 04 ST ANTON AM ARLBERG

In 1901 St Anton am Arlberg founded the first ski club in the Alps and downhill skiing was born. Strung out along the northern bank of the Rosanna River at the foot of 2811m-high Valluga, in winter St Anton is a cross between a ski bum's utopia and Ibiza in fast-forward mode – the terrain fierce, the nightlife hedonistic.

Walking in the mountains through meadows full of wildflowers and grazing cattle is the most popular summertime activity. A handful of cable cars and lifts rise to the major peaks. Pick up the Galzigbahn cable car for the Mutspuren Circular Trail on the Galzig; the Vallugabahn glides up to 2,809m from here for a sweeping serrated panorama. The Rendlbahn is the gateway for the **Alpenrosenweg** (Alpine Rose Path) hike on the opposite side of the valley. Single cable-car tickets can be pricey. Consider a one-day All-in ticket or the hiking Wanderpass, providing unlimited access to all lifts. The St Anton Card also includes access to swimming pools and outdoor activities.

### THE DRIVE
A 25km deep valley drive via the B197 and B316 brings you to Landeck.

## 05 LANDECK

Landeck is an ordinary town with an extraordinary backdrop: framed by an amphitheatre of forested peaks, it's bordered by the fast-flowing Inn and Sanna Rivers, and presided over by a hilltop medieval castle that's visible from afar, 13th-century **Schloss Landeck** (schlosslandeck.at). The castle's museum has exhibitions covering the history of the region, and a contemporary art gallery. Sweeping views over Landeck and the Lechtaler Alps extend from the tower.

In summer, the **Venet** (venet.at) cable car zooms up to Krahberg (2208m), where there's a web of marked walking trails.

A wild run of water thrashes the limestone cliffs at **Zammer Lochputz** (zammer-lochputz.at), a gorge 4km northeast of Landeck, across the Inn River from Zams. Leading up through pine forest, a 2.9km round-trip trail passes viewpoints and interesting rock formations.

### THE DRIVE
Take the B171 40km east to reach Stams. For a detour, travel the B171 for 20km to Imst. Starkenberger Biermythos – a 200-year-old brewery housed in a medieval castle with tours – is 2.3km north of Imst. From here, take the northeast-bound B189 for 22km to the village of Krebsbach, then head south, crossing the Inn River, to reach Stams (29km in total).

## 06 STIFT STAMS

Monumental ochre-and-white abbey **Stift Stams** (stiftstams.at) was founded in 1273 by Elisabeth of Bavaria, the mother of Konradin, the last of the Hohenstaufens. It's set in pristine grounds, with a facade topped by twin silver cupolas, a final flourish added when the abbey was revamped in baroque style in the 17th century. The exuberant church interior is dominated by the high altar: the intertwining branches of this version of the 'tree of life' support 84 saintly figures surrounding an image of the Virgin. Near the entrance is the Rose Grille, an exquisite iron screen made in 1716. Crane your neck to admire the ceiling's elaborate stucco-work, gilding and frescos.

Marmalade, juice, honey, liqueurs and schnapps made on the premises can be bought from the **Kloster shop**, plus bread that's freshly baked here on Wednesday and Friday.

### THE DRIVE
Travel along the eastbound B171 for 37km to Innsbruck. Approaching the city you'll pass its airport – the views of planes descending into the valley are amazing.

### Tiroler Schnapsroute

For another flavour-packed detour, set out on the Tiroler Schnapsroute (schnapsroute.at). Like the Bregenzerwald Käsestrasse, this isn't a single road but instead refers to a region.

On a sunny plateau dotted with apple and plum orchards, the village of Stanz has just 204 residents but over 50 schnapps distilleries where you can taste and buy the local firewater.

From Landeck, it's a 2.5km drive northwest to Stanz. If you're still thirsty, other Schnapsroute villages include Grins, Elbigenalp, Prutz, Pfunds, Imsterberg and Arzl.

**Photo Opportunity**
Innsbruck's Gothic Hofkirche.

**Hofkirche, Innsbruck**

### 07 INNSBRUCK

The mountains surrounding Innsbruck beg to be explored but the city itself is also filled with treasures.

Innsbruck's pride and joy is the Gothic **Hofkirche** (tiroler-landesmuseen.at/haeuser/hofkirche), one of Europe's finest royal court churches. It was commissioned in 1553 by Ferdinand I, who enlisted top artists of the age such as Albrecht Dürer, Alexander Colin and Peter Vischer the Elder. Top billing goes to the empty black-marble sarcophagus of Emperor Maximilian I (1459–1519), a masterpiece of German Renaissance sculpture.

Built for Emperor Maximilian I, **Goldenes Dachl & Museum** (Golden Roof) glitters with 2657 fire-gilt copper tiles. Inside, look for the grotesque tournament helmets designed to resemble the Turks of the rival Ottoman Empire.

The cupola-crowned **Hofburg** (Imperial Palace; hofburg-innsbruck.at) was built as a castle for Archduke Sigmund the Rich in the 15th century, expanded by Emperor Maximilian I in the 16th century and given a baroque makeover by Empress Maria Theresa in the 18th century.

Amid beautiful gardens, Renaissance **Schloss Ambras** (schlossambras-innsbruck.at) was acquired in 1564 by Archduke Ferdinand II, then ruler of Tyrol, who transformed it from a fortress into a palace. Don't miss the Spanische Saal (Spanish Hall), the dazzling armour collection and the gallery's Velázquez and van Dyck originals.

### THE DRIVE

**08**

From Innsbruck it's just a 10km trip east to Hall in Tirol along the B171 on the Inn River's northern bank.

### HALL IN TIROL

Tucked beneath the Alps, medieval Hall prospered from salt in the 13th century. You can visit a reconstructed salt mine, complete with galleries, tools and shafts, on a 45-minute guided tour at the **Bergbaumuseum** (hall-wattens.at).

Hall's winding lanes, lined with pastel-coloured townhouses, are made for ambling. Bordering the main square is Hall's 15th-century **Rathaus** (Town Hall). Its distinctive courtyard is complete with crenellated edges and mosaic crests.

At **Burg Hasegg** (muenze-hall.at), a staircase spirals up 186 steps to the 5th floor for panoramic views. The castle had a 300-year career as a mint for silver *Thalers* (coins; the root of the modern word 'dollar'). Its history is unravelled in the Münze Hall, displaying water-driven and hammer-striking techniques; kids can mint their own coins here.

### THE DRIVE

It's a 92km drive from Hall in Tirol to Kitzbühel. East along the B171 along the widening valley, you'll pass Wattens, home to Austria's Swarovski crystal and the dazzling Swarovski Crystal Worlds attraction (kristallwelten.swarovski.com/en) with bejewelled art installations. From the village of Wörgl the incline ramps up. Turn east on the B178, passing beneath the awe-inspiring Kaisergebirge mountains, before heading south at St Johann on the B161 to Kitzbühel.

### KITZBÜHEL

**09**

Kitzbühel began life in the 16th century as a silver and copper mining town, and preserves a charming medieval centre despite its winter aspect. Ever since Franz Reisch slipped on skis and whizzed down the slopes of Kitzbüheler Horn in 1893, so christening Austria's first Alpine ski run, Kitzbühel has carved out its reputation as one of Europe's foremost ski resorts.

In summer, it's a four-hour (14km) hike one way, or a speedy cable-car ride to the **Alpine Flower Garden**. Arnica, edelweiss and purple bellflowers are among the 400 Alpine blooms flourishing here atop Kitzbüheler Horn. A road also twists up to the mountain.

The **Museum Kitzbühel** (museum-kitzbuehel.at) traces Kitzbühel's heritage from its Bronze Age mining beginnings onwards. The big emphasis is on winter sports, and pays tribute to homegrown legends like ski racing champ Toni Sailer and winter landscape painter Alfons Walde.

### THE DRIVE

Kitzbühel sits 85 fabulously scenic kilometres from Salzburg. Head northeast on the B161 then B178, passing the white-water rafting village of Lofer, and cross the German border (the road becomes the B21). On your left you'll see an opaque turquoise lake, the Saalachsee, before reaching Bad Reichenhall. The road crosses back into Austria and brings you into Salzburg.

### SALZBURG

**10**

Salzburg is storybook Austria, and easily explored on foot. Beside the fast-flowing Salzach River are the Altstadt's mosaic of domes and spires, and the formidable 900-year-old clifftop fortress, the **Festung Hohensalzburg** (festung-hohensalzburg.at/en), reached by the glass **Festungsbahn funicular**, with the mountains beyond. This dazzling backdrop inspired the lordly prince-archbishops and home-grown genius Mozart.

You can visit the great composer's 1756 birthplace, the **Mozarts Geburtshaus** (Mozart's Birthplace; mozarteum.at/mozart-museen/mozarts-geburtshaus#info), as well as his one-time residence, the **Mozart-Wohnhaus** (Mozart's Residence; mozarteum.at/en/mozart-museums/mozarts-residence); both house museums.

Other unmissable stops include Salzburg's baroque cathedral, the **Dom** (salzburger-dom.at), and the **Salzburg Museum** (salzburgmuseum.at), inside the baroque Neue Residenz palace, along with sights from *The Sound of Music*. Visit film-set locations on the sing-along bus tour (panoramatours.com/en/salzburg).

AUSTRIA 25 MOUNTAIN VALLEYS OF TYROL & VORARLBERG

BEST ROAD TRIPS: GERMANY, AUSTRIA & SWITZERLAND

# 26

# Castles of Burgenland & Styria

| DURATION | DISTANCE | GREAT FOR |
|---|---|---|
| 2–4 days | 228km / 141 miles | History & wine |

| BEST TIME TO GO | May to September offers the most idyllic weather. |
|---|---|

Austria's showpiece capital, Vienna, sets the stage for a dramatic voyage through this region's history of conquest, moving from the political centre of the Roman Empire's northeastern territory to a string of hilltop-studded castle strongholds that held against marauding invaders and finishing in the country's second-largest (and spirited) city, Graz. A trail also threaded by the vineyards producing some of Austria's finest wines.

### Link Your Trip

**23 Along the Danube**
From Vienna, you can follow the Danube to Passau, just over the German border, to do this route in reverse.

**28 Carinthian Lakes**
Graz is the starting point for a drive around the crystal-clear Carinthian Lakes.

### 01 VIENNA

The majestic sights of the capital's historic centre are easily explored on foot. The peak of Vienna's splendour, however, is at the Habsburgs' opulent summer palace, UNESCO World Heritage–listed **Schloss Schönbrunn** (schoenbrunn.at). Of its 1441 rooms, 40 are open to the public. The fountain-filled, French-style formal gardens shelter the world's oldest zoo, the 1752-founded **Tiergarten**; a 2700sq m hedge maze with interactive stations; and the Gloriette, whose roof offers panoramas over the palace grounds and beyond.

Grand *Kaffeehäuser* (coffee houses) aside, the

**Naschmarkt, Vienna**

**BEST FOR FOODIES**
Vienna's Naschmarkt.

best place to *nasch* (snack) is the historic **Naschmarkt**, with food-laden stalls, delis, sit-down cafes and takeaway stands.

### THE DRIVE
The 37km drive from Vienna is unavoidably industrial until you clear the city's outskirts. Take the A4 southeast for 19km. After passing the airport, take the exit to the B9 and follow it eastwards for a further 18km.

### 02 PETRONELL-CARNUNTUM

The Roman town of Carnuntum was the most important political and military centre in the empire's northeast; with a population of 50,000 people at its peak, it made Vienna look like a village in comparison. The town developed from the 1st century CE and was abandoned some 400 years later.

The three main Roman attractions are covered by one ticket. Modern-day Petronell-Carnuntum is home to the fascinating open-air museum **Freilichtmuseum Petronell** (carnuntum.at), with buildings painstakingly reconstructed using ancient techniques, including an oil merchant's house, an upper-class city mansion and Roman public baths. Situated 2.7km east, the grass-covered **Amphitheater Militärstadt** (carnuntum.at) seated 8000. The spa town of Bad Deutsch-Altenburg, a further 1km northeast, harbours archaeological finds at the **Museum Carnuntinum** (carnuntum.at). The gladitorial **Amphitheater Zivilstadt**, southwest of the town, hosted 13,000 spectators.

### THE DRIVE
The 49km drive southwest to Rust becomes increasingly picturesque. Travel through farmland via the B211 and B50 to the vast lake Neusiedler See region. Here, you enter wine country, with vineyards covering the hillsides. Wine villages along this stretch of the B50 that offer tastings and cellar-door sales include Purbach am See, Donnerskirchen and Oggau am Neusiedler See.

**Photo Opportunity**
Buttercup-yellow Schloss Esterházy.

**Schloss Esterházy**

### 03 RUST

The picturesque wine hamlet of Rust sits on the western shores of Europe's largest steppe lake, Neusiedl, where you can ferry over to the windy surf shores of Podersdorf. Rust is famed for its white stork residents who find sanctuary in the village, nesting in the chimneys in spring and summer to rear their young.

The tower of the central **Katholische Kirche** is a good vantage point for observing storks. For a close-up view, check out the **stork nest cam** at the Tourism Information Office on Conradplatz, which tracks stork numbers each season.

In 1524 the emperor granted local vintners the right to display the letter 'R' on their wine barrels and today the corks still bear this distinctive insignia. Wineries where you can sample the local drop are scattered through the village's streets.

#### THE DRIVE
Driving northwest along the B52 for 15km through rolling countryside ribboned with vineyards brings you to Eisenstadt's Schloss Esterházy.

### 04 SCHLOSS ESTERHÁZY

Dating from the 14th century, giant, sunny yellow **Schloss Esterházy** (esterhazy.at/schloss-esterhazy), in Burgenland's small capital, Eisenstadt, received one makeover in baroque and a later one in the neoclassical style. Many of the 256 rooms are occupied by the provincial government, but several can be seen on tours. The highlight is the frescoed **Haydn Hall**, where during Joseph Haydn's employment by the Esterházys from 1761 to 1790 the great composer conducted an orchestra on a near-nightly basis.

Kirchschlag in der Buckligen Welt, then head southeast on the B55 (54km in total).

### 06 BURG LOCKENHAUS

**Burg Lockenhaus** (ritterburg.at) is infamous for its former resident Elizabeth Báthory, aka the 'Blood Countess'. During her reign of terror early in the 17th century, she reputedly tortured and murdered over 600 mainly peasant women for her own sadistic pleasure. The castle has long been cleansed of gruesome horrors but still contains an impressive torture chamber, complete with an iron maiden.

#### THE DRIVE
Head south on the B56 for 66km, skirting the Hungarian border, before following the road west to Güssing.

### 07 BURG GÜSSING

Burgenland's oldest castle, dating to 1157, **Burg Güssing** (burgguessing.info) rises dramatically over the Strembach River and peaceful town, reached by a modern 100m **funicular railway**. A mix of ruins and renovations, the castle contains plenty of weapons from the Turks and Hungarians, striking portraits from the 16th century and a tower with 360-degree views of the surrounding countryside.

#### THE DRIVE
You'll traverse hilly forest and farmland on this scenic stretch. Take the B57 southwest to Heiligenkreuz im Lafnitztal. Continue south on the L116, grazing the Hungarian border (literally across the road), and rejoin the B57. The L207 then L224 travel northwest, passing the delightful swimming and pedal-boating lake Seebad Riegersburg, before heading uphill to Burg

Haydn's music accompanies you as you walk past exhibitions on his life and work. Austria's largest **wine museum** is in the palace basement. Taste test local vintages at the contemporary *Vinothek* opposite (selektion-burgenland.at)

#### THE DRIVE
It's 26km through mostly open countryside to Burg Forchtenstein via the B50.

### 05 BURG FORCHTENSTEIN

Straddling a dolomite spur, **Burg Forchtenstein** (esterhazy.at/burg-forchtenstein) was built in the 14th century and enlarged in 1635 by the Esterházys (who still own it today). Apart from a grand view from its ramparts, the castle's highlights include an impressive collection of armour and weapons, portraits of regal Esterházys in the **Ahnengalerie**, and spoils from the Turkish wars (it was the only castle in the area not to fall to the Turks). Its **Schatzkammer** contains a rich collection of jewellery and porcelain.

#### THE DRIVE
From Burg Forchtenstein, head up into heavily forested hills on the L223. Join the southbound L149 to

## Wines of Burgenland

Burgenland's wine is some of Austria's finest, due to the 300 days of sunshine per year, rich soil and excellent drainage. Although classic white varieties have a higher profile, the pick of the local wines is arguably the red *Blaufränkisch*, whose 18th-century pedigree here predates its arrival in the Danube region and Germany.

*Eiswein* (wine made from grapes picked late and shrivelled by frost) and selected late-picking sweet or dessert wines are being complemented by *Schilfwein*, made by placing the grapes on reed (*Schilf*) matting so they shrivel in the heat.

Southern Burgenland is best known for *Uhudler*, a typically rosé-coloured wine with a distinctly fruity taste.

Riegersburg (50km altogether).

### 08 BURG RIEGERSBURG

Perched on a 482m-high rocky outcrop in Stryia, **Burg Riegersburg** (dieriegersburg.at) is a hugely impressive 13th-century castle built to ward off invading Hungarians and Turks. In 1822 it came into the possession of the Liechtenstein family (who still own it today). It houses a Hexenmuseum on witchcraft, a Burgmuseum featuring the history of the Liechtenstein family, who acquired it in 1822, and an impressive collection of weapons. A war memorial is a reminder of fierce fighting in 1945, when Germans occupying the castle were attacked by Russian troops.

A cable car on the north side whisks you up in 90 seconds or you can take the 20-minute walk up the rocky footpath.

 **THE DRIVE**
From Riegersburg, it's just 57km north via the B66 and west via the B65 to the lively city of Graz.

### 09 GRAZ

Austria's second-largest city, spliced by the rushing river Mur, is infused with creativity and the energy of its spirited student population. A protected historic centre of red rooftops and green parkland, Renaissance courtyards and baroque facades is complemented by modern art and architecture, uber-cool neighbourhoods like Lend and a hunger-stirring list of restaurants that cements this southern city's status as Austria's culinary capital.

Rising 473m, **Schlossberg** is the site of the original fortress where Graz was founded. It's topped by the city's most visible icon – the **Uhrturm** (clock tower). Its wooded slopes can be reached by bucolic (and slightly strenuous) paths, by lift or the scenic Schlossbergbahn funicular.

Graz' elegant palace, **Schloss Eggenberg** (museum-joanneum.at), was created for the Eggenberg dynasty in 1625. Admission is via a highly worthwhile guided tour during which you'll learn about each room's idiosyncrasies, the stories portrayed by the frescos and the Eggenberg family itself.

**Schlossberg, Graz**

### Detour
### South Styrian Wine Road
**Start:** 09 **Graz**

Following a loop from Graz, explore a part of the state's largest-growing wine region with a sip-worthy journey along the **South Styrian Wine Road** (Südsteirische Weinstrasse). Undulating roads connect a ribbon of villages between Ehrenhausen (from Graz follow the B67a and B73 south for 50km) and Leutschach to an emerald green swatch of sloping vineyards and terraced meadows. Along the way, stop at local vintners, whose showrooms beckon from the vine rows, or at *Buschenschänken*, the local wine taverns serving cold snacks and regional pumpkin seed oil. The regional specialities to try are Sauvignon Blanc and Morillon whites and Schilcher and Blauer Zweigelt reds.

# 27

# Salz-
# kammergut

**BEST FOR HISTORY**

Salt mine Salzwelten, detailing the area's 'white gold'.

| DURATION | DISTANCE | GREAT FOR |
|---|---|---|
| 5-7 days | 282km / 175 miles | History & nature |

**BEST TIME TO GO** | The lakes are at their sparkling best from June to September.

Wolfgangsee, St Gilgen

On this spectacular loop drive from Salzburg, tour the Salzkammergut's gemstone-coloured lakes that glitter beside enchanting villages and beneath soaring, snow-capped Alps. The landscapes may be the showstopper sights of this trip, but you can also explore beneath the surface in iridescent ice caves and labyrinth salt mines, or take a ramble through movie locations from *The Sound of Music*.

### Link Your Trip

**24 The High Alpine Trio – Grossglockner to Silvretta**
This adventure-filled trip also starts in Salzburg.

**25 Mountain Valleys of Tyrol & Vorarlberg**
Salzburg is the end point for this bucolic Alpine drive.

### 01 SALZBURG

Salzburg is blessed with architectural standouts and outdoor activities, and you might know some of its most magnificent buildings from *The Sound of Music*. These can be visited on a DIY tour and include the stately baroque square, the **Residenzplatz**, with its horse-drawn carriages and palatial **Residenz** (domquartier.at). Another splendid palace, the **Schloss Mirabell**, was built by Prince-Archbishop Wolf Dietrich for his mistress Salome Alt in 1606 and given an early 18th-century baroque makeover that included its lavish, stucco Marmorsaal (Marble Hall). The 1300-year-old **Stift Nonnberg** (Nonnberg Convent), has beautiful Romanesque frescos.

A highlight is Hellbrunn Park at early 17th-century Italianate villa **Schloss Hellbrunn** (hell brunn.at). The summer palace, built by Prince-Archbishop, Markus Sittikus as an escape from his Residenz duties, features whimsical interiors.

### THE DRIVE
It's 28km from Salzburg along the eastbound B158, past the resort lake, Fuschlsee, to St Gilgen.

### ST GILGEN
St Gilgen's historic centre, 400m west of the Wolfgangsee's shore, huddles around Mozartplatz and the photogenic Rathaus (old town).

Mozart's mother was born in St Gilgen and the family is the focus at St Gilgen's **Mozarthaus** (mozarthaus.info;), especially Mozart's sister 'Nannerl', also an accomplished composer and musician.

Cosy little museum **Muzikinstumente-Museum der Völker** (Folk Music Instrument Museum; hoerart.at) is home to 1500 musical instruments from all over the world, collected by a family of music teachers; there are opportunities to hear and play the instruments.

The village **cable car** (zwoelferhorn.at) drifts to the 1522m heights of the Zwölferhorn mountain for a ringside seat of the lake's mighty long stretch. It's also a prime spot for tandem paragliding.

### THE DRIVE
Leaving St Gilgen, take the B154 northeast past the small Krottensee. At its northern end, you'll enter a tight, forested mountain pass, then descend to the Mondsee. Continue northwest along the lakeshore to the town of Mondsee at the lake's northwestern end (14km in total).

### MONDSEE
The lively – if touristy – town of Mondsee extends along the northern tip of the crescent-shaped, warm-water lake of the same name.

A must-see for *The Sound of Music* lovers is the 15th-century Gothic former monastery **Basilica Minor St Michael** (pfarre-mondsee.com). Its lemon-yellow baroque facade (added in 1740) and interior, centred on a soaring high altar, featured in the Captain and Maria's wedding scene in the film. Pope John Paul II upgraded it from a parish church to a *basilica minor* in 2005.

Next door to the basilica, the **Museum Mondseeland und Pfahlbaumuseum** (museum-mondsee.at) has displays on Stone Age finds and the monastic culture of the region.

**Segelschule Mondsee** (segelschule-mondsee.at) offers windsurfing, SUP board and sailing-boat rental as well as courses.

### THE DRIVE
From Mondsee it's a 13km drive, taking the B151 along the Mondsee's northern shoreline, flanked by farmland with picturesque swimming spots en route, to Unterach am Attersee.

### 04 UNTERACH AM ATTERSEE

The Attersee is the largest of the Salzkammergut's lakes. The village of Unterach am Attersee has little in the way of sights but is a relaxing spot to swim or rent a SUP (stand-up paddleboard) from **SUP Attersee** (sup-attersee.at).

From Unterach am Attersee, you can cruise on the lake with **Attersee-Schifffahrt** (atterseeschifffahrt.at) which runs a four-stop northern lake tour, a nine-stop southern lake tour, and an 11-stop full lake tour.

### THE DRIVE
Take the B152 along the Attersee's southern then eastern shores for 24km to Kammer (signposted Kammer-Schörfling am Attersee, with its neighbouring town of Schörfling).

### 05 KAMMER

A treat for art lovers, Kammer, on the shores of the Attersee, is home to the **Gustav Klimt-Themenweg**, a 2km-long (roundtrip) lakeside trail including information boards with prints of works by symbolist painter Gustav Klimt (1862–1918), a seminal Vienna Secession movement member. Klimt spent regular spells on the Attersee, painting many of his renowned landscapes here; the trail passes his summer residences. There are also some boards in other lake settlements.

The **Gustav Klimt Zentrum** (klimt-zentrum.at) is a showcase of Klimt's life and works on the Attersee; temporary exhibitions highlight the works of his contemporaries. There's often an original on-loan work displayed here.

The centre neighbours privately owned **Schloss Kammer**, dating from the mid-13th century.

---

## DIY Salzburg *The Sound of Music* Tour

Did you know that there were 10, not seven, Trapp children, the eldest of whom was Rupert (so long Liesl)? Or that in 1938 the Trapp family left quietly for the United States instead of climbing every mountain to Switzerland?

No matter. Sing as you stroll on a self-guided tour of *The Sound of Music* filming locations. Let's start at the very beginning:

**The Hills Are Alive** The opening scenes were actually filmed around the Salzkammergut lakes. Maria makes her twirling entrance on Alpine pastures of the Untersberg, which also appears briefly at the end of the movie when the family flees the country.

**A Problem Like Maria** Nuns waltzing on their way to mass at Benedictine Stift Nonnberg is fiction, but it's a fact that the real Maria von Trapp intended to become a nun here.

**Have Confidence** Residenzplatz is where Maria playfully splashes the spouting horses of the Residenzbrunnen fountain.

**So Long, Farewell** The grand rococo palace Schloss Leopoldskron, a 15-minute walk from Festung Hohensalzburg, is where the lake scene was filmed. Its Venetian Room was the blueprint for the Trapp's lavish ballroom, where the children bid their farewells.

**Do-Re-Mi** The Pegasus fountain, the steps with fortress views, the gnomes...the Mirabellgarten at Schloss Mirabell might inspire a rendition of 'Do-Re-Mi', especially if there's a drop of golden sun.

**Sixteen Going on Seventeen** Liesl and Rolf's glass-paned pavilion hides out in Hellbrunn Park at Schloss Hellbrunn.

**Edelweiss and Adieu** The Felsenreitschule (Summer Riding School) is the backdrop for the Salzburg Festival in the movie, where the Trapp Family Singers win the audience over with 'Edelweiss' and give the Nazis the slip with 'So Long, Farewell'.

Pavillion, Hellbrunn Park, Schloss Hellbrunn, Salzburg (p182)

From Kammer, you can hop on the Attersee-Schifffahrt northern lake tour.

### THE DRIVE
A 24km drive brings you to Seeschloss Ort. From Kammer, follow the A1 east and exit onto the B145. Just south of Gmunden, as the road descends to the Traunsee, you'll spot Seeschloss Ort out in the lake.

### 06 SEESCHLOSS ORT
On the Traunsee's northern peninsula, pretty nature reserve Toscana Park forms a backdrop to **Seeschloss Ort**. Reached by a pedestrian bridge, this lake-set castle on a small island is believed to have been built on the ruins of a Roman fortress. Dating from 909 or earlier, it was rebuilt in the 17th century after a fire. There's a picturesque courtyard, a late-Gothic external staircase and sgraffiti from 1578. You can walk around the outside for free.

### THE DRIVE
Traunkirchen lies 10km south of Seeschloss Ort on the Traunsee just off the B145.

### 07 TRAUNKIRCHEN
Traunkirchen sits on a picturesque spit of land on the western shore of the **Traunsee**, guarded by immense mountain peaks. A beautiful 450m path wends around the headland. The signposted Kleiner Sonnstein trail tracks 1.8km through the mountain paths of the Alpine foothills; its summit cross marks its most spectacular vantage point over Traunkirchen and the gemstone blue Traunsee sweep.

There are plenty of lake cruises; to explore under your own steam you can rent pedal boats and electric boats from **Schifffahrt Loidl** (schifffahrt-traunsee.at).

### THE DRIVE
It's 22km from Traunkirchen southwest on the B145 to Bad Ischl. As you come into Ebensee, you'll cross the Traun River; 3km south of Ebensee, you'll cross the river again and follow its northern bank.

### 08 BAD ISCHL
This spa town's reputation was enhanced after the Habsburg Princess Sophie took an infertility cure here in 1828. Within two years she had given birth to Emperor Franz Josef I, who made Bad Ischl his

**Photo Opportunity**
D-o-w-n through the glass floor of the 5 Fingers viewing platform.

5 Fingers viewing platform, Krippenstein

summer home for the next 60 years. The fateful letter he signed declaring war on Serbia, sparking WWI, bore a Bad Ischl postmark.

The **Stadtmuseum** (stadt museum.at) showcases Bad Ischl's history inside the building where Franz Josef and Princess Elisabeth of Bavaria were engaged (the day after they met at a ball).

Franz Josef's Italianate **Kaiservilla** (kaiservilla.at) was bought by Sophie as an engagement present for her son and Elisabeth. Tours give illuminating insights into the family's life.

If you want to sample the waters of the town, take a dip in the salt and freshwater pools at the historic Eurothermen Resort (eurothermen.at/bad-ischl) against a backdrop of peaks.

**THE DRIVE**
St Wolfgang sits 16km west from Bad Ischl via the B158 and the L116 and L546.

**09 ST WOLFGANG**
Charming St Wolfgang slinks down the steep banks of the Wolfgangsee. Its narrow streets can get clogged with day-trippers but early evenings offer tranquil strolling along the forested lakeshore past creaking wooden boathouses.

St Wolfgang became famous as a place of pilgrimage, and the faithful still come to the **Wallfahrtskirche** (Pilgrimage Church; pfarre-sankt-wolfgang.at), a 14th-century pilgrim church. It's a spectacular gallery of religious art, with glittering altars (from Gothic to baroque), an extravagant pulpit, a fine organ and countless statues and paintings.

The lovable crimson-coloured steam train that appeared with Maria and the children in *The Sound of Music*, the **Schafbergbahn** (5schaetze.at), chugs from St Wolfgang to the summit of the 783m-high Schafberg. During the season there are up to eight departures daily, starting from 9.15am, with services running every 20 minutes to one hour until 3.30pm.

**THE DRIVE**
The prettiest drive from St Wolfgang back to Bad Ischl is along the narrow L546 through undulating open countryside. From Bad Ischl, head south on the B145 to Bad Aussee, and take the L701 west on a tight, heavily forested descent before crossing the Traun River into Obertraun (53.5km in total).

**THE DRIVE**
From Obertraun it's just 4.5km to Hallstatt via the L547 along the southern edge of the beautiful Hallstätter See.

### 11 HALLSTATT

Hallstatt's pastel-coloured houses cast shimmering reflections onto the glassy waters of the Hallstätter See.

The village is strung along a narrow stretch of land between the towering mountains and lakeshore. The **Beinhaus** (Bone House), a small ossuary, contains rows of neatly stacked skulls, painted with decorative designs and the names of their former owners. It stands in St Michael's Chapel in the grounds of the 15th-century Catholic **Pfarrkirche** (Parish Church), which has some attractive Gothic frescos and three winged altars inside.

Salt in the surrounding hills have made it a centre of salt mining. The Hallstatt Period (800 to 400 BCE) refers to the early Iron Age in Europe, named after the village and the Iron Age settlers and Celts who worked the salt mines here.

The fascinating **Salzwelten** (salzwelten.at), situated high above Hallstatt on Salzberg (Salt Mountain), is accessible via the Salzbergbahn cable car. Tours (in English and German) detail how salt is formed and the history of mining, and take visitors into the depths on miners' slides – the longest is 60m. The Hallstätter Hochtal (Hallstatt High Valley) near the mine was also an Iron Age burial ground.

A free downloadable audio guide (salzwelten.at) details the history of the area with text and augmented reality features.

### TOP TIP:
### Salzkammergut Savings

Save money by picking up a Salzkammergut Erlebnis-Card (Salzkammergut Adventure Card), available from tourist offices and hotels. The non-transferable card offers discounts of up to 25% at popular attractions, sights and activities for 21 days. Details of seasonal savings and conditions are available on the comprehensive website salzkammergut.at.

### 10 OBERTRAUN

Obertraun offers easy access via cable car to the extraordinary **Dachstein Eishöhle** (dachstein-salzkammergut.com). Millions of years old, these glittering ice caves extend into the mountain for almost 80km in places. Dress warmly and wear sturdy shoes. Also here is the non-ice **Mammuthöhle** (dachstein-salzkammergut.com), among the deepest and longest caves in the world.

Another cable car runs up to the 2109m-high **Krippenstein** (dachstein-salzkammergut.com) and its vertigo-inducing **5 Fingers viewing platform**, protruding from a sheer cliff face. Each 'finger' has a different form, with one reminiscent of a diving board. A glass floor allows you to peer below your feet into a gaping void.

Allow a whole day to see one or both caves and the viewpoint.

Next to the mine entrance is the Skywalk - an observation deck that narrows, giving the birdseye feeling of floating over the shore of Hallstatt.

At the time of updating, the Hallstatt funicular was in renovation, due for completion in June 2026.

**THE DRIVE**
Take the L547 north along the cliff-framed Hallstätter See until you reach the Gosaubach River. Then head west on the B166 through the Gschütt mountain pass and the hot-air ballooning town of Gosau to Lindenthal. Take the B162 northwest to Golling an der Salzach, then the B159 north to return to Salzburg (77km in total).

# 28

# Carinthian Lakes

**BEST FOR FAMILIES**

'Miniature world' Minimundus.

Weissensee (p191)

| DURATION | DISTANCE | GREAT FOR |
|---|---|---|
| 2–4 days | 381km / 270 miles | History, nature & families |

| BEST TIME TO GO | May to September offers the best weather for boating and swimming. |
|---|---|

Hit the road for a multi-lake spin through the sunny south of Carinthia, known as the 'Austrian Riviera' for its water-bound beauty. Trip through an Alpine stage that pairs crystal-clear waters perfect for bathing, boating, waterskiing, wakeboarding and scuba diving at Austria's highest swimmable glacial lake, with a cultural hit in shoreline towns with Roman foundations, mountain-top bastions and contemporary art galleries.

### Link Your Trip

**24 The High Alpine Trio – Grossglockner to Silvretta**
Pick up this dizzying Alpine drive in Lienz.

**26 Castles of Burgenland & Styria**
This castle- and winery-lined route ends in Graz.

### 01 GRAZ

Austria's second-largest city might be famed for its historic treasures, including palatial **Schloss Eggenberg**, but you'll find edgy new art and architecture here too.

Inside the Joanneumsviertel museum complex, the **Neue Galerie** (museum-joanneum.at/neue-galerie-graz) packs a stunning collection of paintings and photography, sculptures and installations in its fine arts showcase, from Austrian and international artists.

188  BEST ROAD TRIPS: GERMANY, AUSTRIA & SWITZERLAND

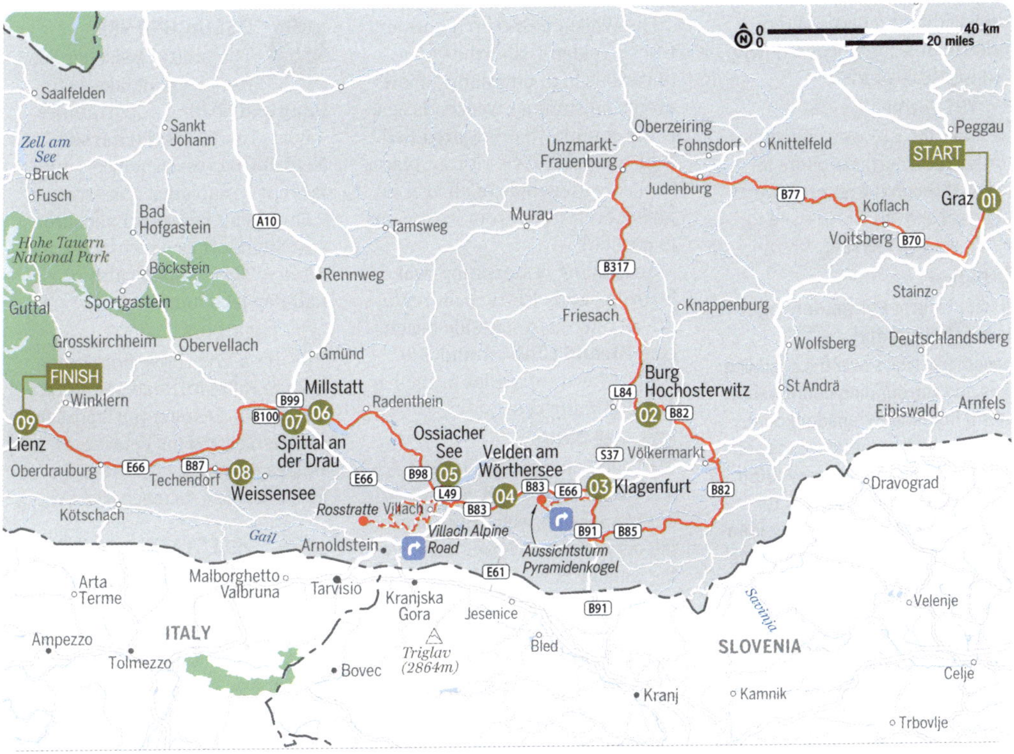

World-class contemporary-art space **Kunsthaus Graz** (museum-joanneum.at/kunsthaus-graz) looks something like a space-age sea slug. Exhibitions here change every three to four months.

In the middle of the Mur River, floating landmark **Murinsel** (murinselgraz.at) is a curvilinear metal and plexiglass island/bridge containing a cafe, outdoor lounge area and a cultural events space.

### THE DRIVE
Avoid the faster but tunnel-dominated highways and drive the scenic 170km to Burg Hochosterwitz through farmland and mountains. Take the B70 then B77 northwest to Judenburg and join the B317. Take the L84 past the Längsee and head east on the B82; the castle's car park is a 3km drive uphill.

### 02 BURG HOCHOSTERWITZ
Storybook fortress **Burg Hochosterwitz** (burg-hochosterwitz.com) rises from the slopes of a Dolomite mountain, with 14 gate towers on the path up to the final bastion. The towers were built between 1570 and 1586 by its former owner, Georg Khevenhüller, to ward off invading Turks. Each gate presented different challenges to attackers – some have embedded spikes, which could be dropped straight through unwary invaders passing underneath.

From the car park a 14-person lift ascends to the castle; otherwise it's a steep but smooth-going 620m walk.

### THE DRIVE
From the base of the hill, head east to Brückl then southeast on the B82, past the Völkermarkter Stausee, to join the westbound B85 to the Ferlacher Stausee. The B91 leads north to Klagenfurt (84km in total).

### 03 KLAGENFURT
Art museum- and gallery-packed Klagenfurt isn't comparable with Graz or Vienna but it's still an enjoyable, sunny city that offers easy access to the beautiful Wörthersee, which, due to its thermal springs, is one of the region's warmer lakes, averaging 21°C in summer.

At the town's western limit is the wide green space of **Europapark**. Its family-friendly *Strandbad* (beach) on the shores of the Wörthersee offers splashy fun. The park's biggest draw is **Minimundus** (minimundus.at), a 'miniature world' with 140 replicas of the world's architectural icons, downsized to a scale of 1:25.

#### 🚗 THE DRIVE
Take the B83 west along the Wörthersee's northern shore for 16.5km, through the resort town of Pörtschach am Wörthersee to Velden am Wörthersee.

#### 📍 Detour
**Aussichtsturm Pyramidenkogel**
**Start:** 03 **Klagenfurt**
Phenomenal views over the sparkling lakes and surrounding countryside extend from the Pyramidenkogel. The 851m-high mountain is topped by a stunning contemporary 100m tower (the world's highest of its kind), the **Aussichtsturm Pyramidenkogel** (pyramidenkogel.info), made of steel with wooden beams spiralling up its exterior. Two of its three viewing platforms are open; one, the lower-level Sky Box, is encased in glass. Its highest is close to 71m; its largest at 64m.

After climbing 441 steps or riding the glass lift and taking in the panoramas, you can return to ground level on Europe's highest covered **slide**, down 120 tube-enclosed metres (on a mat), dropping 52m in about 20 seconds at speeds of up to 25km/h. Recover with a drink in the cafe at the tower's base. In summer, you can fly down via the 100m-long zipline.

From Klagenfurt, it's an 18km side trip: head west to the Wörthersee's southern shore and follow the L96 along the lakefront to Reifnitz. Turn left on the L97B and follow it to the lake, Keutschach See. Take the L97C northwest until you reach the tower.

### 04 VELDEN AM WÖRTHERSEE
The Wörthersee stretches from east to west between Klagenfurt and Velden.

The Wörthersee's top nightlife resort, Velden is also the venue of various high-adrenaline sports events on summer weekends (this is the country that invented Red Bull, after all). It's a vibrant place packed with people of all ages enjoying everything from ice creams to cocktails.

Paragliding, waterskiing, wakeboarding and electric boat rental are all offered by lakeside beach club **Strand Club** (strandclub.com). Afterwards, relax at the bar and adjoining cafe.

#### 🚗 THE DRIVE
Continue west on the B83 and take the L49 north, passing Burg Landskron, which has summer falconry shows, to Annenheim, on the western shores of the Ossiacher See (18km in total).

#### 📍 Detour
**Villach Alpine Road**
**Start:** 04 **Velden am Wörthersee**
While this trip may be firmly grounded on a trail around glittering lakes, this detour through the Roman-rooted, church-dotted Villach ramps up the altitude. From Velden, pick up the B83 west, which heads south into Villach after passing Landskron, turning right onto the B86 to Villach-Möltschach, the start of the Villach Alpine Road (villacher-alpenstrasse.at). It's a curling drive on 11 tight mountain bends on the (high) way to Rosstratte point at 1732m, with viewpoint stations overlooking the historic city and the spiking Slovenia-Italy cradling Julian Alps. On the way down, turn left and follow the Villacher Alpenstrasse, which turns into the Almweg before Heiligengeist. Pick up the L35 east, the B86 north (direction Spittal/Drau) and the B100 (roundabout exit, Ossiacher See; road turns into the B94) northeast to Annenheim. (64km in total).

### 05 OSSIACHER SEE
The pretty Ossiacher See has plenty of lake swimming and boating opportunities.

Boats run by **Ossiachersee Schifffahrt** (ossiachersee-schifffahrt.at) complete a criss-cross 2.5hr circuit between Landskron and Steindorf as part of a regular service. The company also runs half-day lake tours.

#### 🚗 THE DRIVE
It's a 39km drive from Annenheim to Millstatt. Head northwest on the B98. En route you'll pass the Afritzer See and the Feldsee, as well as the northern shore of the Millstätter See, to reach Millstatt.

### 06 MILLSTATT
Stretching 12km long but just 1.5km wide, the Millstätter See, Carinthia's second-largest lake, was gouged out during the Ice Age around 30,000 years ago and has temperatures of 22°C to 26°C in summer. Millstatt is the most appealing of its small towns.

Swimming, boating and water sports aside, Millstatt's main attraction is its Romanesque Benedictine abbey, **Stift Millstatt** (stiftsmuseum.at). Founded in 1070, it contains the Stiftsmuseum, an attractive 11th-century abbey church and a graveyard. The abbey grounds and magnificent arcades and cloisters are free to enter.

#### 🚗 THE DRIVE
The 9km drive from Millstatt follows the Millstätter See shore on the B98 before veering south through a steep forested valley on the B99 to Spittal an der Drau.

### 07 SPITTAL AN DER DRAU
Spittal is a key economic and administrative centre in upper Carinthia. Its name comes from a 12th-century

**Aussichtsturm Pyramidenkogel**

> **Photo Opportunity**
> Lake views from the top of the Aussichtsturm Pyramidenkogel.

hospital and refuge that once succoured travellers here.

Adjoining a small but attractive park with splashing fountains and bright flowerbeds is the impressive Italianate palace **Schloss Porcia** and **Museum für Volkskultur** (Local Heritage Museum; museum-spittal.com). Inside, arcades line a central courtyard used for summer theatre performances. The top floors contain the local museum with 3D exhibits and artefacts illustrating Carinthia's heritage from mining to mountaineering.

**THE DRIVE**
Traversing 44km along a farmed valley framed by towering snow-capped Alps via the B100 and B87 brings you to the least developed of Carinthia's lakes, the Weissensee.

**08 WEISSENSEE**
Wedged within a glacial cleft in the Gailtal Alps, the pristine nature reserve Weissensee holds Austria's highest swimmable glacial lake, with an altitude of 930m and summer temperatures of above 20°C. Just 1km or so wide in most parts, it stretches for almost 12km.

Boat services on Weissensee operated by **Weissensee Schifffahrt** (weissensee-schifffahrt.at) are as much an excursion through the picturesque landscape as a way of getting around the lake.

The crystal-clear waters offer incredible visibility for dazzling views of the lake's 22 fish species. **Yachtdiver** (yachtdiver.at) runs scuba-diving trips for experienced divers and courses for beginners, as well as ice-diving expeditions in winter.

**THE DRIVE**
Take the B87 back to the B100 and head west to lively Lienz (a 48km journey).

**09 LIENZ**
Towering **Dolomite peaks** rise like an amphitheatre around Lienz.

The Romans settled here some 2000 years ago. Their legacy is explored at the regional history museum inside the medieval castle **Schloss Bruck** (museum-schloss bruck.at), and at the archaeological site **Aguntum** (aguntum.at), where excavations are unearthing details of this two-millenia-old municipium, which was a centre of trade and commerce under Emperor Claudius. Visit the museum before exploring the ruins; an 18m-high observation tower overlooks it all.

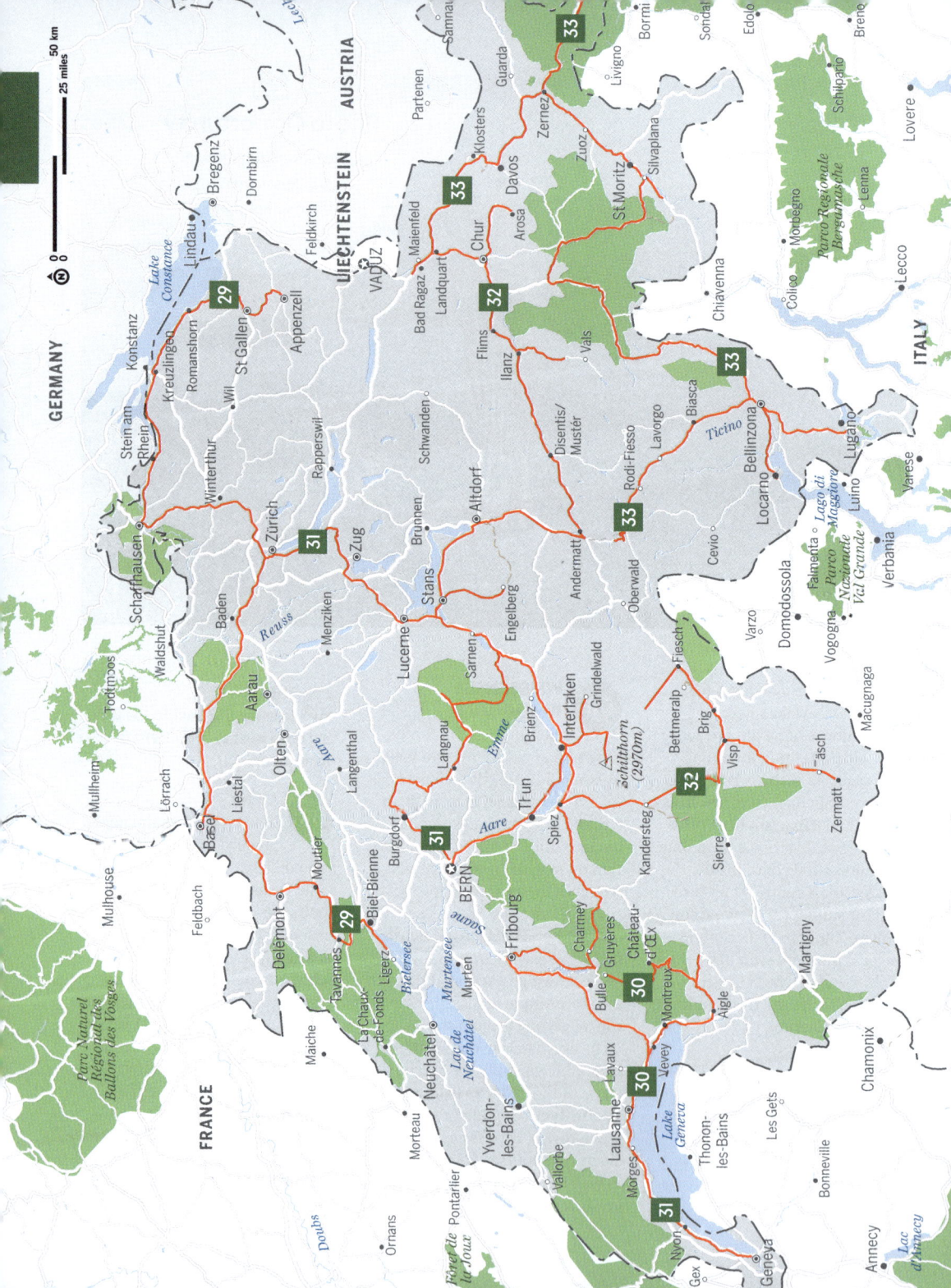

Faulhorn (p214)

# Switzerland

**29** **Northern Switzerland**
Architectural marvels and epic water features are the highlights of this oft-overlooked region. **p196**

**30** **Lake Geneva & Western Switzerland**
A glorious lake, stunning vineyards, enchanting villages and fairy tale castles. **p200**

**31** **Geneva to Zürich**
Mountains, pastures, lakes and small-town charm, bookended by Switzerland's biggest cities. **p204**

**32** **The Swiss Alps**
The greatest of the great outdoors: perfect peaks, gorgeous glaciers, verdant valleys. **p210**

**33** **Graubünden & Ticino**
Big-sky wilderness, off-the-beaten-track beauty, pretty towns and unique local flavours. **p218**

# Explore

# Switzerland

A place of heart-stopping natural beauty and head-spinning efficiency, Switzerland lies in the centre of Europe yet exhibits a unique blend of cultures. Dazzling outdoor scenery – such as the ever-admired Alps, pristine lakes, lush meadows and chocolate-box chalets – combines with local traditions, cosmopolitan cities and smooth infrastructure. In short, Switzerland makes it easy for you to dive deep into its heart: distances are manageable and variety is within easy reach. You can be perusing a farmers market for picnic provisions in the morning, then feasting on them on a mountaintop come lunchtime. At nightfall, try gazing at stars in the night sky from cosy digs or revelling in the cultural offerings of one of Switzerland's sophisticated cities.

## Zürich

Culturally vibrant, efficiently run and attractively set at the meeting of river and lake, Zürich is regularly recognised as one of the world's most liveable cities. Long known as a savvy, hard-working financial centre, Switzerland's largest and wealthiest metropolis has also emerged in the 21st century as one of Central Europe's hippest destinations, with an unexpectedly artsy, postindustrial edge.

Much of the ancient centre, with its winding lanes and tall church steeples, has been kept lovingly intact. Yet Zürich has also embraced contemporary trends, with the conversion of old factories into cultural centres and creative new living spaces. Nowhere is that clearer than in Züri-West, the epicentre of the city's nightlife.

## Geneva

Often mistaken for Switzerland's capital (it isn't), the country's second-largest city is slick and cosmopolitan, its streets awash with chatter in almost every language. Some 200-odd international organisations, including not-for-profits, are headquartered here, along with an overload of luxury hotels, boutiques, jewellers, restaurants and chocolatiers. But beneath this flawless exterior lies a fascinating rough-cut diamond, peopled by artists and activists educated in international schools, drifters and denizens.

## Basel

Basel sits astride the mighty Rhine and at the juncture of the French, German and Swiss borders. A wealthy, global centre for the pharmaceutical industry, this is also a city of art and architecture and a wealth of galleries, museums and iconic buildings. Split in two by the river, the Altstadt in Grossbasel is a warren of cobbled streets while Kleinbasel (Little Basel) has a more 'everyday' vibe and riverside alfresco dining.

### WHEN TO GO

Switzerland is pretty much a year-round destination. June to September is the summer high season, with the most visitors showing up during the European summer holidays. Autumn is a great time to be here as the crowds thin and the forests put on a fiery show. Winter sees another peak with the skiing season lasting from December to April.

## Locarno

With its palm trees and much-hyped 2300 hours of sunshine a year, Locarno's near-Mediterranean setting has been swooned over by visitors since the late 19th century. Switzerland's lowest-altitude town is quite special, for sure, with an air of chic insouciance, a promenade strung along its mountain-facing lakefront and botanical gardens bristling with subtropical flowers and foliage. Beyond Lake Maggiore, there's a pretty Renaissance Old Town which fans out from the Piazza Grande, host of a renowned music and film festival in summer.

## Bern

Wandering through the picture-postcard, UNESCO World Heritage–listed Old Town, with its provincial, laid-back air, it's hard to believe that Bern (Berne in French) is the capital of Switzerland. Its flag-festooned, cobbled centre, rebuilt in distinctive grey-green sandstone after a devastating 1405 fire, is an aesthetic delight, with 6km of covered arcades, cellar shops and bars, and fantastical folk figures frolicking on 16th-century fountains. From the surrounding hills, you're presented with an equally captivating picture of red roofs arrayed on a spit of land within a bend of the Aare River.

### WHERE TO STAY

There is accommodation to suit every taste in Switzerland, though perhaps not every budget. Given the high cost of staying the night, many turn to campsites but are often shocked by the nightly rate for even a small tent. One standout sleeping option is the mountain hut, refuge or chalet, call it what you will. These are usually basic places to stay at altitude in very remote areas are you can choose between a private room or floor space for a sleeping bag. Food is often served and there are cooking facilities. With cash to splash, go for a romantic night in a castle or mansion.

### TRANSPORT

There are major airports in Zürich and Geneva and these are the best gateways when arriving from outside continental Europe. EuroAirport Basel-Mulhouse-Freiburg is also a major airport just outside Basel but actually in France. Switzerland is well linked by rail and by coach with the rest of Europe.

### WHAT'S ON

**Montreux Jazz Festival**

Montreux' best-known festival, established in 1967, takes over the town for two weeks in July. Free concerts take place daily and the music is not just jazz, with many big names from pop and rock having performed here over the decades.

**Art Basel**

One of three international exhibitions (Miami and Hong Kong are the others) showcasing the works of more than 4000 artists from almost 300 galleries, over four days in June.

### Resources

**Switzerland Tourism** (*myswitzerland.com*) High-level overview of what there is to experience across the country.

**SwitzerlandMobility** (*schweizmobil.ch*) Full details of accessible beautiful trails in Switzerland and Liechtenstein.

**Switzerland Travel Centre** (*switzerlandtravelcentre.com*) One-stop shop for hotels, train tickets and packages.

# 29

# Northern Switzerland

**BEST FOR CULTURE**

From St Gallen's rococo ebullience to Basel's myriad museums and architectural gems.

Vitra Design Museum, Basel (p199)

| DURATION | DISTANCE | GREAT FOR |
|---|---|---|
| 3 days | 355km / 220 miles | History |

**BEST TIME TO GO**: Any time of year, although the warmer months are best.

The best of Switzerland is blended to perfection with a little northern exposure. This route allows travellers to tiptoe off the tourist trail and experience lesser-known places such as Appenzell before returning for the heavy-hitting urban pleasures of museum-rich Basel. Impressive natural wonders like the Rheinfall compete with architectural jaw-droppers such as St Gallen's Stiftsbibliothek, while tucked-away vineyards delight the senses.

### Link Your Trip

**30 Lake Geneva & Western Switzerland**
Head south from Ligerz for 77km to Gruyères, the end of Trip 30, which you can easily reverse.

**31 Geneva to Zürich**
Geneva lies 145km southwest of Ligerz, allowing a loop through the country, back to the north.

 **01 ST GALLEN**

St Gallen's riotously beautiful rococo library, **Stiftsbibliothek** (stiftsbezirk.ch), in its Catholic abbey, is a must-see. The 16th-century library (one of the world's oldest), along with the monastery complex, forms a UNESCO World Heritage site. Filled with 170,000 priceless books and manuscripts painstakingly handwritten by monks in the Middle Ages, it's a dimly lit confection of ceiling frescos, stucco, cherubs and parquetry.

 **THE DRIVE**
Driving through the verdant countryside from St Gallen, take gently winding Rte 443 for 19km to Appenzell's centre.

## 02 APPENZELL

Appenzell is a feast for the eyes and the stomach. Behind the gaily decorative pastel-coloured facades of its traditional buildings lie cafes, *confiseries* (sweets and cake shops), cheese shops, delicatessens, butchers and restaurants offering local specialities. It's also perfect for a lazy wander along the **Sitter River** or through the photogenic **Altstadt** (old town) with its **Landsgemeindeplatz** featuring elaborately painted hotels and restaurants. **Brauerei Locher** (appenzellerbier.ch) is great for brew lovers, or come to grips with local history at the **Appenzell Museum** (museum.ai.ch) nearby.

### THE DRIVE
Retrace your drive to St Gallen (Rte 447), then head to Arbon (the A1 and A1.1) on Lake Constance's shore. From Arbon drive to Romanshorn, then take Rte 13 to Schloss Arenenberg, on the Untersee – 70km in all.

## 03 SCHLOSS ARENENBERG

**Lake Constance** (Bodensee) is the German Mediterranean, with a mild climate, gardens and palm trees. Nicknamed the 'Swabian Sea', Central Europe's third-largest lake straddles Switzerland, Germany and Austria. It's a cool place to wind down. The lakeside road (Rte 13) between Kreuzlingen and Stein am Rhein is dotted with quaint half-timbered villages such as **Gottlieben**, **Steckborn** and **Berlingen**. Near the latter is **Schloss Arenenberg** (napoleon museum.tg.ch), a handsome lakefront mansion in beautiful grounds where France's Napoléon III grew up.

### THE DRIVE
Departing the castle, continue on lakeside Rte 13 for 18km to Stein am Rhein.

## 04 STEIN AM RHEIN

Stein am Rhein appears to have leaped from the pages of a fable, with its leafy river promenade and gingerbread houses. The effect is overwhelming in cobblestone **Rathausplatz**, hailed as Switzerland's most

### Photo Opportunity
The half-timbered heart of Stein am Rhein.

Stein am Rhein (p197)

beautiful town square: houses, some half-timbered, others covered in frescos, line up for a permanent photo op with the fresco-festooned **Rathaus** (town hall) soaring above. Situated between the Rathaus and the Rhine is the **Klostermuseum St Georgen** (klostersanktgeorgen.ch), on the site of a Benedictine monastery built in 1007. Today's cloister and magnificent *Festsaal* (grand dining room) are largely a late-Gothic creation.

#### THE DRIVE
It's a straightforward 20km, 20-minute drive along Rte 13 to Schaffhausen, passing small towns and agricultural holdings.

### 05  SCHAFFHAUSEN
Quaint medieval Schaffhausen is known for ornate frescos and oriel bay windows (called *Erker*), which grace its old town houses. The colourful frescos of 17th-century **Zum Goldenen Ochsen** (Vorstadt 17) and 16th-century **Zum Grossen Käfig** (Vorstadt 45) depict the parading of Turkish sultan Bajazet in a cage by the triumphant Mongol conqueror Tamerlane. A block east, eye-catching 1492 **Haus zum Ritter** (Vordergasse 65) boasts a detailed Renaissance-style fresco of a knight. Good city **walking tours** leave the tourist office in summer. The 16th-century circular **Munot** fortress lords it over a vineyard-streaked hill.

Completed in 1103, **Allerheiligen Münster** (All Saints' Cathedral), with its beautifully simple cloister, is a rare Romanesque specimen in Switzerland. The art collection of **Museum zu Allerheiligen** (allerheiligen.ch) has works by Otto Dix and Lucas Cranach the Elder.

#### THE DRIVE
Taking Rte 4, it's a very quick trip (5.5km) to Rheinfall, with parking at Schloss Laufen.

### 06  RHEINFALL
Ensnared in wispy spray, thundering **Rheinfall** (Rhine Falls; rheinfall.ch) might not compete with Niagara in height (23m), width (150m) or

flow (700 cu metres per second in summer), but Europe's largest waterfall is stunning nonetheless. Trails thread up and along its shore, and viewpoints provide photo ops.

The 1000-year-old medieval castle **Schloss Laufen** (schloss laufen.ch) overlooks the falls at closer quarters. Buy a ticket at its souvenir shop to walk or take the lift down to the **Känzeli viewing platform** to fully appreciate the crash-bang spectacle.

During summer, **ferries** (rhyfall-maendli.ch) flit in and out of the water at the falls' bottom. The best is the round trip that stops at the tall rock in the middle of the falls, from where you can climb to the top.

 **THE DRIVE**
Get on the A4, then change to the A1 and eventually the A3 to get to Basel as quickly as possible (128km).

### 07 BASEL

Business-minded Basel's delightful medieval old town is centred on **Marktplatz**, dominated by the astonishingly vivid red facade of the 16th-century **Rathaus** (Town Hall). Blending Gothic exteriors with Romanesque interiors, the 13th-century **Münster** (Cathedral; baslermuenster.ch) was largely rebuilt after a 1356 earthquake. Renaissance humanist Erasmus of Rotterdam (1466–1536) lies buried in the northern aisle. For views, climb the soaring Gothic **towers**, or visit leafy **Münster Pfalz** for sublime Rhine watching.

The astounding private turned public collection, **Fondation Beyeler** (fondationbeyeler.ch), assembled by former art dealers Hildy and Ernst Beyeler, is housed in a light-filled, open-plan building designed by Renzo Piano. It has works by Picasso, Rothko, Miró and Max Ernst.

Built by Ticino architect Mario Botta, **Museum Jean Tinguely** (tinguely.ch) showcases the playful, mischievous and wacky concoctions of sculptor turned mad scientist Tinguely. Pop across the German border to the dazzling **Vitra Design Museum** (design-museum.de). The main building, designed by Frank Gehry, is surrounded by ever-expanding installations by other cutting-edge architects.

 **THE DRIVE**
For this last drive, enjoy the longer and slower (95km, 1¾ hours) route through the lush Jura countryside: Rte 18 to Delémont, Rte 16 to Biel/Bienne and finally scenic Rte 5 along the beautiful vineyard- and village-lined Bielersee to Ligerz.

### 08 LIGERZ

This hidden delight sees lush green vines stagger down the steep hillside towards Lake Biel's northern shore. The quaint lakeside hamlet of Ligerz is, simply put, a heavenly place to savour local wines in relaxed surrounds. There's a small **wine museum** (Rebbaumuseum am Bielersee 'Hof'; rebbaumuseum. ch) and the old-fashioned **Vinifuni funicular** (vinifuni.ch) climbs through the vines to hilltop Prêles. On clear days, views across the vines to the snow-capped Bernese Alps are a revelation. A 30-minute lakeside walk to Twann reaches **Vinothek Viniterra Bielersee** (viniterra-bielersee.ch).

---

## Acid Base

In 1943 a chemist for Sandoz, Albert Hofmann (1906–2008), accidentally absorbed an experimental compound through his fingertips while searching for a migraine cure and took the world's first 'acid trip'. Hofmann's discovery was soon taken up by artists and writers such as Aldous Huxley, and by the 1960s flower-power generation.

Basel remains the epicentre of the Swiss multibillion-franc pharmaceutical industry; industry giants like Roche and Novartis are based here.

# 30

# Lake Geneva & Western Switzerland

**BEST FOR FOODIES**

Lausanne's dining scene has come into its own and fondue is a regional staple.

Fondue

| DURATION | DISTANCE | GREAT FOR |
|---|---|---|
| 4 days | 165km / 108 miles | Wine, nature & families |

**BEST TIME TO GO** — From May to September, when the vineyards put on a show.

Touring Lake Geneva (Western Europe's biggest lake, known as Lac Léman to locals) is a treat; the 570sq-km lake is the region's summer playground, embellished by the Alps, historic vineyards, chic urban centres, *petites plages* (beaches), beautiful villages, classic castles and the constant play of light and wind upon its surface. Plus, this is the perfect spot to enjoy rare wines, fondue and heavenly meringues under double cream.

## Link Your Trip

**31 Geneva to Zürich**
Head north for 32km via the A12 from Gruyères to beautiful bilingual Fribourg, in the same canton.

**32 The Swiss Alps**
The fastest route to Arosa, starting point of the A to Z of Swiss Alps, is 330km, heading west along the A1 then the A3.

### 01 NYON

The wine-producing region between Lausanne and Geneva is known as La Côte (The Coast). From Geneva to Nyon is a 40-minute trip (24km) via Rte 1, which skirts the lake. Of Roman origin, Nyon is a pretty fishing village pierced at its hilltop heart by the white turrets of a textbook castle. **Château de Nyon** (chateaudenyon.ch) was begun in the 12th century, modified 400 years later and now houses the **Le Caveau de Nyon** (caveaudenyon.ch). Don't miss the view of Lake Geneva from the terrace. Nyon's ancient history is on display at the **Musée Romain** (Roman Museum; mrn.ch) in the foundations of a 1st-century basilica.

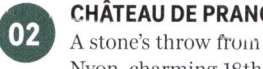

### 🚗 THE DRIVE
From Rte 1 in Nyon, it's a short hop (3km) through the leafy landscape to Château de Prangins. Drive along Rte 1, continuing until the château's car park (make a right turn just after the bus stop named 'Prangins, Les Abériaux'). You'll need to walk from there (signed).

### 02  CHÂTEAU DE PRANGINS
A stone's throw from Nyon, charming 18th-century **Chateâu de Prangins** (chateaudeprangins.ch) houses one of the branches of the **Musée National Suisse**. Swiss history from 1730 to 1920 is covered in satisfying detail, and the lovely *potager* (vegetable garden) and nature trail warrant exploration.

### 🚗 THE DRIVE
Avoid the motorway and stick with Rte 1 for just under an hour (36km). You'll be rewarded with views of the lake, verdant countryside, small towns, orchards and some impressive hedges that stand between you and the discreetly super-rich.

### 03  LAUSANNE
One of Switzerland's lovelier cities, Lausanne has overcome a reputation for culinary stagnation and now has a buzzing food scene, with solid drinking choices. Dominated by the grand Gothic **Cathédrale de Notre Dame** (musees.vd.ch/musees-cantonaux), the city has a full cultural calendar, pretty lakefront, delightful **old town** and fabulous food **market** (Lausanne Market). Must-see sights also include the wonderful **Musée Olympique** (olympics.com/museum) and **Fondation de l'Hermitage** (fondation-hermitage.ch).

### 🚗 THE DRIVE
Take Rte 9 for a few kilometres until just after Lutry. Turn left on Rte Petite Corniche, passing through small medieval towns such as Aran and Epesses. The road becomes Rte de la Corniche, taking you up to Chexbres. From there, drive east back down to the lakeside, then head west along Rte 9 to St Saphorin.

**04 LAVAUX**

East of Lausanne, the 830-hectare serried ranks of 800-plus-year-old **vineyards** stagger up the steep terraced slopes of Lake Geneva to form the Lavaux wine region. They're sufficiently magnificent to be a UNESCO World Heritage site. Walking between vines and tasting wines are key reasons to explore the string of villages beaded along this 40km stretch of fertile and wealthy shore. This drive starts as a loop of sorts once you reach **Lutry**, heading up into the vines and villages, before heading down and back along the shore. The prettiest town here and the focus of untold 'I could live here' fantasies is **St Saphorin**, a little gem with closely packed centuries-old houses, narrow streets, wine cellars, a church dating from 1530 and a great lunch-spot *auberge* (inn).

### Ten O'Clock & All is Well!

From the height of Lausanne's cathedral bell tower, *a guet* (night watchman) still calls out the hours into the night, from 10pm to 2am. Four times after the striking of the hour he calls out: *'C'est le guet! Il a sonné dix, il a sonné dix!'* (Here's the night watchman! It's 10 o'clock, it's 10 o'clock!). In earlier times the *guet* kept a lookout for fires around town and other dangers. He was also charged with making sure that townsfolk were well-behaved during solemn moments of church services.

**THE DRIVE**
It's a 1.4km, two-minute drive from St Saphorin to Vinorama. You may even want to walk it, so that you can take advantage of the wine tasting then walk off its effects.

**05 VINORAMA**

**Lavaux Vinorama** (lavaux-vinorama.ch) marries edgy modern architecture with the region's best tipples (some 260 of them). It sits in a designer bunker fronted by a 15m-long bay window, decorated with 6000 metallic pixels inspired by the veins of a vine leaf. Find it at the foot of a terraced vineyard by the lake.

**THE DRIVE**
It's an easy 14km drive along Rte Cantonal (Rte 9) to Montreux. For the hotel, turn left onto Av de Alpes (100m after Hôtel Villa Toscane). Continue until the roundabout and take the fourth exit for Rue de la Gare (heading up), then continue until you take a slight left onto Rue du Pont, eventually turning left onto Rue du Temple.

**06 MONTREUX**

No place does palm trees and yellow awnings better than Montreux on a sunny day. The town's golden microclimate and prized position belie the fact that the place is fairly quiet outside the **Montreux Jazz Festival** (montreuxjazzfestival.com). The main draw is the **Queen studio experience** (casinosbarriere.com/montreux), where fans of Queen and the beloved Freddie Mercury get a kick out of seeing the studio where Queen recorded numerous albums (they owned the joint from 1979 to 1993). Evocative memorabilia includes Freddie's handwritten lyrics and flamboyant Zandra Rhodes stage wear, plus the original mixing desk. At lakefront Place du Marché, in front of the town's covered market, there's a 3m-tall **statue** of Freddie, 'lover of life, singer of songs'.

**THE DRIVE**
Drive along Rte 9 for 3km until you reach the castle, located in Veytaux (parking available).

**07 CHÂTEAU DE CHILLON**

The magnificent 13th-century fortress **Château de Chillon** (chillon.ch) is a maze of courtyards, towers and halls filled with arms, period furniture and artwork. The landward side is heavily fortified, but lakeside presents a gentler face. Don't miss the medieval frescos in the Chappelle St Georges and the spooky Gothic dungeons. The fortress gained fame in 1816 when Byron wrote 'The Prisoner of Chillon', a poem about François Bonivard, thrown into the dungeon for his seditious ideas and freed by Bernese forces in 1536. Byron carved his name into the pillar to which Bonivard was supposedly chained.

**THE DRIVE**
From Château de Chillon, Rte 9 heads east to exit 17. From here take Rte 11 through Aigle (making sure to catch sight of its castle surrounded by vineyards), before ascending via the same winding road through forested countryside topped with rocky peaks to Col du Pillon (parking), just past Les Diablerets. All told, it's 38km (about 45 minutes).

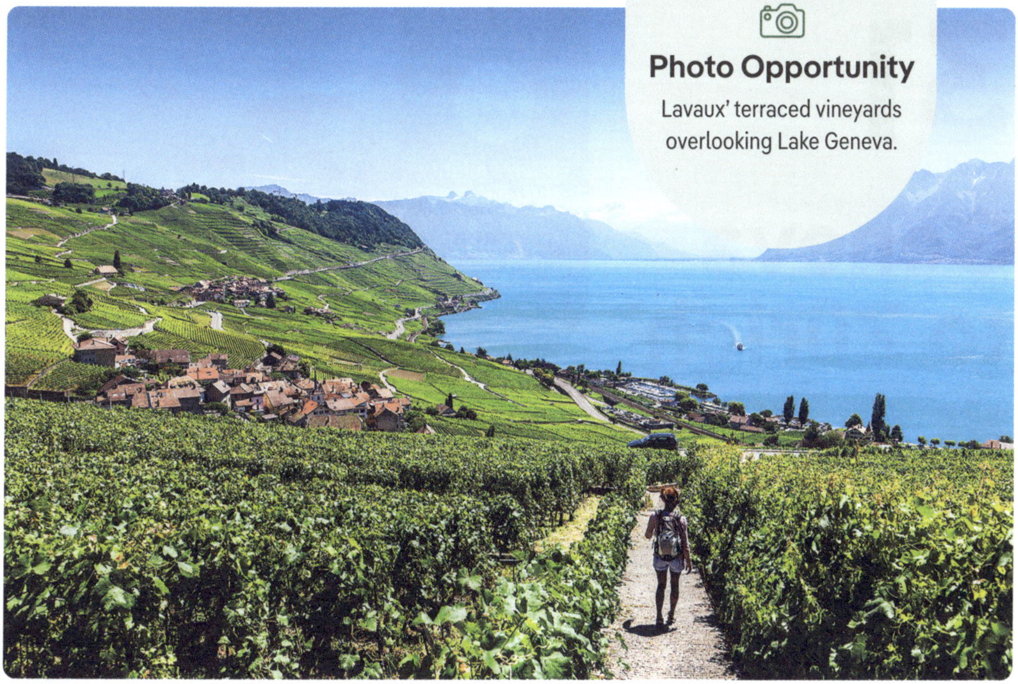

SAMUEL BORGES PHOTOGRAPHY/SHUTTERSTOCK

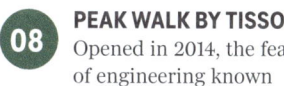

## Photo Opportunity

Lavaux' terraced vineyards overlooking Lake Geneva.

Vineyards, Lavaux

## 08 PEAK WALK BY TISSOT

Opened in 2014, the feat of engineering known as **Peak Walk** (glacier3000.ch) allows you to stroll between sky-scraping peaks and feast on views of iconic mountains such as Eiger, Mönch, Jungfrau, the Matterhorn and Mont Blanc. The 107m-long span has viewfinders (with names of the peaks) that overlook the famous Glacier3000 ski station. From the car park at Col du Pillon, take the **cable car** to Cabane and then to the Mario Botta–designed station at Scex Rouge (15 minutes; 2971m).

### THE DRIVE

Rte 11 and Rte 190 connect Col du Pillon with Gruyères (55km, 70 minutes) through countryside and quaint chalet-filled villages (Les Mosses has a sweet wood-shingled church). From Col du Pillon, retrace your drive on Rte 11 and follow signs to Bulle. From Montbovon, the road skirts the train tracks, but just past Estavannens, take a left (Rte de Gruyères).

## 09 GRUYÈRES

This dreamy village of 15th to 17th-century houses tumbling down a hillock has a cobblestone heart and the postcard-perfect **Château de Gruyères** (chateau-gruyeres.ch) as its crowning glory. The hard AOC Gruyère cheese (the 's' is dropped for the cheese) has been made for centuries in the surrounding Alpine pastures; learn all about it at **La Maison du Gruyère** (lamaisondugruyere.ch), with daily cheesemaking demonstrations, a shop and information about area walks. It's 1.5km from Gruyères, in Pringy.

# 31

# Geneva to Zürich

**BEST FOR CULTURE**

Zürich's mighty museums and relentless nightlife are intoxicating.

Zürich (p208)

| DURATION | DISTANCE | GREAT FOR |
|---|---|---|
| 7 days | 481km / 292 miles | History & nature |

| BEST TIME TO GO | Late spring, summer and autumn, when the light and weather are best. |
|---|---|

Rather than take a straight line from Geneva to Zürich, this trip gives you room to roam some of Switzerland's finest sights: small cities with charming old towns, heaven-sent lakes with dreamy views, winding roads through unspoilt countryside and wild, an adventure centre with the perfect setting, a train ride to the top of Europe, and scenic ascents that will have you gasping – all bookended by Switzerland's cultural capitals.

## Link Your Trip

**29 Northern Switzerland**

From end point Zürich it's an easy one-hour, 85km drive east to start-point St Gallen.

**32 The Swiss Alps**

It's a two-hour (147km) drive eastward from Zürich to Arosa, the starting point of the Alpine whirl.

### 01 GENEVA

Cosmopolitan Geneva is a rare blend: a multicultural population chattering in every language under the sun, a distinctly French feel, one of the world's most expensive cities, a stronghold of the Protestant Reformation, a synonymity with numbered bank accounts and a humanitarian haven.

With a whole day and night, schedule time for Geneva's magnificent **old town**. For waterside attractions, make a beeline for the emblematic **Jet d'Eau** (Quai Gustave-Ador) and the egalitarian **Bains des Pâquis** (aubp.ch).

Plenty of museums will tempt you: among the best are the **Musée d'Art Moderne et Contemporain** (Museum of Modern & Contemporary Art MAMCO); mamco.ch), the **Musée International de la Croix-Rouge et du Croissant-Rouge** (International Red Cross & Red Crescent Museum; redcrossmuseum.ch) and the lavish timepieces of **Patek Philippe Museum** (patek.com/en/museum/the-patek-philippe-museum). For a behind-the-scenes glimpse of the UN or the Large Hadron Collider, prebook a tour of the **Palais des Nations** (Palace of Nations; unog.ch) or **CERN** (home.cern), respectively.

### THE DRIVE
Head west via the A1 until the A9 (follow signs to Vevey/Montreux). Take exit 11 and follow signs for Lutry. From Lutry, take Rte 9 (direction Vevey) until Cully, then head up Rte de la Corniche to Chexbres. Next follow Rte du Genevrex and get on the A9, followed by the A12 to Fribourg (143km total).

### 02 FRIBOURG
Nowhere is Switzerland's language divide felt more keenly than in Fribourg (Freiburg or 'Free Town'), a medieval city where inhabitants on the west bank of the Sarine speak French, and those on the east bank of the Sanne speak German. Sights that merit a look-see include the bohemian **Espace Jean Tinguely – Niki de Saint Phalle** (mahf.ch), the evocative **old town** filled with Gothic facades, the **Musée d'Art et d'Histoire** (Museum of Art & History; mahf.ch) and the outsize **Cathédrale de St Nicolas de Myre** (St Nicolas Cathedral; stnicolas.ch) with its 74m-tall **tower**. Make time for a couple of the city's bohemian cafe-bars, such as **Le Port** or **Café Culturel de l'Ancienne Gare** (CCAG; nouveaumonde.ch/cafe).

### THE DRIVE
It's a longish (103km, one hour and 50 minutes) scenic route along winding roads through lovely small towns and unspoiled countryside in Fribourg and Bern cantons. Head to the village of Charmey via Rte 189, then to Boltingen. Take Rte 11 to Speiz on Lake Thun, then follow Rte 8 to Interlaken.

### 03 INTERLAKEN
Once Interlaken made the Victorians swoon with mountain vistas from the chandelier-lit confines of grand hotels; today it makes daredevils scream with adrenaline-loaded adventures. Straddling the glittering Lakes Thun and Brienz and dazzled by the pearly whites of Eiger, Mönch and Jungfrau, the scenery is mind-blowing. Check out views from **Harder Kulm** (jungfrau.ch/harderkulm), or try daredevil activities with **Outdoor Interlaken** (outdoor-interlaken.ch), organised in advance.

Leave the car in Interlaken after overnighting and head to the **Jungfraujoch**, a glacier saddle between two dizzying peaks, very early the next morning.

### THE DRIVE
From Interlaken it's a one-hour (54km) drive via Lake Thun's Seestrasse, past turreted Schloss Oberhoffen and, where Art Nouveau meets neo-Renaissance, Schloss Hünegg. After Thun, you'll get to Bern quickly via the A6.

## Photo Opportunity

The verdant Emmental region exemplifies pastoral perfection.

Emmental region

**Detour**
**Jungfraujoch**
Start: **03** Interlaken

Presided over by monolithic Eiger, Mönch and Jungfrau (Ogre, Monk and Virgin), the crown jewels of Bernese Oberland's Alpine scenery will make your heart skip a beat.

The 'big three' peaks have an enduring place in mountaineering legend, particularly the 3970m Eiger, whose fearsome north wall remained unconquered until 1938. Today, it takes only 2½ hours from Interlaken Ost by train to **Jungfraujoch** (3454m), Europe's highest station.

From Kleine Scheidegg (the last stage of the journey), the train burrows through the Eiger before arriving at the **Sphinx meteorological station**. Opened in 1912, the tunnel took 3000 men 16 years to drill. Along the way, the Eigerwand and Eismeer stops have panoramic windows offering glimpses across rivers of crevassed ice.

Good weather is essential for this journey; check beforehand on jungfrau.ch and always take warm clothing, sunglasses and sunscreen. Within the Sphinx weather station there's a nice sculpture gallery, restaurants, indoor viewpoints and a souvenir shop. Outside there are views of the 23km-long **Aletsch Glacier**. On cloudless days, the views stretch as far as the Black Forest in Germany.

When you tire (as if) of the view, you can zip across the frozen plateau on a flying fox, dash downhill on a sled or snow disc, or enjoy a bit of tame skiing or boarding at the **Snow Fun Park**.

If you cross the glacier along the prepared path, in around an hour you reach the **Mönchsjochhütte** (moenchsjoch.ch) at 3650m, where rock climbers psych themselves up to tackle Eiger or Mönch.

**BERN**

Wandering through the picture-postcard **old town**, with its laid-back, riverside air, it's hard to believe that Bern (Berne in French) is the Swiss capital, but it is, and a UNESCO World Heritage site to boot. The flag-festooned, cobbled centre, rebuilt in grey-green sandstone after a devastating 1405 fire, is a delight, with 6km of covered arcades, cellar shops and bars, and fantastical folk figures frolicking on 16th-century fountains, such as the **Kindlifresserbrunnen** (on the Kornhausplatz). Be sure to visit Bern's **Münster** (berner muenster.ch); the famous **Bären Park** (Bear Park; tierpark-bern.ch), the architecturally daring **Zentrum Paul Klee** (zpk.org); and the well-endowed **Kunstmuseum** (Museum of Fine Arts; kunstmuseumbern.ch).

### THE DRIVE
Leave via the A6 and take Krauchthalstrasse (35 minutes, about 24km) through leafy countryside to Burgdorf. From Burgdorf to Affoltern im Emmental, 6km to the east, is a scenic drive past old farmsteads bedecked with flower boxes, neat woodpiles and kitchen gardens. Rte 23 between Affoltern and Langnau im Emmental is 21km (25 minutes).

### 05 EMMENTAL REGION
After so much city time, the postcard-perfect landscapes of rural Switzerland beckon: time for the bucolic idyll of the Emmental region, where holey Emmental (Swiss) cheese is produced. To see the iconic cheese being made, head to **Emmentaler Schaukäserei** (Emmental Open Cheese Dairy; emmentaler-schaukaeserei.ch) in Affoltern.

The region's gateway towns of Burgdorf and Langnau im Emmental preside over a mellow patchwork of quiet villages, grazing cows and fabulous farm chalets with vast barns and overhanging roofs, strung out along the Emme's banks. Burgdorf (literally 'castle village') is split into an Upper and Lower Town. The natural highlight of the Oberstadt (Upper Town) is the 12th-century **Schloss** (castle), with its drawbridge, thick stone walls and trio of museums.

### THE DRIVE
From Langnau im Emmental, take Rte 10 for 30 minutes (23km), crossing from Bern canton to Lucerne canton, to reach Schüpfheim, the heart of the Entlebuch biosphere.

### 06 UNESCO BIOSPHERE ENTLEBUCH

The 39,000-plus-sq-km **Entlebuch area** (biosphaere.ch), a mixed mountain-and-highland ecosystem, was declared a UNESCO Biosphere Reserve in 2001. Far from being a lonely wilderness outpost, the reserve is home to some 17,000 people keen to preserve their traditional dairy-farming lifestyle. The landscape of karst formations, sprawling moors (some 25% of the area), Alpine pastures and mountain streams, which rise from 600m to some 2350m above sea level, makes for stirring scenery. The park office is in Schüpfheim.

### THE DRIVE
Driving from Schüpfheim, take the Panoramastrasse (which deserves to be more famous) to the town of Giswil (Obwalden canton; 50 minutes, 37km). Next, follow the signs to Lucerne (Luzern in German) along the A8 (30 minutes, 30km).

---

## Island Dining in Geneva

Genevan living is easy in summer: a constant crowd throngs the lakefront quays to hang out in pop-up terrace bars such as **La Terrasse** (laterrasse.ch), the fashionista spot by the water to see and be seen. Meander away from Quai du Mont-Blanc to uncover a beloved trio of summertime shacks on the water's edge – alfresco and effortlessly cool.

The right-bank address is refreshingly casual: Rhône-side **Terrasse Le Paradis** (terrasse-paradis.ch) is the type of cafe that practically begs you to pull out a book and stay all day in deckchairs arranged down steps to the water, while sipping beakers of homemade *citronnade* (lemonade). 'Paradise' does not serve alcohol, but green mint tea flows and the wholly affordable sandwiches, salads and legendary tabbouleh hit the spot.

**Le Bateau Lavoir** (bateaulavoir.ch) is an eye-catching boat with rooftop terrace moored between the old market hall and Pont de la Coulouvrenière. Its cabin-size dining area cooks fondue and basic local dishes, the crowd is hip and there is a 360-degree lake view. Its design and name evoke the wash-house boats – yes, where undies and so on were washed – that floated here in the 17th century.

Then there is **La Barje** (labarje.ch), not a barge at all but a vintage caravan with tin roof and candy-striped facade, parked on the grassy banks of the Rhône near the Bâtiment des Forces Motrices. The beer and music are plentiful, outside concerts and art performances pull huge crowds, and proceeds go towards helping young people in difficulty.

## Fribourg's Filthy Funicular

Nowhere else in Europe does a funicular lurch up the mountainside with the aid of sewage water (on certain days it smells as you'd expect). Constructed in 1899 and managed by the Cardinal Brewery until 1965 (when the municipality took over), the **Funiculaire de Fribourg** links the lower town with the upper. It runs every six minutes, and the ride in one of two counterbalancing water-powered carriages from the lower Pertuis station (121m; Place du Pertuis) to the upper station (618m; Rte des Alpes) takes two minutes.

### 07 LUCERNE

Recipe for a gorgeous Swiss city: take a cobalt lake ringed by mountains of myth (Pilatus, Rigi), add a well-preserved medieval **old town** (Altstadt), then sprinkle with covered bridges **Kapellbrücke** (Chapel Bridge) and **Spreuerbrücke** (Spreuer Bridge), sunny plazas, candy-coloured houses and waterfront promenades. Legend has it that an angel with a light showed the first settlers where to build a chapel in Lucerne, and today it still has amazing grace.

One minute it's nostalgic – its emotive **lion monument** (Löwendenkmal) – the next highbrow, with concerts at acoustic marvel **Kultur und Kongresszentrum** (KKL; kkl-luzern.ch) and the peerless Picasso collection of **Museum Sammlung Rosengart** (rosengart.ch). Crowd-pleasers such as **Verkehrshaus** (Swiss Museum of Transport; verkehrshaus.ch) and the surrounding natural wonders never fail to impress, while balmy summers and golden autumns ensure this 'city of lights' shines constantly.

#### THE DRIVE
A fast 15-minute, 15km journey along the A2 will get you from Lucerne to Stans' Stansstaderstrasse 19, for the journey up to Stanserhorn.

### 08 STANSERHORN

Looming above the lake, 1898m Stanserhorn (stanserhorn.ch) boasts 360-degree vistas of **Lake Lucerne**, **Mt Titlis**, **Mt Pilatus** and the **Bernese Alps**, among others. Getting to the summit is half the fun. The journey starts with a ride on a vintage 19th-century funicular from Stans to Kälti; from here, the nearly transparent **CabriO** (cabrio.ch), launched in 2012 as the world's first cable car with an open upper deck, takes you the rest of the way, offering amazing on-the-go views.

On sunny days or when many travellers are expected, book an online 'boarding pass' to confirm your time of departure and subsequent return.

At the summit there's the star-shaped **Rondorama**, the region's only revolving restaurant, which rotates 360 degrees every 43 minutes. Kids love the nearby **marmot park**, where the critters can be observed in a near-natural habitat.

#### THE DRIVE
Retrace your route along the A2 and head toward Lucerne before changing to the A4 and following the signs to Zürich (50 minutes, 65km).

### 09 ZÜRICH

Culturally vibrant, efficiently run and set at the meeting of river and lake, Zürich is constantly recognised as one of the world's most liveable cities. It's a savvy, hard-working financial centre, yet Switzerland's largest and wealthiest metropolis has an artsy, post-industrial edge. Much of the old town, with its winding lanes and quaint squares, is lovingly intact. Must-see sights include the glorious **Fraumünster** (fraumuenster.ch), with its Marc Chagall stained-glass windows; the **Grossmünster** (grossmuenster.ch) with its salt-and-pepper-shaker steeples; and the excellent **Kunsthaus** (kunsthaus.ch), which holds an impressive permanent collection. For contemporary cool, walk around Züri-West. In summer, the fun revolves around lake and river pools like **Seebad Utoquai** (seebadutoquai.ch), **Frauenbad** and **Männerbad**.

# 32
# The Swiss Alps

**BEST FOR OUTDOORS**

Whatever the season, the Alps offer activities galore.

| DURATION | DISTANCE | GREAT FOR |
|---|---|---|
| 7 days | 612km / 333 miles | Nature & families |

| BEST TIME TO GO | Year-round, but some mountain passes may be closed to vehicular traffic. |
|---|---|

Cable car, Mt Titlis, Engelberg (p213)

A natural barrier, the Alps are both a blessing and a burden when it comes to tripping around Switzerland. The soul-stirring views are stupendous, but you have to either go over, around or through them to get to the next one. Starting in Graubünden's Arosa and finishing in Valais' Zermatt, this trip visits five cantons via hairpin bends, valley highways, tunnels, passes and cable cars to bring you the best.

### Link Your Trip

**30 Lake Geneva & Western Switzerland**

Zermatt is three hours (245km) east of Geneva, the starting point of Trip 30.

**31 Geneva to Zürich**

Arosa is a two-hour drive east (147km) on the A3 from Zürich, the end point of Trip 31.

### 01 AROSA

Framed by the peaks of **Weisshorn**, **Hörnli** and moraine-streaked **Schiesshorn**, Arosa is a great Alpine all-rounder: perfect for downhill and cross-country skiing in winter, hiking and downhill biking in summer, and heaps of family activities year-round. Although only 30km southeast of Chur (Switzerland's oldest city), getting here involves 180-degree hairpin bends so challenging that Arosa cannot be reached by postal buses. Once here, you may want to revel in the beauty of the Mario Botta–designed **Tschuggen Bergoase Spa** (tschuggencollection.ch), an architectural statement built at the foot of the mountains. The structure's recurring leaf-shaped motifs look particularly striking when illuminated at night.

### 🚗 THE DRIVE
The trip from Arosa to Vals takes 79km and 1¾ hours. Head back towards Chur, then take Rte 19 to Ilanz for the delightful road that passes through Uors and St Martin before arriving at Vals (1252m). About 2km short of the village, you emerge into Alpine pastures, liberally scattered with chalets and shepherds' huts.

### 02 THERME VALS
Shadowing the course of the babbling Glogn (Glenner) stream south, the luxuriantly green Valsertal (Vals Valley) is full of sleepy hamlets and thundering waterfalls. **Vals** stretches 2km along its glittering stream. The secret of this chocolate-box village and its soothing waters is out since Basel-born architect Peter Zumthor transformed **Therme Vals** (7132therme.com) into a temple of cutting-edge cool. Using 60,000 slabs of local quartzite, Zumthor created one of the country's most enchanting thermal spas. Aside from heated indoor and outdoor pools, this grey-stone labyrinth hides watery nooks and crannies, cleverly lit and full of cavernous atmosphere. Drift away in the bath-warm Feuerbad (42°C) and perfumed Blütenbad, sweat it out in the steam room, and cool down in the teeth-chattering Eisbad.

### 🚗 THE DRIVE
Return to Ilanz, then continue on Rte 19 to Disentis/Mustér (50km, 55 minutes).

---

### WHY I LOVE THIS TRIP
**Sally O'Brien**, writer

Even though I now call Switzerland home, the Alpine scenery still has an other-worldly effect on me. The abundance of snow-capped peaks, mountains with fairy tale names that 'pop up' at numerous vantage points, time-defying glaciers, gravity-defying railways. And then there's the moment you catch sight of the Matterhorn...

Cliff Walk, Mt Titlis, Engelberg

## Wine Time

The canton of Valais, which features so much of Switzerland's stunning Alpine scenery, is also the country's largest and best wine producer. Sampling the wine in situ at the end of a day's driving is a great idea.

Drenched in extra sunshine and light from above the southern Alps, much of the land north of the Rhône river in western Valais is planted with vines. Unique to the Valais are the *bisses* (narrow irrigation channels) that traverse the vineyards.

Dryish white Fendant, the perfect accompaniment to fondue and raclette, and best served crisp cold, is the region's best-known wine, accounting for two-thirds of Valais wine production. Dôle, made from Pinot noir and Gamay grapes, is the principal red blend and is full-bodied, with a firm fruit flavour.

When ordering wine in a wine bar or restaurant, use the uniquely Swiss approach of *deci* (decilitre – ie a 10th of a litre) multiples. Or just order a bottle...

 **03 DISENTIS/MUSTÉR**

Disentis/Mustér's Benedictine monastery, **Kloster Disentis** (kloster-disentis.ch), rising like a vision above town, has a lavishly stuccoed baroque church attached. A monastery has stood here since the 8th century, but the present immense complex dates from the 18th century. Enter the **Klostermuseum**, crammed with memorabilia, left of the church entrance. Head left upstairs to the **Marienkirche**, a chapel with Romanesque origins now filled with *ex votos* from people seeking (or giving thanks for) a miraculous intervention from the Virgin Mary. If you're peckish, a handy (and very good-value) on-site cafe/takeaway has soups, salads and local specialities.

**THE DRIVE**
Disentis is an exhilarating (40-minute, 32km) drive along Rte 19 and the twisting Oberalp Pass (2044m), which connects Graubünden and Uri cantons. In winter, the pass is closed to cars, but a car train connects Sedrun on Rte 19 and Andermatt (three services daily in winter, two in spring). Reservations are essential (matterhorngotthardbahn.ch).

## 04 ANDERMATT

Blessed with austere mountain appeal, Andermatt (Uri canton) contrasts low-key village charm with big wilderness. Once an important staging-post on the north–south St Gotthard route, it's now bypassed by the tunnel. It remains a key crossroads near four major passes (Susten, Oberalp, St Gotthard and Furka), making it a terrific base for **hiking** and **cycling**. The tourist office supplies free booklets.

One popular hike leads from the Oberalp Pass to sparkly **Lai da Tuma**, the source of the Rhine; the 11km round trip takes three to four hours, with 500m elevation gain. A walk around and along **Gotthardstrasse** reveals textbook dark-wood central-Swiss architecture, often weighed down with either geraniums or snow.

Skiers in the know flock to 2963m **Gemsstock** (skiarena.ch), reached by the Gemsstockbahn cable car, for the snow-sure winter slopes.

 **THE DRIVE**
Take Rte 2 to Göschenen, then get on the A2/E35 and follow the signs for Lucerne. The road skirts the bottom of Lake Uri for lovely water views. Continue to exit 33 (Stans-Süd), then follow Rte 374 to Engelberg (one hour, 77km in total).

## 05 ENGELBERG

Wonderful **Engelberg** (literally 'Angel Mountain'), backed by the glacial bulk of **Mt Titlis** (titlis.ch; central Switzerland's tallest mountain) and frosted peaks, which feature in many a Bollywood production, is divine. After visiting the 12th-century Benedictine **Engelberg Monastery** (Kloster Engelberg; kloster-engelberg.ch), get closer to the heavens via the world's first revolving **cable car** (titlis.ch/en/activities/titlis-rotair). It pirouettes over the dazzling **Titlis Glacier**, peaks rising like shark fins ahead, before you step out onto Titlis station's **terrace** (3020m), with a panorama that stretches to Eiger, Mönch and Jungfrau in the Bernese Oberland. For even more thrilling views, take the adjacent **Cliff Walk** (titlis.ch/en/glacier/cliff-walk) – opened in 2012, this 100m-long, 1m-wide, cable-supported swinging walkway is Europe's highest suspension bridge.

There are some 360km of marked hiking trails in and around Engelberg. For gentle ambles and gorgeous scenery, head for **Brunni** across the valley. Its **cable car** (brunni.ch) goes up to Ristis at 1600m, where a chairlift takes you to the Swiss Alpine Club's refurbished **Brunni Hütte**. From here, you can choose to watch a magnificent sunset before spending the night.

 **THE DRIVE**
Retrace your route to the A2, heading west, before turning onto the A8 (direction Interlaken), and continuing alongside bright-blue Brienzersee to Giessbachfälle. One hour and 10 minutes, 71km.

**TOP TIP:**

## Zumdorf

If the grand scale of this trip seems overwhelming, the antidote surely lies in a quick detour to Switzerland's smallest village, Zumdorf: little more than a cluster of small buildings on the Furkastrasse and a population counted on one hand. Despite its diminutive size, it has **Restaurant Zum Dörfli** (zumdoerfli.ch), specialising in Swiss dishes (especially rösti) and venison (in season). Find it 6km southwest of Andermatt.

## 06 GIESSBACHFÄLLE

Illuminating the firs like a spotlight in the dark, the misty **Giessbachfälle** (Giessbach Falls) plummet 500m over 14 rocky ridges. **Europe's oldest funicular**, dating to 1879, creaks up from the boat station, but it's only a 15-minute walk up to the most striking section of the falls.

 **THE DRIVE**
Get back onto the A8 and follow it along the Brienzersee until exit 25 (Wilderswil/Grindelwald), then continue as the road winds its way through countryside up to Grindelwald (39km, 45 minutes).

**07 GRINDELWALD**

Grindelwald's sublime natural assets are film-set stuff – the chiselled north-face features of **Eiger**, the glinting tongues of **Oberer** and **Unterer Glaciers**, and the crown-like peak of **Wetterhorn**. Skiers and hikers cottoned onto its charms in the late 19th century, making it one of Switzerland's oldest resorts. It has lost none of its appeal, with geranium-studded chalets and verdant pastures aplenty.

Turbulent waters carve a path through craggy **Gletscherchlucht** (Glacier Gorge; grindelwaldsports.ch), a 30-minute walk south of the centre. A footpath weaves through tunnels hacked into cliffs veined with pink and green marble. It's justifiably a popular spot for canyon and bungee-jumping expeditions.

Grindelwald is outstanding **hiking** territory, veined with trails that command arresting views to massive north faces, crevasse-filled glaciers and snow-capped peaks. Reach high-altitude walks by taking cable cars from the village.

 **THE DRIVE**

Follow the signs to Lauterbrunnen, which is 20km (15 minutes) away by car.

**08 LAUTERBRUNNEN**

Laid-back Lauterbrunnen's wispy **Staubbachfall** (Staubbach Falls) inspired both Goethe and Byron to write poems to their ethereal beauty.

Bachalpsee

## Around Grindelwald: First

From Grindelwald, a cable car zooms up to **First**, the trailhead for 100km of paths, half of which stay open in winter. You can trudge up to **Faulhorn** (2681m; 2½ hours), even in winter, via the cobalt **Bachalpsee** (Lake Bachalp). As you march along the ridge, the unfolding views of the Jungfrau massif are entrancing. Stop for lunch and 360-degree views at Faulhorn. You might like to continue to Schynige Platte (another three hours) and return by train.

Other great walks head to **Schwarzhorn** (three hours), **Grosse Scheidegg** (1½ hours), **Unterer Gletscher** (1½ hours) and **Grindelwald** itself (2½ hours).

First has 60km of well-groomed pistes, which are mostly wide, meandering reds suited to intermediates. The south-facing slopes make for interesting skiing through meadows and forests. Freestylers should check out the kickers and rails at **Bärgelegg** or have a go on the superpipe at **Schreckfeld station**.

Faulhorn happens to be the starting point for **Europe's longest toboggan run**, accessible only on foot. Bring a sled to bump and glide 15km over icy pastures and through glittering woodlands all the way to Grindelwald via Bussalp. Nicknamed 'Big Pintenfritz', the track lasts around 1½ hours, depending how fast you slide.

Year-round, you can get your pulse racing on the **First Flyer**, a staggeringly fast zip line from First to Schreckfeld. The mountains are but a blur as, secure in your harness, you pick up speeds of around 84km/h.

The **First Cliff Walk** is a summit trail with a 40m-long suspension bridge, climbing stairs and an observation deck, with suitably impressive views of the local landscape and the jaw-dropping mountains.

Today the postcard-perfect village, nestled in the valley of 72 waterfalls – including the **Trümmelbachfälle** (Trümmelbach Falls; truemmelbachfaelle.ch) – attracts a less highfalutin crowd. Hikes heading into the mountains from the waterfall-laced valley include a 2½-hour uphill trudge to car-free **Mürren** and a more gentle 1¾-hour walk to **Stechelberg**. In winter, glide past frozen waterfalls on a well-prepared 12km cross-country trail.

### THE DRIVE
Head to Stechelberg (10 minutes, 6km), where you'll leave the car (paid parking available) and take the cable car to Schiltorn.

### 09 SCHILTHORN
There's a tremendous 360-degree, 200-peak panorama from the 2970m Schilthorn, best appreciated from the **Skyline viewing platform** or **Piz Gloria revolving restaurant** (schilthorn.ch). On a clear day, you can see from **Titlis** around to **Mont Blanc**, and across to the German Black Forest.

## Photo Opportunity
The Matterhorn.

**Matterhorn**

Some visitors seem more preoccupied with practising their delivery of the line, 'The name's Bond, James Bond', because scenes from *On Her Majesty's Secret Service* were shot here in 1968–69. The **Bond World 007** interactive exhibition gives you the chance to pose for photos secret-agent style, and relive movie moments in a helicopter and bobsled.

### THE DRIVE
When you descend to Stechelberg, head to Kandersteg via the road down to Interlaken. Get on the A8/Rte 11, then take exit 19 (direction Spiez/Kandersteg/Adelboden). The 60km trip takes one hour.

### 10 KANDERSTEG
Turn up in Kandersteg in anything but muddy boots and you'll attract a few odd looks. Hiking is the town's raison d'être, with 550km of surrounding trails. An amphitheatre of spiky peaks studded with glaciers and jewel-coloured lakes, such as **Blausee** (blausee.ch) and **Oeschinensee** (oeschinensee.ch), creates a sublime natural backdrop to the rustic village of dark-timber chalets.

In winter there are more than 50km of cross-country ski trails, including the iced-over Oeschinensee. The limited 15km of downhill skiing suits beginners and Kandersteg's frozen waterfalls attract ice climbers.

### THE DRIVE
Take the BLS Lötschberg Tunnel, which connects with Goppenstein (in Valais) at regular intervals daily; it takes 15 minutes. From Goppenstein, head east from Rte 9. Once past Brig, the deep valley narrows and the landscape switches to rugged wilderness, with a string of bucolic villages of timber chalets and onion-domed churches. It's 47km in total.

### 11 ALETSCH GLACIER
The Aletsch Glacier is a seemingly never-ending, 23km-long swirl of ice with deep crevasses that slices past thundering falls, jagged spires of rock and pine forest. It stretches from Jungfrau in the Bernese Oberland to a plateau above the Rhône and is, justly so, a UNESCO World Heritage site.

Picture-postcard riverside **Fiesch** on the valley floor is the best place to access it. From

## The High Life

Charming as Zermatt is, heading out of town and up to the mountains is a rush like no other. Europe's highest cogwheel railway, the **Gornergratbahn** (gornergrat.ch), has climbed picture-postcard scenery to Gornergrat (3089m) – a 30-minute journey – since 1898. Sit on the right-hand side to gawp at the Matterhorn. Tickets allow you to get on and off en route; there are restaurants at **Riffelalp** (2211m) and **Riffelberg** (2582m). In summer an extra train runs once a week at sunrise and sunset – the most spectacular trips of all.

Views from Zermatt's cable cars are all remarkable, but the **Matterhorn Glacier Paradise** (matterhornparadise.ch) is the icing on the cake. Ride Europe's highest-altitude cable car to 3883m and marvel at 14 glaciers and 38 mountain peaks over 4000m from the Panoramic Platform (only open in good weather). Don't miss the **Glacier Palace**, an ice palace complete with glittering ice sculptures and an ice slide to swoosh down bum first. End with exhilarating snow tubing outside in the wintery surrounds.

the village, ride the **cable car** (eggishorn.ch) up to **Fiescheralp** and continue up to **Eggishorn** (2927m). Streaming down in a broad curve around the **Aletschhorn** (4195m), the glacier is just like a frozen six-lane superhighway. In the distance to the north rise the glistening summits of Jungfrau (4158m), Mönch (4107m), Eiger (3970m) and Finsteraarhorn (4274m). To the southwest of the cable-car exit, you can spy Mont Blanc and the Matterhorn.

### THE DRIVE
It takes one hour (56km) to get from Fiesch to Täsch via Rte 19 to Visp, then the winding rural road to Täsch itself. Park the car here before boarding the train to car-free Zermatt.

### 12 ZERMATT

You can almost sense the anticipation on the train from Täsch. As you arrive in car-free Zermatt, the pop-up-book effect of the one-of-a-kind Matterhorn (4478m) works its magic. Like a shark's fin it rises above the town, with moods that swing from pretty and pink to dark and mysterious. Since the mid-19th century, Zermatt has starred among Switzerland's glitziest resorts. Today skiers cruise along well-kept pistes, spellbound by the scenery, while style-conscious wannabe celebs flash designer threads in the town's swish lounge bars.

Meander main-strip **Bahnhofstrasse** with its boutiques and stream of horse-drawn sleds or carriages and electric taxis, then head towards the noisy Vispa River along **Hinterdorfstrasse**. This old-world street is crammed with archetypal Valaisian timber granaries propped up on stone discs and stilts to keep out pesky rats; look for the fountain commemorating Ulrich Inderbinen (1900–2004), a Zermatt-born mountaineer who climbed the Matterhorn 370 times, the last time at age 90.

A walk in Zermatt's **Mountaineers' Cemetery** in the garden of St Mauritius Church is sobering. Numerous gravestones tell of untimely deaths on Monte Rosa, the Matterhorn and Breithorn. In July 2015 a **memorial** to 'the unknown climber' was unveiled to mark the 150th anniversary of the Matterhorn's first ascent.

The **Matterhorn Museum** provides a fascinating insight into Valaisian village life, the dawn of tourism in Zermatt and the lives the Matterhorn has claimed. Short films portray the first successful ascent of the Matterhorn on 14 July 1865, led by Edward Whymper, a feat marred by tragedy on the descent when four team members crashed to their deaths in a 1200m fall down the North Wall. The infamous rope that broke is on display.

# 33
# Graubünden & Ticino

**BEST FOR CULTURE**

Graubünden is home to Romansch, an official Swiss language spoken regularly by only 60,000 people.

18th-century house, Graubünden

| DURATION | DISTANCE | GREAT FOR |
|---|---|---|
| 5 days | 490km / 345 miles | Wine & nature |

| BEST TIME TO GO | Spring or summer. |
|---|---|

The wild beauty of Switzerland dominates, tracing valley floors sheltered by hulking mountains, pristine forests and brilliantly blue lakes. Cities on this route are reassuringly relaxed and even slightly retro, the villages embrace their quiet appeal, and at the end of it all climbs one of Europe's most exciting drives. Start in Graubünden, with its unique language and identity, then finish with a hearty *ciao bella* in riviera-rich Ticino.

### Link Your Trip

**29 Northern Switzerland**
End point St Gotthard Pass is a 2½-hour drive northeast from St Gallen, starting point of Trip 29.

**31 Geneva to Zürich**
Starting point Chur is only a 75-minute (120km) drive southeast from Zürich, end point of Trip 31.

### 01 CHUR

The Alps rise like an amphitheatre around Chur, Switzerland's oldest city, inhabited since 3000 BC.

The **Bündner Kunstmuseum** (Museum of Fine Arts; buendner-kunstmuseum.ch) in the neoclassical Villa Planta gives an insight into the artistic legacy of Graubünden-born Alberto Giacometti (1877–1947) and his talented contemporaries, including Giovanni Segantini and Ernst Ludwig Kirchner.

The city's most iconic landmark is **Martinskirche** (St Martin's Church), with its distinctive spire and clock face. The 8th-century church was rebuilt in the

## THE DRIVE

From Maienfeld, take Landstrasse for 5km to turn left onto the N28 road east from Landquart. Here you enter the broad Prättigau Valley, which stretches east to Davos for 39km. This high Alpine country is punctuated by villages and burned-wood Walser houses built by these rural folk since migrating here from eastern Valais from the 13th century onward.

### 03 DAVOS

Davos is more cool than quaint, but what the resort lacks in Alpine prettiness, it makes up for with seductive skiing and a great après-ski scene. It is also the annual meeting point for the crème de la crème of global capitalism, the World Economic Forum. Davos also inspired Thomas Mann to write *The Magic Mountain*.

Davos' giant cube of a museum, **Kirchner Museum** (kirchner museum.ch), showcases the world's largest Ernst Ludwig Kirchner (1880–1938) collection, with some 50 paintings. The German expressionist painted extraordinary scenes of the area around Davos, which he called home from 1918. When the Nazis classified Kirchner a 'degenerate artist' and emptied galleries of his works, he was overcome with despair and took his own life in 1938.

## THE DRIVE

Turn onto Rte 28 (Flüelastrasse), continuing for 34km (40 minutes) until you reach Zernez, where the headquarters of the Swiss National Park are located. This route includes, weather permitting, the Flüela Pass (2383m). If the pass is closed, you'll need to travel through the Vereina Tunnel (car train) from Selfranga to Sagliains (rhb.ch/en/car-transporter).

late-Gothic style in 1491 and is dramatically lit by a trio of Augusto Giacometti **stained-glass windows**.

Chur is a 1¼-hour drive from Zürich along the A3, passing the fantastically fjord-like **Walensee**. The limestone Churfirsten mountains rise like an iron backdrop along the lake's north flank, occasionally interrupted by a coastal hamlet or upland pasture and, about halfway along the lakefront, seemingly cracked open by **Seerenbachfälle**, Switzerland's highest waterfall.

## THE DRIVE

Chur to Tamina Therme is a simple 18-minute, 20km drive along the A13.

### 02 BAD RAGAZ

The graceful little spa town of Bad Ragaz opened in 1840 and attracted the bath-loving likes of Douglas Fairbanks and Mary Pickford. The fabled waters are said to boost the immune system and improve circulation. The sleek and stylish **Tamina Therme** (taminatherme. ch), a couple of kilometres south of Bad Ragaz, has several pools for wallowing in the 36.5°C thermal waters, as well as massage jets, whirlpools, saunas and an assortment of treatments and massages, not to mention Alp views and a good cafe. Dine and sleep in nearby Maienfeld.

## 04 SWISS NATIONAL PARK

Spanning 172 sq km, Switzerland's first and only national park (established 1 August 1914) is a nature-gone-wild swathe of dolomitic peaks, shimmering glaciers, larch woodlands, pastures, waterfalls and high moors strung with topaz-blue lakes. It's a real glimpse of the Alps before the dawn of tourism.

Some 80km of well-marked hiking trails lead through the park, where, with a little luck and decent binoculars, ibex, chamois, marmot and golden eagle can be sighted. The **Swiss National Park Centre** (nationalpark.ch) in **Zernez** should be your first port of call for information on activities and accommodation. An audioguide gives you the lowdown on conservation, wildlife and environmental change. The tourist office here can also provide details on park hikes.

Zernez itself is an attractive cluster of stone chalets, outlined by the profile of its baroque church and the stout medieval tower of its castle, **Schloss Wildenberg**.

### THE DRIVE
The views between Zernez and Müstair along Rte 28 are stupendous, with wild Alpine scenery and the Ofen/Fuorn Pass (2149m). The drive takes 40 minutes (39km).

## 05 MÜSTAIR

Nestled in a remote corner of Switzerland, just before the Italian border, **Müstair** is one of Europe's early Christian treasures and a UNESCO World Heritage site. When Charlemagne supposedly founded a monastery and a church here in the 8th century, this was a strategically placed spot below the Ofen Pass, separating northern Europe from Italy and the heart of Christendom.

Vibrant Carolingian (9th century) and Romanesque (12th century) frescos line the interior of the church of Benedictine **Kloster St Johann** (St John's Convent; muestair.ch). Beneath Carolingian representations of Christ in Glory in the apses are Romanesque stories depicting the grisly ends of St Peter (crucified), St Paul (decapitated) and St Stephen (stoned). The **museum** next door takes you through part of the monastery complex, with Carolingian art and other relics.

### THE DRIVE
From Müstair to Zuoz is 56km (one hour). This is mostly retracing your drive back to Zernez along Rte 28, before heading southwest along Rte 27, which sticks close to the Inn River as it snakes through the valley floor.

## 06 ZUOZ

Little Zuoz is a quintessential Engadine town, with colourful **sgraffito houses**, flower boxes bursting with geraniums and Augusto Giacometti **stained-glass windows** illuminating the church chancel. Though skiing is fairly limited (albeit good), Zuoz is unquestionably one of the Oberengadin's prettiest towns, and a great place to unwind for a night.

### THE DRIVE
Follow Rte 27 for 18km along the valley path, admiring the landscape of broad-shouldered mountains and small towns.

## 07 ST MORITZ

Switzerland's original winter wonderland and the cradle of Alpine tourism, St Moritz has been luring royals, celebrities and serious money since 1864. With its shimmering aquamarine lake, emerald forests and aloof mountains, the town looks a million dollars, which you could probably drop during a quick shopping spree on **Via Serlas**.

The real riches lie outdoors with superb carving on **Corviglia** (2486m), tricky black runs on **Diavolezza** (2978m) and miles of **hiking** and **biking** trails when the snow melts.

---

### Must-Try Bündner Specialities

**Pizokel** Stubby wheat-and-egg noodles, seasoned with parsley and often served with speck, cheese and onions.

**Bündnerfleisch** Seasoned and air-dried beef or game.

**Capuns** A hearty dish consisting of egg pasta and sausage or Bündnerfleisch, which is wrapped in chard, flavoured with herbs and cooked in milky water.

**Maluns** Potatoes soaked for 24 hours, then grated and slowly roasted in butter and flour. Apple mousse and Alpine cheese add flavour.

**Nusstorte** Caramelised nut tart usually made with walnuts.

**Bündner Gerstensuppe** Creamy barley soup with smoked pork, beef, speck, leeks, celery, cabbage, carrots and potatoes.

> **Photo Opportunity**
> Sublimely pretty Val Fex.

Val Fex

### THE DRIVE
Part of the 10km-long drive (take Rte 27, then Rte 3) from St Moritz to Sils-Maria skirts the startlingly turquoise, wind-buffeted Silvaplanersee, a kitesurfing and windsurfing mecca. Sils-Maria is situated between Silvaplanersee and another equally beautiful lake, the Silsersee.

### 08 SILS-MARIA
Sils-Maria (Segl in Romansch) is a cluster of pastel-painted, slate-roofed chalets set against a backdrop of rugged, glacier-capped mountains. German philosopher Friedrich Nietzsche spent his summers here from 1881 to 1888 writing, including *Thus Spake Zarathustra*. A geranium-bedecked chalet, the little memorabilia-filled **Nietzsche Haus** (nietzschehaus.ch) was his summer retreat.

Nearby car-free **Val Fex** features high pastures freckled with wildflowers in summer and streaked gold with larch forests in autumn, and a glacier crowning a host of rocky peaks. Nietzsche, Thomas Mann and Marc Chagall were among those who found the space here to think and dream.

Reaching the valley is an experience in itself, whether you hike (around 2½ hours from Sils-Maria) or arrive by horse-drawn carriage. For the latter, head to Dorfplatz in Sils-Maria from where carriages depart.

### THE DRIVE
Head back past the Silvaplanersee, then turn left onto Rte 3. This takes you to the Julier Pass (open year-round; 2284m) and then up towards Thusis. Next head south on Rte 13, which you drive along for just under 5km to get to Via Mala (64km total, one hour and 10 minutes).

### 09 VIA MALA
The narrow, breathtakingly sheer and narrow gorge Via Mala ('Bad Path') was once part of a pack-mule trail to Italy. Today you can descend to its depths (some cliffs reach 300m) via 321 steps and try to imagine what an arduous and inhospitable slog this must have been back in the day.

### THE DRIVE
Head to Lake Lugano via Rte 13 and watch as the landscape

**Schloss Schauenstein**

changes from stoic Graubünden mountains to the velvety hills of Ticino, via the San Bernardino Pass (2066m). It takes around two hours and 130km.

### 10 LUGANO

Ticino's lush, mountain-rimmed Lago di Lugano (Lake Lugano) isn't its only liquid asset. The largest city in the canton is also the country's third-most-important banking centre. Suits aside, Lugano is a vivacious city, with chic boutiques, bars and pavement cafes, all huddling in the spaghetti maze of steep cobblestone streets that untangle at the edge of the lake and along the flowery promenade.

For a bird's-eye view of Lugano and the lake, head for the hills. A funicular from Cassarate hauls you to the summit of the 925m **Monte Brè** (montebre.ch) from March to December. The peak is the trailhead for hiking and mountain-biking trails that grant expansive views of the lake and reach deep into the Alps.

### THE DRIVE

Hop on the A2 heading north. Take exit 48 (Monte Ceneri) and then Rte 2 and A13, following the signs to Locarno (45 minutes, 43km).

### 11 LOCARNO

With its palm trees and much-vaunted 2300 hours of sunshine a year, Locarno, the lowest town in Switzerland, attracts sun lovers to its warm, Mediterranean-style setting, and has done so since the late 19th century.

The impossibly photogenic **Santuario della Madonna del Sasso** (madonnadelsasso.org) overlooks the town and is a must-see. It was built after the Virgin Mary supposedly appeared in a vision to a monk, Bartolomeo d'Ivrea, in 1480. There's a highly adorned church and several rather rough, near-life-size statue groups (including one of the Last Supper) in niches on the stairway. The best-known painting in the church is La Fuga in Egitto (Flight to Egypt), painted in 1522 by Bramantino. A **funicular** runs every 15 minutes from the town centre past the sanctuary to Orselina, but a more scenic, pilgrim-style approach is the 20-minute walk up the chapel-lined Via Crucis (take Via al Sasso off Via Cappuccini).

## Schloss Schauenstein

Lauded as one of Switzerland's greatest chefs, Michelin-starred Andreas Caminada is king of fairy tale **Schloss Schauenstein** (schauenstein.ch), which has featured in the World's 50 Best Restaurants list.. The rarefied experience belies the simplicity of many of the ingredients, often local, all handled with imagination and exquisite technique. The excellent wine list features many of Switzerland's best vintages, along with international offerings.

The castle's **guesthouse** features three rooms decorated with sleek contemporary furnishings and three suites that combine period fixtures and modern features. The manicured grounds come with an outdoor pool and terrace.

Reserve well in advance for both (up to eight months), or try your luck with listings of last-minute table cancellations via the website. Find it in Fürstenau, just off Rte 13 from Chur, before Thusis and Via Mala.

### THE DRIVE
Take the A13 then Rte 13; follow the signs to Bellinzona (30 minutes, 24km).

### 12 BELLINZONA

At the convergence of several Alpine valleys, Bellinzona is visually striking. Its three grey-stone medieval castles have attracted everyone from Swiss invaders to British painter William Turner.

The main castle, **Castelgrande** (fortezzabellinzona.ch), rising from a rocky central hill, was a Roman frontier post and Lombard defensive tower. It's now one of Bellinzona's best places to eat, and wandering the vineyard-surrounded grounds is unforgettable.

The three castles didn't stop Swiss-German confederate troops from overwhelming the city in 1503, thus deciding Ticino's fate for the following three centuries. Castelgrande is the easiest castle to access, but both **Castello di Montebello** (fortezzabellinzona.ch) and **Castello di Sasso Corbaro** (fortezzabellinzona.ch) reward the effort.

### THE DRIVE
On the A2, take exit 41 (direction Nufenen/Bedretto/Passo San Gottardo) before continuing on Rte 2 towards San Gottardo (one hour, 72km).

### 13 ST GOTTHARD PASS

An exhilarating drive if ever there was one, this famous mountain pass (2108m) at the heart of Europe connects cantons Ticino and Uri (namely, Andermatt). It can be bypassed by the tunnel (road and train), but if you want spectacular scenery and a sense of really getting over the Alps, then take the famous cobblestone **Tremola Road**. On the southern side of the pass, it connects the highest point with the Italian-speaking town of Airolo via 37 tortuous twists, and is a must. Once at the top, visit the **Museo Nazionale San Gottardo** (passosangottardo.ch). This museum covers the commercial, political and cultural significance of the pass and is housed in a former customs house and hotel. From here, you can connect with Andermatt easily.

# TOOLKIT

The chapters in this section cover the most important topics you'll need to know about in Germany, Austria and Switzerland. They're full of nuts-and-bolts information and valuable insights to help you understand and navigate Germany, Austria and Switzerland and get the most out of your trip.

**Arriving**
p226

**Getting Around**
p227

**Accommodation**
p228

**Cars**
p229

**Health & Safe Travel**
p230

**Responsible Travel**
p231

**Nuts & Bolts**
p232

**Grossglockner High Alpine Road, Austria (p166)**
DRONETOP/SHUTTERSTOCK

# Arriving

Germany, Switzerland and Austria are well connected to the rest of Europe and, indeed, the world, with major airports in the countries' capitals as well as Frankfurt, Munich and Zürich. Major European roads and railway lines criss-cross the region.

### Hiring & Sharing Cars

Across the region, it's always cheaper to pre-book a car than hire one on arrival. You'll find all the major car-hire companies at airports, including Sixt, Hertz and Enterprise. The minimum age for hiring small cars is 19; for prestige models, 25 years and a valid licence issued at least one year prior is necessary. An economy-size vehicle could cost anywhere from about €40 to €60 per day, plus insurance and taxes, though you may find cheaper deals at quiet times.

Car-sharing schemes have become popular in recent years as the cost of hiring has increased. For instance, the **Mobility** (mobility.ch) scheme in Switzerland is an excellent deal. You'll need to register for membership on its website, then make a booking. Cars can be hired for as little time as an hour. Day packages include an allowance of 100km within 24 hours.

### Airports to City Centres

| | Berlin | Vienna | Zürich |
|---|---|---|---|
|  **TRAIN** | €5 | €5 | Chf10 |
|  **BUS** | €4.70 | €11 | Chf7 |
|  **TAXI** | €60 | €60 | Chf60 |

---

**EU & SCHENGEN**

Germany and Austria are in the EU and the Schengen Zone; Switzerland isn't in the EU but is in the Schengen Zone. Travellers should always have their passports with them as border checks are becoming more frequent, even between Schengen countries.

**ETIAS**

From late 2026, new EU entry rules require nationals from 60 countries (including the US, UK, Canada) to apply and pay for travel authorisation (European Travel Information & Authorisation System, €20) before entering Schengen countries.

**CASH**

Cash is readily available from ATMs at entry points and card and contactless payment methods are commonplace everywhere. Germany and Austria use the euro, Switzerland's currency is the franc.

**PHONES IN SWITZERLAND**

Switzerland is not part of the EU roaming-free zone, so your phone, while still working as normal, will stack up a hefty 'world roaming' bill quickly. Buy a Swiss SIM or, even better, download an e-SIM.

# Getting Around

### SWISS MOTORWAY VIGNETTES
One of the biggest official motoring swindles in Europe is the Swiss motorway vignette. No matter whether you are passing through the country in a few hours or moving permanently to Switzerland, you must buy an annual pass for Chf40. No day, week or month tickets are available, and the pass is only valid until the end of January the following year. Using the back roads to avoid this hefty fee is very impractical and sometimes impossible.

## DRIVING INFO

Drive on the right in all three countries

Winter tyres compulsory from November to March

Buy motorway vignettes online in advance to save time

Although you'll be driving in the region, there may still be times, especially in big cities, when you'll need to use public transport.

## Transport Apps
Almost all big cities in the region have a transport app you can download onto your smartphone. These enable you to buy tickets and plan journeys, making travel on public transport a lot simpler and cash- paper ticket-free.

## Navigation
Many fall back on Google Maps for navigation but there are other, sometimes better options. One of these is **mapy.com**, a Czech map app that provides a much greater level of detail than Google and includes hiking trails.

## Free Rides
It may come a surprise to some, but in the Alps, staying in a town overnight often gives you free access to public transport and sometimes cable cars. Ask your accommodation about this as it is usually they who issue the pass.

## Buses
Austria and Switzerland have a system of postbuses that link remote mountain villages to large cities and train lines. Bus is also the best way to get around the German Alps but elsewhere the train is better.

## TRAVEL COSTS

**Petrol (Euro 95)**
Austria/Germany/Switzerland per litre €1.50/€1.70/Chf1.80

**Ten-day Austrian motorway vignette (permit)**
€12.40

**Cost to use Germany's entire autobahn system**
free

FROM LEFT: NIKADA/GETTY IMAGES, FOOTTOO/SHUTTERSTOCK

# Accommodation

### HIGH & LOW SEASON

High season in the Alps goes with the sun and snow, spiking price-wise around the summer holidays (July and August) across the region and in winter (especially Christmas). Outside peak periods, there are better deals on rooms, especially in shoulder season. On top of the room rate, you are very likely to pay an *Ortstaxe* (local tax), a certain percentage of your accommodation cost. But, before you grumble, this often goes towards paying for the invaluable *Gästekarte* (guest card), which usually covers local public transport and offers discounts on attractions.

**HOW MUCH FOR A NIGHT IN...**

An Alpine hut
€60

A pitch for two in a campground
€40

A historic hotel
from €150

## Mountain Huts

The Alps have hundreds of mountain chalets and huts, some luxurious with gourmet food, others bunkhouses at high altitude. They are open from mid-June to early October and bookings are essential if you want more than just floor space for a sleeping bag. They are administered by the Österreichischer Alpenverein (alpenverein.at), the German Alpine Club (alpenverein.de) and the Swiss Alpine Club (sac-cas.ch).

## Camping

Camping is a great way to explore most of the region though in some parts of the Alps it's certainly no longer cheap. Campgrounds are usually well maintained and scenically located near national parks, reserves and beauty spots. Most close in winter. Wild camping is officially not permitted, but bivouacking is often overlooked, especially above the tree line.

## Farm Stays

*Bauernhöfe* (farmhouses) are great for a slice of rural life, with serene views and often very welcoming hosts. Many are ideal for families, with animals to pet, farm-fresh eggs, plenty of fresh air, and hiking and cycling trails on the doorstep. Most rent out apartments for a minimum of three nights. You'll often need your own transport to reach them.

## Million Stars Stays

With stays ranging from transparent igloos and converted feed silos to 'floating' tree tents and even a very comfortable alfresco bed in a field, Switzerland takes camping and glamping to the next level. The common feature of the country's scattered 'Million Stars Hotels' is their unobstructed view of the night skies. See myswitzerland.com for details.

### FAIRY TALE STAYS

Consider a fairy tale getaway in a castle or manor. Remote countryside settings, from craggy rocks to rivers and rolling hills, are splurge-worthy getaways. Most blend modern amenities with old-fashioned trappings – maybe even a family descendant as host. Though most are luxury stays, budget-friendly exceptions exist; for example, around 30 castles have been converted into DJH youth hostels.

# Cars

## HOW MUCH TO HIRE A...

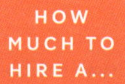

**Small car**
€50/day

**EV**
€60-80/day

**Campervan**
€90-170/day

### Car Rental

Cars in this region are normally rented from airports and train stations. You need to be at least 19 years of age and have a held a licence for a year.

Collision damage waivers vary immensely and can sometimes add hundreds of euros to the final bill. Deals that involve limited kilometres should also be avoided.

Make sure your car has a motorway vignette (permit) for the country in which you are hiring. Also check conditions for taking vehicles over borders.

To get a vehicle with automatic transmission you will need to specify this when you book.

Any parking tickets or fines are added to the final bill plus a hefty admin fee on top.

### Electric Vehicles (EVs)

Hiring an EV in Germany, Austria and Switzerland is possible, though some hire companies are reviewing how many such vehicles they should have available as the option has not proved particularly popular.

These three countries have relatively decent charging possibilities though nothing like Scandinavia or the US. Range anxiety is only an issue in Germany where distances are large.

Be aware that subzero temperatures in the winter Alps reduce range. A lot of uphill driving also drains batteries fast.

EVs still need a motorway vignette in Austria and Switzerland. You do not need one if driving from Austria to Saxony in the part of the journey through Czechia.

### OTHER GEAR

Child seats, sat-navs, in-car wi-fi and other add-ons can bump up the cost considerably and it is always best to bring your own gear if you can. Most of these need to be booked in advance as availability is limited, especially in summer and during the skiing season.

FROM LEFT: MICAËL CHEVALLEY/500PX, RONALD RAMPSCH/SHUTTERSTOCK

# Health & Safe Travel

### Ticks & Mozzies

Mosquitoes can be a pest around lakes but pose no real danger. Ticks, however, can carry Lyme disease (*Borreliose* in German) and encephalitis (TBE). They are usually found below 1200m, in undergrowth at the forest edge and long grass. Long trousers tucked into boots or socks and a DEET-based insect repellent are the best preventions.

### Tap Water

The region's tap water is clean, drinkable and well filtered, especially in rural areas. After all, consider the source: Alpine and mountain springs. Despite this drinkable purity, asking for tap water in a restaurant is generally a no-no. Germans, Austrians and the Swiss prefer bottled mineral or spring water at mealtimes.

### Mountain Safety

Every year people die in landslides, avalanches and from getting lost in the Alps. Always check weather conditions before heading out. Before going on challenging hikes, ensure you have the proper equipment, clothes and fitness levels. Inform someone at your hotel or guesthouse where you're going and when you intend to return. Consider hiring a guide when skiing off-piste.

### INSURANCE

For UK and EU citizens, a UK Global Health Insurance Card (GHIC) or European Health Insurance Card (EHIC) from your healthcare provider covers most emergency medical care in Austria. This is no substitute for good insurance. Many standard policies don't cover outdoor activities (especially higher-risk activities like skiing). You'll need to pay a premium for winter sports and adventure sports.

### CAR BREAKDOWNS

If your hire car breaks down, your first call should be to the hire company who will sort out a tow or fix and a replacement vehicle. If you do suffer a fault and you have to stop, put on reflective vests immediately and place the warning triangle a sensible distance behind the car. Don't wait in your car on the motorway hard shoulder.

# Responsible Travel

## Climate Change & Travel

Lonely Planet urges all travellers to engage with their travel carbon footprint, which will mainly come from air travel. While there often isn't an alternative, travellers can look to minimise the number of flights they take, opt for newer aircrafts and use cleaner ground transport, such as trains.

One proposed solution — purchasing carbon offsets — unfortunately does not cancel out the impact of individual flights. While most destinations will depend on air travel for the foreseeable future, for now, pursuing ground-based travel where possible is the best course of action.

The **UN Carbon Offset Calculator** shows how flying impacts a household's emissions:

The **ICAO's carbon emissions calculator** allows visitors to analyse the $CO_2$ generated by point-to-point journeys:

## Resources

**umweltbundesamt.de/en**
German Federal Environmental Agency

**www.umweltbundesamt.at**
Austrian Environment Agency

**bafu.admin.ch**
Swiss Federal Office for the Environment

---

### SWISSTAINABLE

The Swiss tourism website has tips on travelling in the country more responsibly, such as staying in accommodation featuring the Swisstainable logo, as this means it is committed to environmental protection and social justice.

### STAYING ON A FARM

You can't get much closer to nature than taking a holiday on a farm. FeBa (bauernhof-ferien.ch), the Swiss holiday farms association, has around 100 members offering a variety of accommodation.

### EMISSIONS STICKER

To decrease air pollution caused by fine particles, most German cities now have low-emission environmental zones that only cars displaying an *Umweltplakette* (emissions sticker, sometimes *Feinstaubplakette*) may enter – even foreign ones.

FROM LEFT: PAVLO GLAZKOV/SHUTTERSTOCK, ROBERTO MOIOLA/SYSAWORLD/GETTY IMAGES

# Nuts & Bolts

**GOOD TO KNOW**

**Time zone** CET

**Country code** (+49) Germany, (+43) Austria, (+41) Switzerland

**Emergency number** 112

### Cash

Cash is still king in Germany. Always carry some and plan to pay cash at places like cafes and pubs. Since the pandemic, e-payments are catching on, but setting aside smaller bills for tips and emergencies is always a good idea. Barkeepers and kiosks may gripe about big notes.

### Euros in Switzerland

As with the other non-euro-zone countries of Central and Eastern Europe, businesses throughout Switzerland will accept payment in euros, but only notes. Change will be given in Swiss francs either at the official rate of exchange calculated on the day or slightly lower.

### Tipping

Tipping is not automatically expected in the region (especially in Switzerland). Round up the bill in restaurants to the nearest €10, to €5 in taxis and in bars. Always tip in cash directly to the server and never reward huffy service. Payment terminals with the option to tip are making an unwelcome appearance.

### Opening Hours

Except in transport terminals, supermarkets in all three countries are closed on Sundays.

**CURRENCY: EURO (€), SWISS FRANC (CHF)**

### Toilets

Free public toilets are now a rare thing in this region (except in Switzerland). Use hotel, cafe and museum facilities. Even shopping centre bathrooms in Germany now charge something.

### Smoking

Bans apply in public spaces in all three countries but in Germany smoking is tolerated more.

**ELECTRICITY 230V/50HZ**

Germany and Austria

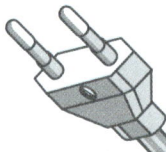

**Type C** 220V/50Hz

Switzerland

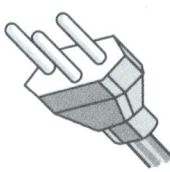

**Type J** 230V/50Hz

**HOW MUCH FOR A...**

**Museum entry** €5-10

**Coffee** €3-7

**Glass of wine** €6-15

**Cable-car ride** €15-80

# Index

5 Fingers viewing platform 187

## A

accommodation 15, 228
activities 15
Ahrenshoop 27
airports 226
Alfeld 32
Alken 105
Along the Baltic Coast 24-9, **25**
Along the Danube 160-3, **161**
Andermatt 213
Annweiler 107-8
apps 227
Appenzell 197
archaeological sites & ruins
   Aguntum 191
   Amphitheater 102
   Archäologische Zone 91
   Archäologischer Park 91
   Burg Metternich 105
   Denghoog 80
   Grevenburg 104
   Kaiserthermen 102
   Konstantin Basilika 102
   Kuenringerburg 163
Arosa 210-11
Augsburg 128
Aussichtsturm Pyramidenkogel 190
Austria 156-91, **156**
   accommodation 159
   climate 158
   festivals & events 159
   resources 159
   transport 159

Routes 000
**Map Pages 000** 000

## B

Bach, Johann Sebastian 47, 56, 58, 66
Bacharach 99-100
Bad Dürkheim 109
Bad Ischl 185-6
Bad Karlshafen 87
Bad Schandau 41
Bad Tölz 140
Baden-Baden 151, 152-3
Bamberg 122
Basel 194, 199
Bastei 41
Bauhausgebäude 31, 60
Bautzen 39
Bayreuth 123
Beethoven, Ludwig van 95
Beilstein 105
Beinhaus 187
Bellinzona 223
Berchtesgaden 143
Bergstrasse 114-17, **114**
Berlin 22, 48-9
Berlin & the Jewels of Eastern Brandenburg 48-51, **49**
Bern 195, 206-7
Bernau am Chiemsee 142
Bernese Alps 208
Bernkastel-Kues 103
Bertha Benz Memorial Route 117
Binz 29
Bockenheim an der Weinstrasse 109
Bodenmais 134
Bodenwerder 87
Bonn 95-6
books 17
Bootsverleih Richter 49
border control 226
Bregenz 147, 159, 169, 170-1

Breisach 151
Bremen 79, 89
Brothers Grimm 54, 83, 85, 86
bus 227

## C

camping 228
Carinthian Lakes 188-91, **189**
car hire 226, 229
castles & fortresses 12-13
   Albrechtsburg 43
   Altes Schloss (Dornburger) 46
   Altes Schloss (Meersburg) 145, 150
   Barockschloss Mannheim 118
   Bergpalais 42
   Burg Eltz 105
   Burg Forchtenstein 179
   Burg Frankenstein 115-16
   Burg Gleichen 47
   Burg Güssing 179
   Burg Guttenberg 119-20
   Burg Hasegg 175
   Burg Hochosterwitz 189
   Burg Hohenwerfen 165
   Burg Hohenzollern 150
   Burg Katz 97
   Burg Landshut 103
   Burg Lockenhaus 179
   Burg Maus 97
   Burg Neukatzenelnbogen 97
   Burg Rheinfels 97
   Burg Riegersburg 180
   Burg Thurant 105
   Burg Trifels 107-8, 163
   Castelgrande 223
   Castello di Montebello 223
   Castello di Sasso Corbaro 223
   Château de Chillon 202
   Château de Gruyères 203

castles & fortresses continued
  Château de Nyon 200
  Chateâu de Prangins 201
  Felsenburg Neurathen 41
  Festung Ehrenbreitstein 97
  Festung Hohensalzburg 175
  Festung Königstein 41
  Fürstbischöfliche Residenz 128
  Hambacher Schloss 108
  Hofburg (Innsbruck) 174
  Hohes Schloss 130
  Jagdschloss Granitz 29
  Kaiserburg 121
  Kaiserpfalz 63
  Landgrafenschloss 85
  Löwenburg 47
  Mühlburg 47
  Munot 198
  Neues Schloss (Bayreuth) 123
  Neues Schloss (Meersburg) 145, 150
  Pfalzgrafstein 98-9
  Reichsburg 105
  Renaissance Palace 46
  Residenz (Salzburg) 182
  Residenzschloss 42
  Rococo Palace 46
  Schloss (Burgdorf) 207
  Schloss (Darmstadt) 114
  Schloss Ambras 174
  Schloss Arenenberg 197
  Schloss Belvedere 46
  Schloss Branitz 49
  Schloss Bruck 191
  Schloss Eggenberg 180, 188
  Schloss Ehrenburg 122
  Schloss Esterházy 178
  Schloss Friedenstein 56-7
  Schloss Güstrow 36
  Schloss Harburg 128
  Schloss Heidelberg 117, 119
  Schloss Hellbrunn 183
  Schloss Herrenchiemsee 142

Schloss Hohenschwangau 131
Schloss Hohentübingen 149-50
Schloss Kammer 184
Schloss Landeck 173
Schloss Laufen 199
Schloss Linderhof 139
Schloss Ludwigslust 35
Schloss Mirabell 182
Schloss Moritzburg 42
Schloss Mosigkau 61
Schloss Neuenburg 45
Schloss Neuschwanstein 130
Schloss Pillnitz 41-2
Schloss Porcia 191
Schloss Schattenburg 171
Schloss Schauenstein 223
Schloss Schönbrunn 176
Schloss Schwerin 35
Schloss Weesenstein 41
Schloss Weikersheim 125, 127
Schloss Wernigerode 63
Schloss Wildenberg 220
Schloss Wilhelmsburg 67
Schloss Wilhelmshöhe 47, 86
Schloss Wilhelmsthal 47
Schloss Wörlitz 31, 60-1
Schlossberg (Graz) 180
Seeschloss Ort 185
Stadtschloss 56
Stiftskirche 109
Wartburg 47
Willibaldsburg 128
Würzburg Residenz 124
Zitadelle Petersberg 47
Zwinger 42, 59
Castles of Burgenland & Styria 176-81, **176**
Central Germany's Castles & Palaces 44-7, **45**
CERN 205
Chemnitz 68, 70
Chur 218-19
churches & cathedrals
  Bamberger Dom 122
  Basilica Minor St Michael 183-4
  Basilika St Emmeram 134
  Basilika St Johann 53

Berner Münster 207
Cathédrale de Notre Dame (Lausanne) 201
Cathédrale de St Nicolas de Myre 205
Church of Maria Himmelfahrt 129
Dom (Cologne) 95
Dom (Fulda) 56
Dom (Naumburg) 58
Dom (Paderborn) 93
Dom St Kilian 125
Dom St Nikolai 27
Dom St Paul 92
Dom St Petri 89
Dom St Stephan (Passau) 133, 160
Domkirche St Nikolauas 171
Eiskapelle 143
Erfurter Dom 67
Frauenkirche (Dresden) 42, 59, 70
Fraumünster 208
Gertrudenkapelle 36
Grossmünster 208
Güstrow Dom 36
Hofkirche 174
Johanniskirche 129
Kaiserdom (Frankfurt) 54
Kalvarienberg 140
Karmeliterkirche St Josef 105
Katholische Kirche 178
Kloster Chorin 51
Kloster St Johann 220
Liebfraukirche 128
Lorsch Abbey 116
Magdeburg Dom 32
Mainzer Dom 53, 100
Mariendom (Erfurt) 57
Mariendom (Linz) 161
Marienkirche (Disentis/Mustér) 212
Marienkirche (Frankfurt (Oder)) 50
Marienkirche (Lübeck) 24-5
Marienkirche (Rostock) 26
Martinskirche 218-19
Münster (Basel) 199
Münster (Konstanz) 147
Münster Bad Doberan 26
Münster Basilica (Bonn) 95

Nikolaikirche (Leipzig) 71
Nikolaikirche (Stralsund) 28
Peterskirche (Görlitz) 59
Peterskirche (Lindau) 144
Petrikirche 25
Pfarrkirche (Hallstatt) 187
Pfarrkirche St Ulrich 109
Salzburger Dom 175
Santuario della Madonna del Sasso 222
Schlosskirche 119
Stadtkirche (Freudenstadt) 155
Stadtkirche St Georg 66
Stadtschloss Weimar 57
St Anna Kirche 128
St Bartholomä 143
St Maria zur Wiese 93
St Patrokli 93
St-Nikolai-Kirche 26
St-Stephan-Kirche (Mainz) 53, 100
St Stephansmünster 151
Thomaskirche 43
Trierer Dom 102
Wallfahrtskirche 186
Wallfahrtskirche Basilika Birnau 147
Wieskirche 130
climate 14-15, 22, 74, 112, 158, 194, 231
clothes 16
Coburg 122-3
Cochem 105
Cologne 75, 90-1, 95
Cologne & the Ruhr Valley 90-3, **91**
costs 227, 228, 229, 232
Cottbus 49
Czechia 122

## D

Dachstein Eishöhle 187
Darmstadt 114-15
Darss-Zingst Peninsula 27
Davos 219
Deidesheim 109
Design for Life: Bauhaus to VW 30-3, **31**
Dessau-Rosslau 31, 60-1
Deutsches Eck 97, 105

Dinkelsbühl 127
Donauinselfest 15
Donauwörth 128
Dornburger Schlösser 45-6
Dortmund 92
Drei Gleichen 47
Dresden 22, 42, 59, 70-1
driving 227
Dürkheimer Riesenfass 109
Dürnstein 163
Düsseldorf 94

## E

Eagle's Nest 143
East Frisian Islands 77-8
Eisenach 47, 56, 66
electricity 232
electric vehicles 229
Emden 76-7
Engelberg 213
Engelhartszell an der Donau 161
Erfurt 23, 47, 57, 67
Erlebniswelt Haus Meissen 43
Essen 91-2
events, see festivals & events

## F

Fahrgastschifffahrt Neumann 50
Fantastic Road 148-51, **148**
farm stays 228, 231
festivals & events 15
 Austria 159
 Bregenzer Festspiele 170-1
 Dürkheimer Wurstmarkt 109
 Montreux Jazz Festival 202
 Northeastern Germany 23
 Northwestern Germany 75
 Queen studio experience 202
 Schlossgartenfestspiele 37
 Southern Germany 113
 Switzerland 195
Fiesch 216
films 16
food 6-7
Frankfurt 54

Frankfurt (Oder) 50
Frauenau 133
Freudenstadt 155
Freyburg 45
Fribourg 205
Friedrichshafen 145
Fulda 54, 56
Füssen 130, 137

## G

Garmisch-Partenkirchen 139
Gedenkstätte Berliner Mauer 49
Gedenkstätte Buchenwald 46
Gedenkstätte Seelower Höhen 50
Geneva 194, 204-5
Geneva to Zürich 204-9, **205**
Gengenbach 151
Gerlos Alpine Road 166, 168
German Alpine Road 136-43, **137**
German Avenues Route 60-71, **61**
German Castle Road 118-23, **119**
German Fairy Tale Road 82-9, **82**
German Wine Route 106-9, **106**
Glass Route 132-5, **133**
Goethe 58, 67
Görlitz 38-9, 59
Gotha 56-7
Göttingen 86
Graubünden & Ticino 218-23, **219**
Graz 158, 180, 188-9
Greifswald 27, 37
Grimmwelt 85
Grindelwald 214
Grossglockner High Alpine Road 166
Gruyères 203

## H

Hallstatt 187
Hamburg 74, 80
Hanau 54, 82
Hanover 23, 32, 89
Hanseatic League, the 29
health 230
Heidelberg 112, 117, 119, 148-9
Helgoland 79

Herzogin Anna Amalia Bibliothek 46, 57, 67
High Alpine Trio – Grossglockner to Silvretta, The 164-9, **165**
highlights 6-13
Highlights of Saxony 38-43, **39**
hiking
   Alpenrosenweg 173
   Alpine Flower Garden 175
   Andermatt 213
   Eiskapelle 143
   Füssen 130
   Gotthardstrasse 213
   Grindelwald 214
   Gustav Klimt-Themenweg 184
   Hunsrück Trails 97
   Jodel Wanderweg 168
   Lai da Tuma 213
   Lauterbrunnen 214-15
   Lugano 222
   Malerwinkel 143
   Mürren 215
   Partnachklamm 139
   Philosophenweg 117
   Schlangenweg 117
   Schrammsteinaussicht 41
   St Moritz 220
   Stechelberg 215
   Vierseenblick 97
   Wasserfallweg 166
   Wildewasserweg 169
history 11
Hitler, Adolf 64, 129, 143
HockenheimRing 117
Hohenschwangau Castle 130-1

## I

Innsbruck 158-9, 168-9, 174
insurance 230
Interlaken 205

Routes 000
**Map Pages 000** **000**

## J

Jena 57, 68
Jever 78
Jugendstilbad 115
Jungfraujoch 205, 206

## K

Kammer 184-5
Kandersteg 216
Kapuzinerberg 165
Karls 26
Kassel 47, 74, 85-6
Kaub 98-9
Kitzbühel 175
Klagenfurt 159, 189-90
Kniebis 154
Koblenz 97, 105
Konstanz 147, 151
Krems an der Donau 163
Krippenstein 187
Krupp Dynasty 92
Kühlungsborn 26

## L

Lake Constance 144-7, **145**
Lake Geneva & Western Switzerland 200-3, **201**
lakes & rivers 10
   Ammersee 139
   Attersee 184
   Bavarian Sea 140
   Blausee 216
   Chiemsee 140, 142
   Edersee 85
   Kochelsee 140
   Kölpinsee 37
   Königssee 143
   Lago di Lugano 222
   Lake Constance 147, 151, 197
   Lake Lucerne 208
   Lake Müritz 36
   Mummelsee 154
   Oeschinensee 216
   Pfaffentiech 36
   Rhine 98, 100
   Segelschule Mondsee 184
   Sitter River 197
   Starnberger See 138
   Tiefwarensee 37
   Traunsee 185
   Walchensee 140
   Walensee 219
Lakes & Treasures of Mecklenburg-Western Pomerania 34-7, **35**
Landeck 173
Landsberg am Lech 129
language 17
Lausanne 201
Lauterbrunnen 214-15
Lavaux 202
Leipzig 22, 43, 44-5, 58, 71
Lienz 166, 191
Lindau 112, 136-7, 144
Linz 161
Locarno 195, 222
Loreley 98
Lübbenau & the Spreewald 49
Lübeck 24-5
Lucerne 208
Lugano 222
Lüneburg 34-5
Luther, Martin 47, 56, 57, 66, 128

## M

Magdeburg 32
Mahnmal St-Nikolai 80
Mainau Island 151
Mainz 53, 75, 100
Mammuthöhle 187
Mannheim 118-19
Marburg 85
Märchenstrasse 84
Mathildenhöhe 114
Mauthausen Memorial 162
Meersburg 145, 150
Mehliskopf 153
Meissen 42-3
Mendelssohn 58
Melk 163

Millstatt 190
Miniatur Wunderland 80
Mittenwald 139-40
Mönchsberg 164
Mondsee 183-4
money 226, 232
Mont Blanc 215
Monte Brè 222
Montreux 202
Montreux Jazz Festival 15
Moritzburg 42
Moselle Valley 102-5, **103**
mosquitoes 230
mountain huts 228
Mountain Valleys of Tyrol & Vorarlberg 170-5, **171**
mountains 8-9
Mozart, Wolfgang Amadeus 175, 183
Mühlhausen 64
Mummelsee 154
Munich 140
Münster 92
museums & galleries
　Angelika Kauffmann Museum 172
　Angermuseum 67
　Appenzell Museum 197
　Atelierhaus 36
　Automobile Welt Eisenach 47, 56, 66
　AutoMuseum 32
　Autostadt 32
　Bachhaus 47, 56, 66
　Bach-Museum 58
　Barockhaus 38
　Bauhaus Museum 30
　Bayerisches Eisenbahnmuseum 128
　Bergbaumuseum 175
　Brechthaus 128
　Brüder Grimm-Haus & Museum Steinau 54, 83
　Bündner Kunstmuseum 218
　Bunkermuseum 76
　Children & Young People's Museum 121
　DDR Museum 41
　Deutsche Bahn Museum 121
　Deutsches Auswandererhaus 79, 89
　Deutsches Hugenotten Museum 87

　Deutsches Hygiene-Museum 59
　Deutsches Museum für Foto-, Film- und Fernsehtechnik 109
　Deutsches Weihnachtsmuseum 121
　DFB-Museum 92
　East Side Gallery 49
　Erlebniszentrum Naturgewalten 80
　Europäisches Hansemuseum 25
　Fachwerkmuseum im Ständerbau 61
　Fagus Werk 32
　Festung Königstein 41
　Freilandmuseum 49
　Freilichtmuseum Petronell 177
　Friedensmuseum Brücke von Remagen 96
　Fuggereimuseum 128
　Galerie für Zeitgenössische Kunst 71
　Galerie Neue Meister 70
　Gedenkstätte 39
　Geigenbaumuseum 140
　Gemäldegalerie 86
　Germanisches Nationalmuseum 121
　Glasmuseum 133
　Goethe-Nationalmuseum 46, 67
　Goldenes Dachl & Museum 174
　Goslarer Museum 63
　Grimmwelt 47
　Gustav Klimt Zentrum 184
　Gutenberg-Museum Mainz 53, 100
　Hamburger Kunsthalle 80
　Harzmuseum 63
　Haus der Deutschen Weinstrasse 109
　Haus der Geschichte 95-6, 127
　Heimat Museum 172
　Hessisches Landesmuseum 115
　Historisches Grünes Gewölbe 42
　Historisches Museum Saar 52
　Historisches Museum Schloss Philippsruhe 54, 82
　Historisch-Technisches Museum 28
　Hohenloher Freilandmuseum 120
　Junges Museum 57
　Käthe-Kruse-Puppen-Museum 128
　Kirchner Museum 219
　Klimahaus Bremerhaven 8° Ost 79
　Klostermuseum 212

　Klostermuseum St Georgen 198
　Kunstgewerbemuseum 42
　Kunsthalle (Bremen) 79
　Kunsthalle Würth 120
　Kunsthaus 208
　Kunsthaus Graz 189
　Kunstmuseum 32, 207
　Kunstmuseum Moritzburg 58
　Landesmuseum für Vorgeschichte 58
　Landesmuseum Mainz 53
　LWL-Museum für Kunst und Kultur 92
　Lyonel Feininger Galerie 61
　Matterhorn Museum 217
　Mendelssohn-Haus 58
　Mercedes-Benz Museum 149
　Messel Museum 115
　Mittelalterliches Kriminalmuseum 121
　Mittelrhein-Museum 97
　Motor Sport Museum 117
　Mozarthaus 183
　Mozarts Geburtshaus 175
　Mozart-Wohnhaus 175
　Münchhausen Museum 87
　Musée d'Art et d'Histoire 205
　Musée d'Art Moderne et Contemporain 205
　Musée International de la Croix-Rouge et du Croissant-Rouge 205
　Musée National Suisse 201
　Musée Olympique 201
　Musée Romain 200
　Museen im Grassi 58
　Museo Nazionale San Gottardo 223
　Museum Alte Kulturen 150
　Museum Carnuntium 177
　Museum der Bildenden Künste 43
　Museum Folkwang 91
　Museum Frieder Burda 152-3
　Museum für Musikinstrumente 58
　Museum für Naturkunde 70
　Museum für Sepulkralkultur 86
　Museum für Volkskultur 191
　Museum für Weinkultur 109
　Museum Gunzenhauser 70
　Museum Hamelin 89

*museums & galleries continued*
Museum Junge Kunst 50
Museum Mondseeland und Pfahlbaumuseum 184
Museum Sammlung Rosengart 208
Museumsdorf Bayerischer Wald 133
Muzikinstumente-Museum der Völker 183
Neue Galerie (Graz) 188
Neue Sächsische Galerie 70
Neues Museum (Berlin) 48
Neues Stadtmuseum 129
Nietzsche Archiv 67
Nietzsche Haus 58
Oberammergau Museum 138
Ostfriesisches Landesmuseum 76
Passat 25
Passauer Glasmuseum 132
Patek Philippe Museum 205
Pergamonmuseum 49
Poppenspäler Museum 80
Porsche Museum 149
Rammelsberg Museum & Besucherbergwerk 63
Rebbaumuseum 199
Rieskrater Museum 128
Römisch-Germanisches Museum 90-1, 95
Ruhr Museum 92
Salzburg Museum 175
Schlesisches Museum zu Görlitz 59
Schloss Museum (Jever) 78
Schloss Museum (Mannheim) 118
Schlossmuseum (Quedlinburg) 61
Seelow Heights Memorial Exhibit 50
Senckenberg Museum 57, 115
Sorbisches Museum 39
Sprengel Museum 32
Städel Museum 54
Stadtgeschichtliches Museum 45
Stadtmuseum (Bad Ischl) 186
Stadtmuseum (Nördlingen) 128
Stadtmuseum (Saalfeld) 68
Stadtmuseum & Kunstsammlung Jena 68
Stasi Museum 43
Tauberfränkisches Landschaftsmuseum 125
Theodor-Storm-Haus 80
Übersee Museum 79
Universitätsmuseum 148
Universum Science Center 79
Verkehrshaus 208
Vitra Design Museum 199
Vorarlberg Museum 147, 170
Waldmuseum 133
Zeiss Planetarium 57, 68
Zeitgeschichtliches Forum 43
Zeppelin Museum 145
Zollverein Coal Mine 92
Zwinger 59
music 17
Müstair 220

# N

Naumburg 58
Neubrandenburg 37
Neuschwanstein Castle 130-1
Neustadt an der Weinstrasse 108-9
Nietzsche 67, 221
Norddeich 77
Nördlingen 128
North Sea Coast 76-81, **77**
Northeastern Germany 20-71, **20**
  accommodation 23
  climate 22
  festivals & events 23
  resources 23
  transport 23
Northern Switzerland 196-9, **197**
Northwestern Germany 72-109, **72**
  accommodation 75
  climate 74
  festivals & events 75
  resources 75
  transport 75
Nuremberg 112, 121
Nyon 200

# O

Oberammergau 138
Obertraun 187
Oktoberfest 15
opening hours 232

# P

Paderborn 93
parks & gardens
  Alpine Flower Garden 175
  Alpine Wildlife Park 169
  Altmühltal Nature Park 128
  Bavarian Forest National Park 134
  Bergpark Wilhelmshöhe 47, 86
  Botanischer Garten 68
  Burggarten 35
  Gartenreich Dessau-Wörlitz 60
  Goethe Gartenhaus 67
  Grosser Garten 89
  Herrenhäuser Gärten 32, 89
  Kurgarten 109
  Landschaftspark Duisburg-Nord 91
  Müritz National Park 37
  Nationalpark Kellerwald-Edersee 85
  Nationalpark Schwarzwald 155
  PalmenGarten 57
  Park & Schloss Branitz 49
  Prater Park 163
  Saxon Switzerland National Par 39
  Schiller's Gartenhaus 57
  Schloss & Park Mosigkau 61
  Schloss & Park Pillnitz 41-2
  Schloss Güstrow 36
  Schlossgarten (Neustrelitz) 37
  Schlossgarten (Schwerin) 35
  Schlosspark (Marburg) 85
  Swiss National Park 220
  Weinbergpark 85
  Wörlitz Park 31, 60-1
Passau 132-3, 160
Passion of Christ 50
Passionstheater 138
Petronell-Carnuntum 177
Pillnitz 41-2
Plönlein 127

## Q

Quedlinburg 61, 64

## R

Rappenlochschlucht 169
responsible travel 231
Rheinfall 198-9
Romantic Rhine 94-101, **94**
Romantic Road, The 124-31, **124**
Rorschach 147
Rostock 26
Rothenburg ob der Tauber 120-1, 127

## S

Saalfeld 68
Saarbrücken 52-3
Sachsenhausen 51
safe travel 230
Salzburg 158, 164-5, 175, 182-3
Salzkammergut 182-7, **183**
Salzwelten 187
Saxon Switzerland National Park 39
Schaffhausen 198
Schilthorn 215-16
Schmalkalden 66-7
Schönau 143
Schongau 129
Schoppernau 171
Schwarzwaldhochstrasse 152-5, **153**
Silvretta High Alpine Road 169
smoking 232
Soest 92-3
*Sound of Music, The* 175, 184, 186
Southern Germany 110-55, **110**
   accommodation 113
   climate 112
   festivals & events 113
   resources 113
   transport 113
Spittal an der Drau 190-1
St Anton am Arlberg 173
Stanserhorn 208
Stein am Rhein 197-8
Steinau 54, 83
St Florian 162
St Gallen 196
St Gilgen 183
St Goar 97
St Wolfgang 159, 186
Stralsund 28
Stuttgart 113, 149
sustainability 231
Swiss Alps, The 210-17, **211**
Swiss National Park 220
Switzerland 192-223, **192**
   accommodation 195
   climate 194
   festivals & events 195
   resources 195
   transport 195
Sylt 80

## T

ticks 230
tipping 232
Tittling 133
toilets 232
Traunkirchen 185
travel seasons 14-15, 22, 74, 112, 158, 194
travel to/from Germany, Austria & Switzerland 226
travel within Germany, Austria & Switzerland 227
Travemünde 25
Trier 102-3
Tübingen 149-50

## U

Unesco Biosphere Entlebuch 207
Unterach am Attersee 184-5

## V

Velden am Wörthersee 190
Venet 173
Via Mala 221
Via Regia 52-9, **53**
Vienna 158, 163, 176-7
vignettes 227
Villach Alpine Road 190
visas 226

## W

Wagner 47, 66
Wallfahrtskirche Birnau 147
Waren 36-7
Warnemünde 26
Wartburg 66
water 230
weather 14-15
Weiden 134
Weikersheim 125, 127
Weimar 30-1, 46, 57, 67
Wilhelmshöhe 86
wine 6-7, 212
   Burgenland 180
   Dürkheimer Wurstmarkt 109
   Haus der Deutschen Weinstrasse 109
   Lavaux 202
   Museum für Weinkultur 109
   Rotkäppchen Sektkellerei 45
   Schloss Esterházy 179
   South Styrian Wine Road 181
Wismar 25-6
Wolfsburg 32
Wurstelprater 163
Würzburg 113, 124-5

## Z

Zammer Lochputz 173
Zell 104
Zell am See 166
Zell am Ziller 168
Zermatt 217
Zugspitze 139
Zuoz 220
Zürich 194, 208
Zwiesel 133

## THE WRITERS

**Marc Di Duca**
Marc has been a travel guide author for over two decades, covering destinations as diverse as Siberia and the Caribbean for Lonely Planet. @marcdiduca

**Becki Enright**
Becki is a travel writer penning guidebooks and articles on culture, adventure and responsible tourism. She has called Vienna home for ten years. @bordersofadventure

**Anthony Ham**
Anthony has been visiting Germany since he was a child, speaks the language and has travelled the world to research and write nearly 200 guidebooks for Lonely Planet. He has written two books of narrative non-fiction, including *The Last Lions of Africa*. anthonyham.com; @AnthonyHamWrite

## BEHIND THE SCENES

This book was researched and written by Marc Di Duca, Becki Enright and Anthony Ham.

The previous edition was written by Marc Di Duca, Anthony Ham, Anthony Haywood, Catherine Le Nevez, Ali Lemer, Craig McLachlan, Hugh McNaughtan, Leonid Ragozin, Andrea Schulte-Peevers, Benedict Walker and Kerry Walker.

This edition was produced by the following:

**Production Editor** Amy Lysen
**Destination Editor** Sandie Kestell
**Coordinating Editor** Bridget Blair
**Image Editor** Hannah Blackie
**Cartographer** Hunor Csutoros
**Cover Researcher** Daisy Korpics
**Assisting Editor** Sally Davies
**Thanks** Fergal Condon, Gwen Cotter, Melanie Dankel, Darren O'Connell, Saralinda Turner

## ACKNOWLEDGMENTS

**Digital Model Elevation Data**
Contains public sector information licensed under the Open Government Licence v3.0 website http://www.nationalarchives.gov.uk/doc/open-government-licence/version/3/

**Cover photograph**
Alps, Switzerland; Plpictures By Paedii Luchs/Stocksy